An Illustrated History of England

An illustrated

History of England

John Burke

Foreword by Sir Arthur Bryant

David McKay Company, Inc.
New York

Devised by David Burnett
Designed by Harold Bartram
Picture research by Marian Berman
Production Director John Ford

First American Edition, 1976

Library of Congress Catalog Card Number: 75–29533
ISBN: 0–679–50585–7
Printed in Great Britain

Contents

Foreword

What is the history of England? It is that part of a little island lying off the western shores of the vast continental bloc of Europe and Asia. Situated athwart the European Atlantic trade-routes, its geographical potential for commercial and strategical opportunities has been exceptional. Much of its history and impact on the world has turned on the degree to which those opportunities were taken. It has turned, too, on the character and ideals of the English peoples.

For the English are an amalgam of many races—the little dark Iberian and neolithic men; the Bronze Age pastoral warriors; the warlike Celts, who settled in the island before the Roman military occupation; the Saxon invaders who overran and destroyed that civilisation; the Norse pirates who followed them; the Norman conquerors who gave law and unity to the whole. All of them had two things in common: they were originally seafarers who had invaded the island across the stormy tidal waters which surround it, and all contrived, somehow, to live together, the earlier invaders sheltering from the more powerful late-comers in the hilly and rainy western districts or in pockets of inaccessible fenland. In later centuries, Flemings, Hugenots, Jews, West Indians and Asiatics, many of them fugitives from persecution, continued the process. All ultimately intermarried to produce a race of many strains, which may account for the paradox that a people famed for stolid, patient, practical common-sense—a nation, as Napoleon said, of 'shop-keepers'—has produced more adventurers, explorers and poets than probably any other in history.

Living in an island the English have enjoyed an island climate— aqueous, changeable and invigorating for plant, beast and man. Its very unpredictability has tended to make them adaptable and versatile, distrustful of long-term planning, yet good at making the best of the unexpected and unwelcome. 'Now,' wrote an 18th-century traveller, 'in as hot a climate as that of the East or West Indies, and sometimes in winter feel the cold of Greenland, up and down; hence we are precarious, uncertain, wild, enduring mortals.'

Two factors shaped England's political development. One was the strong, unifying rule of her Norman and Angevin kings and the native Tudors who followed them. By making the representative leaders of her provinces part of the central royal government they established a rule of common law for the whole island and made respect for law a national characteristic. The other was the libertarian instinct of her people—an inheritance, perhaps, of their sea-faring ancestors—which made it increasingly difficult for her kings to rule them without 'counsel and consent'—the principle enshrined in Edward I's adage 'that that which concerns all should be approved by all'. From this arose the English parliamentary system of govern-

Stonehenge.

ment, that 'supremacy of the Crown in Parliament' which ensures that the latter, exercising the authority of the Crown, can do anything it pleases except one thing, which is to prevent a future Parliament from doing the same. This has ensured that the English, while enjoying strong government, have always been able to change their rulers when they wearied of them.

The discovery of the ocean-routes to America and the Far East placed England in the centre of the world. By taking advantage of it, her sea-farers and traders, with their Scottish, Welsh and Irish compatriots, carried British commerce, colonies and libertarian ideas into every continent of the world. Freedom of the seas for their trade—and everyone else's—was preserved by a strong and invincible Navy. This enabled Great Britain, not to impose her will on the world, but to prevent anyone else from doing so. Five times by her mastery of the sea she has prevented a continental military conqueror from imposing a despotic authoritarian rule on Europe and the world.

Perhaps the most important element in England's history has been the continuity of her Christian tradition. The value set by her people on the freedom and sanctity of the individual, on justice and fair play, on mercy and tenderness towards the weak, and their dislike of lawless violence and their capacity to tolerate, forget and forgive have been, for all England's past mistakes and faults, a very real factor in human evolution. 'By this sacredness of individuals,' wrote Emerson, 'the English have in seven hundred years evolved the principles of freedom.' The Spanish-American philosopher, George Santayana, writing after the 1914–18 War, put it in another way. 'Never since the heroic days of Greece has the world had such a sweet, just, boyish master. It will be a black day for the human race when scientific blackguards, conspirators, churls and fanatics manage to supplant him.' 'We must choose our friends for the future,' declared General Smuts in 1940: 'I choose the country under which we suffered 40 to 50 years ago, but who when we were at their mercy treated us as a Christian people.'

ARTHUR BRYANT

The Uffington White Horse, Berkshire, a place of ritual and legend since prehistoric times. In the 9th century it was the site of a great Saxon victory over the Danes.

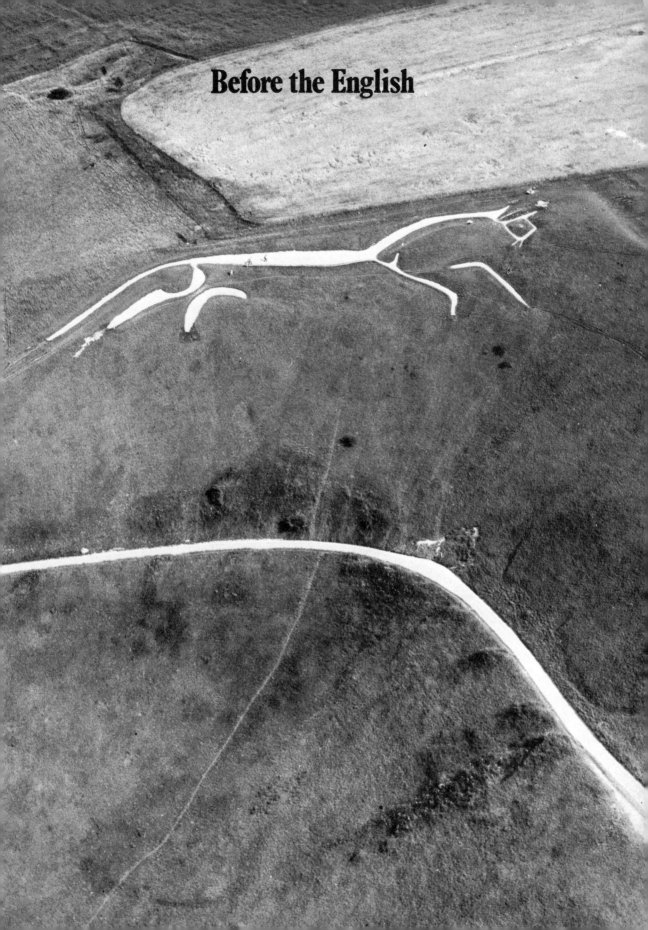

Before the English

Before the English

(1) West Kennet long barrow, Wiltshire; prehistoric burial chamber.

(2) Cerne giant, Dorset; possibly a Romano-British Hercules of the 2nd century A.D.

(3) Gold cup from a tomb at Rillaton, Cornwall; Bronze Age.

The first men to arrive in Britain from the eastern land mass were probably Old Stone Age hunters, seeking fertile tracts here during a lull in the Ice Age half a million years ago. Relics of their stone tools and axes are found in eastern England, especially East Anglia and the Thames valley.

Other immigrants followed over the centuries during periods when the country was linked to Europe by a land bridge. The final inundation of this causeway did not take place until the last melting of the ice drove a permanent seaway through it in about 5000 B.C.

By Neolithic (New Stone Age) times, the cave-dwellers and semi-nomadic hunters had given way to more settled farming communities in causewayed camps such as that at Windmill Hill, near Avebury. Near their settlements they set up large communal tombs for their dead. These long barrows are still to be seen across the southern counties, the most impressive being West Kennet in Wiltshire: the mound, 350 feet long, was dug out of its two parallel ditches, and piled over a chamber of stone slabs. Successive generations of corpses were packed in until the tomb was full, when its east end was sealed with huge standing stones.

With the arrival of newcomers from the western Mediterranean,

(1)

(2)

(1)

(2)

(1) Bronze Age necklace from a barrow tomb at Upton Lovell, Wiltshire.

(2) Early Bronze Age gold plate, 1800–1400 B.C. from Wilsford barrow cemetery, Wiltshire.

these communal graves gave way to individual burials. Each body was buried in a crouching position, accompanied by a stylised drinking-pot—a ritual which has led to the group of peoples being called the Beaker Folk. They brought with them simple bronze tools but seem to have done little metal-working themselves, continuing to rely on knapped flint for domestic and farm implements, daggers and arrowheads.

Stonehenge

It was at this time that Britain's most awe-inspiring megalithic monument, Stonehenge, began to take the shape we know today. The earliest construction was no more than a ring of pits, many containing cremated human bones, encircled by a bank and shallow ditch, with three stones guarding an entrance through the bank. Some five hundred years passed before the Beaker Folk set up inside these earthworks a double circle of bluestones whose appearance on Salisbury Plain has fascinated conflicting theorists ever since.

These four-ton slabs originated in the Prescelly Hills of South Wales, and could have been shipped across the Bristol Channel and up the river Avon on rafts, and then dragged twenty miles overland on tree-trunk rollers. Recent findings about this region during the Ice Age suggest the alternative possibility that the bluestone could have been carried from Wales by the ice flow; but it is doubtful that this controversy can ever be happily settled.

Another wave of invaders crossed the Channel about 1500 B.C. and, though few in number, by force of superior weapons dispossessed or assimilated the Beaker Folk. These founders of the Wessex Culture were traders and designers of some discernment. They sported Scandinavian amber, Egyptian beads, and wrought gold from Ireland; their ornaments show influences of the craftsmanship of Mycenae, one of the most ancient Greek cultures. In Britain they developed the skills of the new Bronze Age. The prehistoric industrial revolution had begun with the extraction and working of copper from hillside mines, but experiment soon produced a superior alloy when tin was added to make bronze. Each community now would have its smith, and other itinerant craftsmen shared their knowledge between the communities. And Britain was rich in tin.

It was this more advanced society which brought fifty-ton sarsen (local sandstone) blocks from the Marlborough Downs and erected a circle and horseshoe at Stonehenge, dressing and arranging the stones with a precision also testifying to Greek influence. Finally there was a rearrangement of the bluestones within the sarsen pattern.

At each stage of its history the monument has undoubtedly been a site of great religious significance. The alignment of the central bluestone, known as the Altar Stone, with the Heel Stone or Hele Stone over which the sun rises on midsummer morning indicates some primitive sun-worship rite. Attempts have been made to demonstrate its function as a calendar, incorporating astronomical and even astrological features, but the many remodellings of the stone patterns at one time and another make it difficult to draw any firm conclusions. The so-called Slaughter Stone at the entrance to the earthwork is unlikely ever to have been used for human sacrifice,

(1) Maiden Castle hill-fort, Dorset. Parts of the defences date from 3000 B.C.

(2) Celtic field system and farming settlement, Smacam Down, Dorset.

(3) Iron Age craftsmanship: gold and silver alloy collar, 1st century B.C.

(1)

(2)

and there is little evidence for its popular association with rituals of the Druids, the priestly caste of the next tide to break on these shores.

The Celts

The Celts of Central Europe had for some time been seizing territories in the south or retreating westwards under the harassment of expanding Germanic tribes. Between 1000 and 500 B.C. they began to seek refuge in Britain, first in isolated groups causing little trouble to their neighbours, and then in more aggressive formations. Their warrior chiefs were formidably armed with iron swords and daggers, often with lavish bronze ornamentation, and led their troops in two-wheeled chariots of Etruscan style, which were buried with them when they died.

They established tribal centres in the Yorkshire Wolds and Northumberland, across southern England, and as far west as Wales. In some areas there was intermarriage with the people they were supplanting; and a lot of less peaceful absorption. From stockaded hill-forts with multiple grass or stone ramparts such as Maiden Castle in Dorset the invaders launched attacks on earlier settlers and rival tribes. Other strongholds were the crannogs or lake villages shielded by water instead of earthworks, of which the most celebrated is Glastonbury.

Celtic farmers imposed great changes on the face of the countryside. In place of the small, haphazard areas cultivated by their predecessors, they laid out large rectangular fields and terraces. The boundaries of these Celtic fields, or lynchets, were marked by double

(1) Roman mosaic showing cupids as gladiators, Bignor, Sussex.

(2) Hadrian's Wall at Housesteads, Northumberland. It is named after the Roman Emperor Hadrian who ordered 73 miles of wall to be built in A.D. 122–30 as a defence against the Picts.

(1)

(2)

ditches or occasionally, as in Cornwall, by rough drystone walls, and traces of their basic pattern are still easy to detect today.

Industry also flourished. From a country roughly corresponding to modern Syria and the Lebanon came the Phoenicians in search of tin, rare in the eastern Mediterranean and now being mined and smelted in south-west Britain for export via the busy trading centre of Ictis—probably St Michael's Mount.

By the time the Roman greed for conquest and colonisation was threatening the westernmost rim of Europe, iron was more in demand than tin. Britain was rich in iron ore also; but this was not the main reason for the first Roman assault on the country.

The Romans

Among those continuing to seek land in Britain were the Belgae, one of the most warlike of the Celtic tribes. In Gaul they had fought bitterly against the Romans, and when Julius Caesar finally subdued them he decided to teach a sharp lesson to those kinsmen who had helped them from Britain.

In 55 B.C. a force of ten thousand men landed in Kent. The cavalry transports which formed part of the invasion fleet were prevented from joining the main force by the tides, and the waiting tribesmen fought a number of battles with the legionaries. Although the Celts were no match for the Romans, Caesar was forced to withdraw; a storm had wrecked many of his beached ships, and he sailed for France as soon as he had carried out repairs. He spent a year in further preparations and then tried again with picked soldiers from five legions. In perfect weather he sailed from Boulogne and made an unopposed landing. Again his ships were badly damaged in a storm while at anchor, but this time he did not retreat but marched on Wheathampstead, the hill-fort of Cassivellaunus, most powerful of the Celtic kings, harried all the way by guerrilla tactics.

After savage fighting the Britons asked for peace. Caesar demanded guarantees of a regular tribute to be paid to Rome; promised protection to other tribes oppressed by the Belgae; and took a number of prisoners back as hostages. The campaign had been little more than a gesture: during the ensuing century the only Romans who visited Britain were peaceful traders.

The serious business of bringing the country completely under Roman rule did not begin until A.D. 43, when an army sent by Claudius landed near Richborough. It was a good time to strike. The Belgic warlords had grown more aggressive and were even more cordially detested by neighbouring tribes. The greatest of them was Cunobelinus (Shakespeare's Cymbeline), the chief of the Catuvellauni in Hertfordshire and the Trinovantes in Essex, who set up his capital and trading centre at Camulodunum (Colchester) and was the acknowledged overlord of a large part of southern England. When he died his riches attracted the envy both of the Romans and of an exiled prince called Bericus, who appealed to Claudius for Roman aid in restoring him to his birthright.

When the Romans responded, their main opposition came from the two sons of Cunobelinus, Togodumnus and Caratacus. Togodumnus died early in the campaign, but Caratacus made a gallant

15

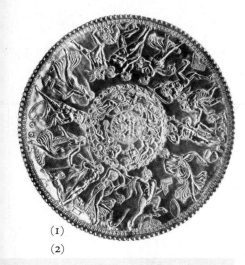

stand at the river Medway, where the battle raged for two days, a rare thing in ancient warfare. After his defeat he fled to Wales, where he organised opposition to Rome for eight years, but was eventually captured and taken in chains with his family to Rome. There his proud bearing and refusal to be cowed impressed even Claudius, who granted him his life, and Caratacus lived thereafter in honourable captivity in Rome.

Two independent states in southern England, who had taken no part in the war, immediately submitted to Claudius. The first of these client kingdoms was that of the Regni, ruled by a king named Cogidubnus from his capital of Noviomagus (Chichester). So co-operative was Cogidubnus with the Romans that Claudius enlarged his kingdom and conferred on him the title of King and Legate to the Emperor in Britain, an unusual honour for a minor client king. Cogidubnus himself became a Roman citizen and took the name of Tiberius Claudius Cogidubnus. The esteem in which he was held is shown by the sumptuous palace he was able to build for himself at Fishbourne, where he held court until his death at the age of about eighty.

The warrior queen
The other Celtic tribe to settle for peaceful co-existence with the invaders was that of the Iceni in East Anglia. When their king died in A.D. 60 he nominated the Emperor Nero co-heir with his widow and daughters. By now, however, the Romans felt secure enough to flout their dead ally's wishes, and plundered both his kingdom and his household, raping his daughters and flogging his widow.

The tribe rose in outrage and stormed Camulodunum, where retired legionaries lived in veterans' homes with small plots of land. Led by the vengeful widow, Queen Boudicca or Boadicea, with her daughters beside her in a chariot whose axles sprouted knife-blades, they massacred the small community and its inadequate garrison, marched on Londinium and completely destroyed it, and then went on to further destruction in Verulam (St Albans). Some seventy thousand people are said to have died in these three towns. Suetonius Paulinus, governor of Britain at the time, was in Anglesey destroying the Druid community there, but hastened back to deal with this threat.

'Win the battle or perish!' So, according to the Roman historian Tacitus, Boudicca exhorted her troops. 'That is what I, a woman, intend to do. Let the men live in slavery if they wish!'

The trained legionaries, with a large cavalry force, proved too much for the over-confident Britons, and boasted later of slaughtering eighty thousand, including women and children who had come to enjoy the spectacle. Boudicca took poison. Many a mysterious hummock in eastern England is reputed to be her secret burial place.

The Brigantes in the Pennines, after more than twenty years of uneasy peace and co-operation with Rome under their queen, Cartimandua, eventually revolted, while the Silures in southern Wales were always a thorn in the Roman side. Between A.D. 71 and 74 the Brigantes were systematically conquered, and it was then the turn first of the Silures and then of the Ordovices in central and northern Wales. Agricola, who became governor of Britain in A.D. 78, com-

(1) 4th-century A.D. silver Neptune dish from Mildenhall, Suffolk.

(2) Roman pottery from Aldborough, Yorkshire.

(3) Detail from Trajan's column showing Roman ships.

(1)

pleted the conquest of the Ordovices in the same year, planted a network of forts and roads in Brigantia the following year, and in A.D. 80 began to advance into Scotland. Building forts to hold the countryside as he went, his campaign reached its climax in 83, when he fought and destroyed the assembled armies of Scotland at the battle of Mons Graupius. In 84, however, he was recalled by the Emperor Domitian and the chance of making the whole of Britain a province of the Roman Empire was lost for ever.

The Picts in Scotland made continual forays for a number of years over the frontier into Roman Britain until, during a visit in A.D. 121 or 122, the Emperor Hadrian decreed the building of a barrier ten feet thick across the country between what are now Wallsend-on-Tyne and Bowness-on-Solway. This wall had a castle every mile, and sixteen larger forts with sizeable garrisons at irregular intervals.

Later, fortifications were built even further north between the Forth and the Clyde in A.D. 142, but this Antonine Wall, a smaller and weaker defence, was overrun so easily and so often that little more than forty years later it was evacuated and its defenders fell back to Hadrian's Wall, which remained in use until the late fourth century. In 368 the Picts, Scots, Saxons and Franks joined forces to invade Britain, and the wall was overrun; it was restored, with some of its buildings, the following year, but in 383 the wall was again overwhelmed and then abandoned, and Rome was never again able to re-establish full control in Britain.

Imperial Province

Within the occupied zone itself the Romans adapted old settlements to their own tastes and designed new ones. Their cities were built on a grid plan and linked by straight roads, often raised on firm embankments with drainage ditches on either side. In these garrison and administrative centres were established shops, temples, amphitheatres, barracks, potteries, glassworks, mints and bath-houses. Wide areas of the Fens were drained by a network of channels to facilitate large-scale farming. Sheep imported from Gaul multiplied

(1) Bronze head of Hadrian, A.D. 117–38, found in the Thames at London Bridge.

(2) Roman road at Wensleydale, Yorkshire.

(3)

on the South Downs. Lead was mined in the Pennines, Derbyshire and Flintshire; lead and silver in the Mendips. Ironworks flourished in the Weald: one battery of more than thirty small furnaces was excavated in the early 1970s near Broadfield in Sussex.

Eboracum (York) was the military capital, important enough for Constantine to be proclaimed Emperor there in A.D. 306. The Multi-angular Tower, one of the corner towers in the town wall built by the Emperor Septimius Severus in about A.D. 200, survives to this day. Caerleon watched over the southern stretches of the Welsh Marches; on the northern border was Chester, then known as Deva, head-quarters of a legion from A.D. 70 until the end of Roman rule. London grew fast as a trading centre. A luxurious spa grew up around the warm springs of Aquae Sulis (Bath), with a forum and a temple dedicated jointly to the Celtic and Roman deities, Sul and Minerva.

Shrewd Britons soon found the advantages of collaboration. The Roman régime offered security and a fair degree of everyday physical comfort. Even slaves lived under conditions which serfs of later centuries would have envied. Agricola thought it good policy to encourage sons of native chiefs to study Roman arts and crafts and, according to Tacitus, 'expressed a preference for British natural ability over the trained skill of the Gauls'. Free-born men granted Imperial citizenship were increasingly encouraged to handle their own local government. Taxes were levied for national defence against barbarians within and without, doubtless accompanied by a Latin version of twentieth-century grumbling on the value of what was received or not received in exchange for these dues.

(1) The Great Bath at Bath, Somerset, where the Romans bathed in hot mineral-spring water. It was to be roofed and surrounded by dressing-rooms.

(2) Head of the Roman goddess Minerva from Bath. It is made of bronze, hollow-cast and gilded.

(3) Stone head of Medusa from Bath, originally the centrepiece of the Roman temple pediment.

(1)

(2)

(1) Roman relief from Walbrook showing the god Mithras slaying a sacrificial bull.

(2) Forts of the Saxon Shore in the 5th century: Bradwell, Dover, Lympne, Brancaster, Burgh, Reculver, Richborough, Pevensey, Portchester.

In the second century each community had also to raise auxiliary troops, or *numeri*, to supplement the legions. For the recruits this meant a posting away from home. To avoid any clash of loyalties, British soldiers were sent to central Europe, while the auxiliaries in Britain itself came from provinces as far away as Africa and Asia Minor. Many married local women and settled down with them after discharge from the army.

By the early fourth century Britain might have been described as a model protectorate. Successful officials and businessmen built luxury villas, gave their sons a Latin education, and worshipped alongside the Romans. Apart from their virulent hatred of the Druids, whom they rapidly exterminated, the Romans tolerated the religious beliefs of others and allowed tribal gods to be revered beside their own. Then Constantine fostered the spread of Christianity throughout the Empire, and before long the Celtic peasantry were the only large group of pagans remaining in the British provinces.

Decline and fall

The orderly way of life was menaced by disorder when Germanic barbarians, already harassing the Romans on the mainland, began to send raiders down the British coast. Theodosius, a general who was later to become emperor, was given the title of Count of the Saxon Shore and set to work renewing old fortifications and setting up new forts along the eastern seaboard. To strengthen the garrisons he took the dangerous step of hiring Angles and Saxons as mercenaries. The pick of the legions were already being recalled to deal with the threat

(1)

to Rome and its nearer provinces. Now, fatally, the main defenders of Britain were brothers and cousins of those most likely to be Britain's enemies.

Picts and Scots seized the opportunity to renew their attacks. The Irish raided Wales and the north-west. In one of their swoops they carried away from his father's villa near the Severn a young man later to be canonised as St Patrick. He was sold into slavery, but escaped after six years and returned to study for the priesthood. Because of his knowledge of the Irish language, the Pope sent him back to the land of his captivity as a missionary. Patrick must have been a persuasive preacher, for within a decade he had converted almost the entire island to Christianity.

In the rest of Britain, the Christian religion and all else that had been achieved in more than three and a half centuries of Roman rule were at the mercy of imported mercenaries, deserters from the demoralised remnant of the regular army, and the expected wave of new invaders. The Romans had transformed a warrior race into a fairly peaceable society of complacent colonials, and now left them to cope as best they could with another race of warriors.

(1) Portchester castle, Hampshire: an important stronghold originally built by the Romans. Today the grandeur of Henry I's keep, built about 1120, is still intact.

(2) The Venerable Bede: the great scholar and historian of Anglo-Saxon England.

The Anglo~Saxons

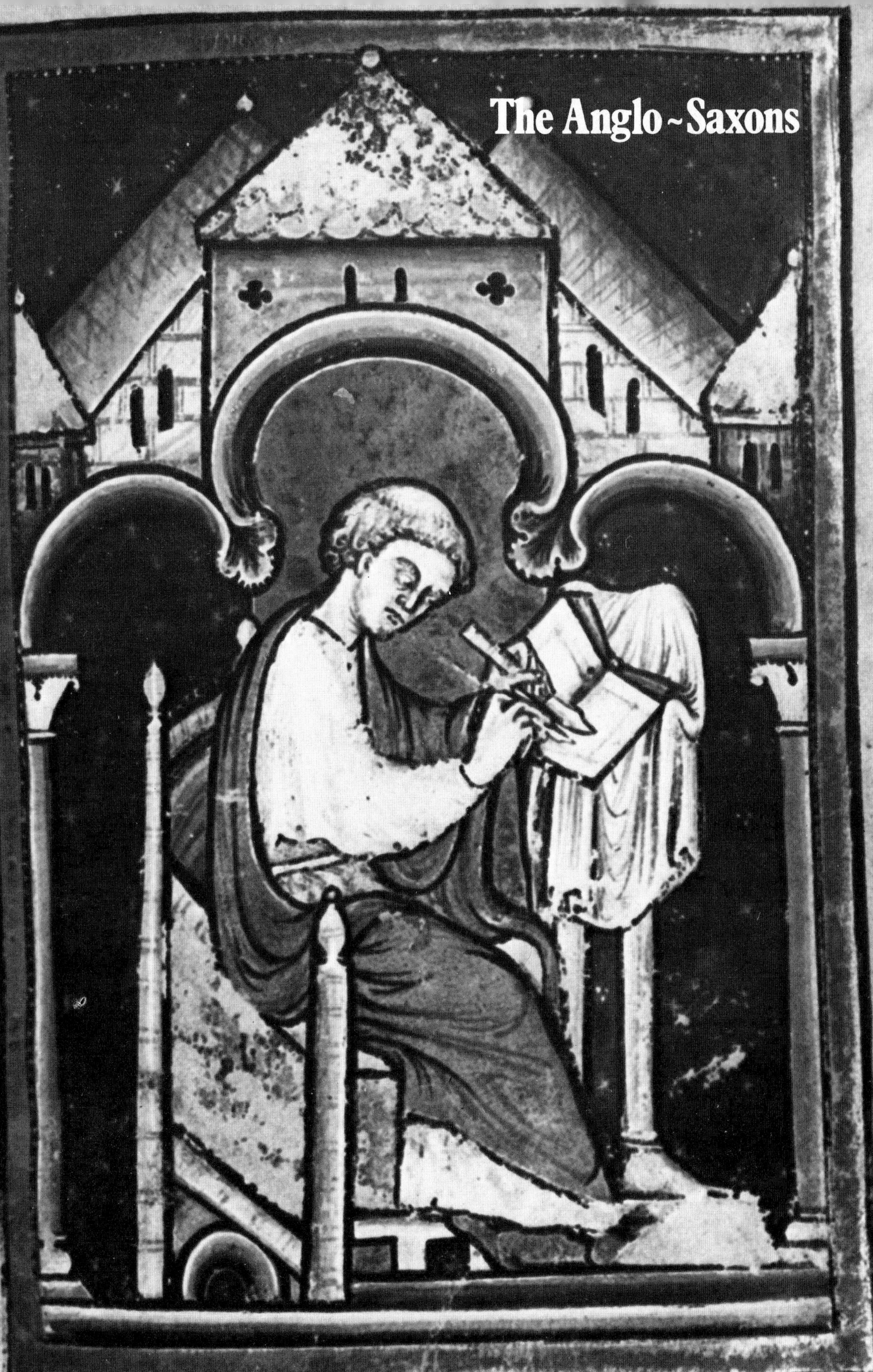

The Anglo~Saxons

Anglo-Saxon building, showing construction of the biblical Tower of Babel.

The years between about 450 and 1066 seem, from our distant viewpoint, to have been dark ages of almost unabated conflict, of squabbles between petty kingdoms and sudden assaults by new invaders. Into the power vacuum left by the Romans there came new tribes no longer content with sporadic coastal raids but eager to take permanent possession of fertile land.

In fact many of the newcomers were in favour of quiet infiltration and settlement if they could achieve this without fighting. But each lull, during which they ploughed their land, cleared the forest, pastured their swine, wove their homespun clothes and drank their ale and mead in hall or hut, was inexorably followed by some outbreak of hostilities against an aggressive neighbour, a fresh intruder, or the war-band of an ambitious leader attempting to shape individual communities into a new kingdom.

Angles, Saxons and Jutes

Hengist and Horsa were two chieftains of the Jutes, a tribe originating, according to the most likely view, from Frisia, the coastal districts of northern Holland and north-western Germany. Their arrival on the Kent coast with three longships full of fighting men was not, initially, an invasion: they came by invitation. Vortigern, originally a local Welsh king, ruled a large tract of the south of England, with his authority stretching as far east as Kent. He became alarmed by the anarchy in the north, and to counter the growing danger from the Picts he offered the Jutes a grant of land on the Isle of Thanet in return for their military services in the protection of that part of the coast.

The newcomers did repel an enemy attack but also noted, according to the Venerable Bede in his eighth-century *History of the English Church and People*, that the other defenders were a cowardly lot. They therefore sent messages to friends and relations at home regarding the land and loot which were there for the taking. There was a clash with Vortigern in which Horsa was killed, but Hengist soon took over the whole of Kent.

Angles from Schleswig-Holstein and Saxons from the region between the Elbe and the Rhine now arrived in force. The Saxons established themselves in Essex, Middlesex, Sussex and Wessex (East, Middle, South and West Saxons), while the Angles occupied Norfolk and Suffolk (North Folk and South Folk). At the same time they were pushing further inland up the navigable reaches of the Thames, the Trent, the Ouse and the Humber with small squadrons of ships whose crews became the founders of new communities. Lighter craft found their way across the Fens, reverting to swamp since being abandoned by the Romans, to firmer ground beyond.

(1)

Although the Angles gave their name to the country, Angle-land becoming England, they were by no means the dominant partners. In spite of inter-tribal strife, the Angles, Saxons and Jutes shared a common background and culture which make it reasonable to refer to this strain in our ancestry as Anglo-Saxon.

If the Britons, both Romano-British and Celts, had been united they might have mounted an effective opposition to these various factions. Instead, they offered only scattered, unco-ordinated resistance and were butchered or driven into the extreme fastnesses of Wales and Cornwall. Many fled over the Channel and gave their name to Brittany, where the Breton tongue still has close affinities with Welsh and the remaining echoes of old Cornish idiom.

There was only one period during which it looked as if the steady mopping-up of land and people by the invaders might be checked. A survivor of the last days of Roman influence and education, Ambrosius Aurelianus, rallied some of his more courageous countrymen and inflicted some telling defeats on the enemy. He was followed by another leader about whose name—if it was indeed his true name —has accrued the most stirring and poetic collection of legends in the history of the British Isles.

The once and future king

This 'King' Arthur was credited with well-nigh magical powers. He was in Wales one moment, on Hadrian's Wall the next. He struck at the Angles this week, at the Saxons in the far west of the country next week. Later medieval chroniclers, particularly Geoffrey of Monmouth in the mid-twelfth century, as well as troubadours in France, where the legend was extremely popular, added chivalrous touches and gave names to his gallant company of knights. This overcolourful myth, however, seems to be based upon fact. Arthur could well have maintained a contingent of mailed cavalry on Roman lines, and with the memory of Roman training and discipline behind them they would have presented a fearsome appearance to Anglo-Saxon foot soldiers, who relied on brute force rather than strategy.

Whoever this Arthur may have been, and whether he was one leader or a symbolic fusion of several still defending Christianised

(2)

(1) A Tudor representation of King Arthur's round table hangs in the Castle Hall, Winchester.

(2) Tintagel castle: upper and lower ward from the island. The castle was built in the 12th century on a site linked in legend with King Arthur.

(1) Silver penny with head of King Offa of Mercia, *c.* A.D. 790.

(2) Saxon woman seeking justice from the king.

(3) Fields at Braunton, Devon, showing strip divisions of early farming.

Roman Britain against the barbarism of the Dark Ages, it is certain that old hill-forts were repaired and that a mighty battle took place at Mons Badonicus somewhere between 490 and 516 which routed the pagans so decisively that there was a breathing-space of some forty years before they reasserted themselves.

Arthur was said to have died in battle against one of his own knights, Medraut, at Camlann, a site never satisfactorily identified, and to have been borne away to the Isle of Avalon. There he will lie until recalled by his country in the hour of its greatest need.

Glastonbury has long been associated with this ghostly island. Shortly after the death of Henry II in 1189 it was reported that the monks had found a coffin containing the bones of King Arthur and Queen Guinevere and had placed them in a casket among the abbey's treasures. But then in 1278 another tomb opened in the presence of Edward I and Queen Eleanor was declared to hold the bones of Arthur and his queen, which were wrapped in silk and once more interred. The tomb was destroyed during the Reformation, but its base was rediscovered in 1931.

Many kingdoms

With organised resistance ended, new federations shaped themselves out of the old British and Roman regions. Between Forth and Humber, two minor kingdoms were amalgamated by Ethelfrith early in the seventh century into one Northumbria, also incorporating large areas of the north-west. For a long time it was the most powerful grouping in the land but was gradually superseded by the Midland kingdom of Mercia, whose eighth-century ruler, Offa, built the huge earthwork of Offa's Dyke to keep the Welsh at bay and grandiloquently styled himself king of the English.

In the south the Saxons quarrelled among themselves for supremacy, until in the ninth century Egbert of Wessex finally annexed Kent and the lands of the south and east Saxons. For a time Egbert also ruled over Mercia and exercised a vague suzerainty over Northumberland. From then on the prestige of Wessex rose until it became usual to recognise its king as *Bretwalda*, the ruler of Britain with seniority over his northern fellows.

(1)

(2)

(1) Saxon king and council showing hangman and victim.

(2) Anglo-Saxon war-bands in action.

(2)

Britons who were prepared to accept the Anglo-Saxon way of life, as their forebears had accepted Roman dominion, worked warily alongside the new rulers or, if circumstances allowed, kept their distance and hoped to be left alone. The Saxons were by custom lowland farmers, developing open strip fields on land reclaimed from the forest, while the Britons took to the hills. The two strands could survive side by side without too much troublesome tangling. Some British merchants and landowners rebuilt their fortunes and even began to play a part in the royal households.

Kings depended on the allegiance and physical strength of followers who gave their services in return for gifts of land and a share in plunder. The king maintained his prestige and prosperity by ensuring that his own share was always the largest. He settled feuds, led hunting expeditions, supervised the administration of laws and of military ventures, collected rents and dues to keep up his retinue, and offered bounteous hospitality in his royal hall.

The king was not an absolute monarch. Although the Saxons revered the tradition of royal lineage, the advisory council, or *Witan*, had the power to choose one member of a royal family rather than another if this seemed better for the future of the realm. *Ealdormen*, the earliest lords-lieutenant, watched over the king's domains but also assessed the worth of his patronage to themselves. His immediate attendants, *gesiths* or companions, were chosen from high-ranking military or landowning families; in later times, when rulers had increased in power and prestige, these retainers were known as *thegnes*. Below came the *ceorls*, who raised duties and, when necessary, an army for their earl or king.

There was no large standing army. Many leaders relied on small, highly trained, well-equipped war-bands for immediate action at any time. When a more substantial force was needed it was supplied by the part-time services of able-bodied men working the land: to conscript too many at one time, or draw too many from one area at a time, would dislocate the farming cycle on which the Anglo-Saxon economy largely depended. Nevertheless, every freeman knew that in an emergency, such as an invasion, he would be expected to down tools and pick up weapons for service in the fighting forces, or *fyrd*, for in such circumstances he knew that defeat meant slavery for himself and his family.

(2)

(1)

(3)

Other obligations included two or three days' work a week for the lord from whom the yeoman received his land, livestock and supplies. If he fell out with one master, there was no bar to his seeking another. Hardship arose only when, after some acute drought or famine, or after defeat in some local conflict, farm-workers and defeated soldiers found themselves with no home and no master. Then a man and his family might seek shelter with any new lord prepared to take them in, not as freemen but all too often as slaves. If such a slave were killed, by accident or outright murder, the only charge in law was that of destruction of property.

The king and his attendants might base themselves on some strategically placed town, but there was rarely a formal court. Instead, the king travelled the country, dispensing justice as he went and collecting his rents and dues. Where these were paid in kind, he ate what was owed to him. This peripatetic administration allowed him to keep a weather-eye on what was going on throughout his kingdom.

The revival of Christianity

Paganism had driven most British Christians into hiding or had sapped their faith. Only on the fringes of the new barbarism did monkish communities keep belief alive. St Columba built churches in Ireland, and then with a few chosen companions founded a monastery on the island of Iona, off the western coast of Scotland, from which he operated as 'Apostle of the Highlands'. Rome, beset by Vandals and other destroyers, had neither the time nor the resources to succour the remoter members of its flock. It was not until the end of the sixth century that Pope Gregory I thought the time propitious to send a missionary expedition into the heart of England itself.

He chose a prior, Augustine, to lead forty monks and preach the word of God to the heathen. They set out in good heart, but while crossing Europe heard such terrifying reports of the ferocity of the English that his companions sent Augustine back to Rome to plead for their release from the task. The Pope, regretting that his own office prevented his working at their side, wrote an encouraging

(1) Reconstructed helmet and (2) clasp worked in gold, garnets and glass from the ship burial at Sutton Hoo, Suffolk, 7th century A.D.

(3) St Cuthbert receives a book from King Aethelstan; title-page from Bede's Life of St Cuthbert.

26

(1)

(2)

(3)

letter and urged them to continue, at the same time giving the monks letters requesting aid from the kings and clergy through whose lands they would pass in Gaul.

They landed in the Isle of Thanet and were met by King Ethelbert of Kent, who fortunately had a Christian wife. Impressed by Augustine's preaching, he granted the evangelists freedom to make converts if they could do so. They were provided with accommodation in Canterbury, and so impressed Ethelbert with their holy lives and teaching that in due course he succumbed and was baptised. On the Pope's command, Augustine visited Arles in 597 in order to be consecrated archbishop of the English nation, and returned to carry on his work.

The Celtic missionaries took advantage of the favourable religious climate. By 634 the monk Aidan from Iona was preaching throughout Northumbria, whose King Oswald had become a Christian during years of exile on the island. One of Aidan's disciples, St Chad, bore the gospel on through Mercia. Further missionaries were trained in the monastery of Lindisfarne, which Aidan built and of which he became abbot.

There were some awkward sectarian differences between the Celts and the teachers from Rome. One body owed ultimate allegiance to the Pope; the other consisted of a number of independent monasteries, with quite different rules from those of the Roman orders. They even celebrated Easter according to different calendars. At the Synod of Whitby in 663 the two factions met. Powerful arguments for the Pope's divine authority were advanced, opposed by the then abbot of Lindisfarne and others favouring Celtic independence. The meeting ended with general agreement with Rome on the points at issue, though it was followed by the withdrawal of many of the Celtic missionaries to Iona. A final tidying up of outstanding problems was achieved by Theodore of Tarsus, appointed by the Pope as archbishop in 668, who restored ecclesiastical order in England and called the first Council of the whole of the English Church at Hertford in 672.

The Celts continued to make outstanding contributions to the work of the Church. St Cuthbert, born in Northumbria of Scottish parents,

(1) Muireadach's Cross, Monasterboice, Co. Louth, is 17ft. 8in. tall and was carved from a single piece of sandstone in the 10th century.

(2) The early Celtic monastery on Skellig Michael, Co. Kerry, an island seven miles west of Bollus Head.

(3) Carved panel of a 7th-century casket from Northumbria, showing both pagan and Christian scenes.

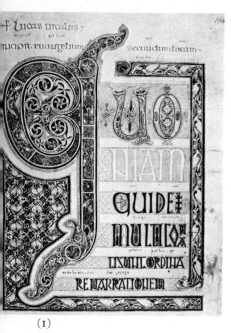

(1)

was for a time a hermit before becoming bishop of Lindisfarne—a post which he then resigned in favour of the solitary, meditative life. In his memory his successor, Eadfrith, began the compilation of the Lindisfarne Gospels, a richly illuminated book with decoration of extraordinary beauty and intricacy, bound in gold with an inlay of precious stones by a hermit named Billfrith. Later still a priest named Aldred added a Saxon rendering of the original Latin. But by then the book was no longer at Lindisfarne: it had been carried away with other treasures and holy relics, including the body of St Cuthbert in his coffin, by monks fleeing before yet another wave of pagans.

The Vikings

The Anglo-Saxon Chronicle, a collection of annals written by various monastic scholars between the ninth and twelfth centuries, in English rather than the customary Latin, recorded that in early 793 there had been grim portents through the land. There were high winds and lightning flashes, fiery dragons were seen flying in the air, and drops of blood dripped from the roof of St Peter's church in York. After all this came a famine.

In June came the Norsemen.

In a sudden pirate raid on the Holy Island, Lindisfarne, these Vikings drowned or beat in the skulls of some monks and carried others away to slavery, along with a rich haul of valuables. Attracted by the wealth of other religious foundations, the dragon-prowed longships sought out Wearmouth and Jarrow, where the Venerable Bede had worked on his histories; fell upon the shrine of St Patrick in the Isle of Man; and several times ravaged Iona, derisive of all gods save Odin and his warlike comrades in the Nordic pantheon.

Most of these early attacks were private-enterprise forays by petty chieftains who, unable to provide well enough for families and re-

(2)

(3)

(4)

tainers on their bleak Scandinavian lands, sought easy loot from prospering England. They roved bloodily in the summer, and wintered in their *viks* or *fjords*. Then larger forces, greedy for the land itself, were launched in more sustained assaults.

King Godfred of Denmark plunged deep into Europe, forcing Charlemagne to set up a whole new system of land and sea defences. Danes, Swedes and Norwegians robbed and traded as far as the Mediterranean and Constantinople. The Orkneys, Shetlands and Faeroes were annexed, and from them prolonged attacks were directed at Scotland and Ireland. In 839 Turgeis, a Norwegian chieftain, founded Dublin and proclaimed himself 'king of all foreigners in Ireland'. He tried to substitute pagan rites for those in the archbishopric of Armagh, but aroused such antagonism that he was drowned in a loch. For a while the Irish succeeded in playing off Danes and Norwegians against each other, but in the end the country was shared out between two Norwegian brothers who kept the Irish firmly subjugated.

From 835 onwards the Danes had been making regular sallies up the Thames, and during the next two decades used Thanet and Sheppey as bases for deeper penetration. Soon they were also coming in through East Anglia. The Saxon kingdoms proved incapable of assembling a powerful enough communal force to stem the onslaught of the 'great heathen host' of 865. Northumbria fell, and from York the great army marched into Mercia, which made several attempts to buy them off before being finally overrun.

In 870 the pious young King Edmund of East Anglia was defeated in a battle near Thetford and forced to flee into Suffolk. Legend has it that, hotly pursued, he hid under a bridge by what is now the village of Hoxne, but was betrayed by a young bride on her way from her wedding-feast who saw the flash of his golden spurs in the

(1) Lindisfarne Gospels: St Luke's Gospel title-page. These beautiful Gospels were written and illuminated by Eadfrith, bishop of Lindisfarne from 698 to 721.

(2) St Dunstan as a scribe. As archbishop of Canterbury in the 10th century he encouraged the reform of the monasteries.

(3) Carved head from the Viking ceremonial wagon found at Oseberg, Norway.

(4) Prow of the famous Oseberg Viking ship during excavation.

(5) Picture-stone from Tjängvide, Sweden, 9th century A.D. The lower panel shows a Viking warship with armed men aboard; the upper panel depicts figures from Norse mythology, including the god Odin's eight-legged steed, Sleipnir.

(5)

29

stream. Dragged out, Edmund was offered his life if he would recant his Christian beliefs and swear fealty to the Danish leader and his gods. He refused and so was bound to an oak tree and used for target practice by Danish archers. After this his head was cut off and thrown into a bush. His followers, finding only the decapitated body, reported that they were led to the missing head by a wolf. The remains were eventually housed in the town which from then on carried the martyr's name: St Edmundsbury, later Bury St Edmunds.

Alfred the Great

With eastern and middle England overrun, the Danes turned their full energies towards Wessex, whose King Ethelred marched to meet them at Reading. Forced to retreat, he prepared a new stand at Ashdown, but insisted on completing lengthy prayers before giving battle. His younger brother Alfred impatiently took charge, fought 'like a wild boar', and was already beating the Danes off when Ethelred arrived to complete the rout.

When Ethelred died soon after, Alfred was unanimously acclaimed king. A devout young man who would have preferred to devote his life to scholarship rather than warfare, he realised that the survival of his beliefs depended upon the military survival of his country, and that the Danes had to be brought to a standstill if not wholly expelled.

His victory at Ashdown was not soon to be repeated. An influx of settlers swelled the ranks of the invaders, and Alfred was driven into hiding on the Isle of Athelney in the Somerset marshes. Slowly and stealthily he assembled an army and came out at last to defeat the Danes at the battle of Edington in 878, driving them back into Chippenham and besieging them there until King Guthrum surrendered.

Guthrum and his leading supporters, impressed by Alfred's clemency after the submission, agreed to be baptised, with Alfred acting as godfather. By the Peace of Wedmore the two kings agreed

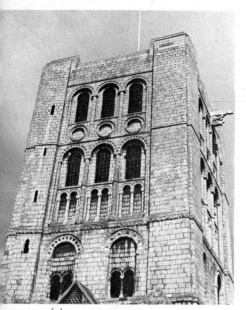

(1)

(2)

(1) Norman tower at Bury St Edmunds, Suffolk.

(2) Ethelred 'the Unready', 978–1016.

(3) Anglo-Saxon silver brooch depicting the five senses (the Fuller brooch); 9th century.

(3)

The 10th-century Saxon church of St Lawrence, Bradford-on-Avon.

on a rough division of England which represented their respective spheres of interest. Most of the Danes were glad to settle down to farm their new lands and develop trade with the continent. However, a new Danish army arrived in 884 which posed a new threat, and the help it received from the Danes of East Anglia convinced Alfred that further steps had to be taken. In 886 he moved forward and captured London, which immediately became a symbolic national centre of resistance to the Danes. Its capture also led to Alfred becoming the natural leader of all the Anglo-Saxons, and to an acceptance of his overlordship by the rulers outside Wessex.

The treaty resulting from the war of 886, known as 'Alfred and Guthrum's Peace', defined the boundary between the two kingdoms, the eastern frontier of Alfred's territory being formed by the river Lea and Watling Street. The area to the east of this line was known as the 'Danelaw'. Within the Danelaw many Danish words and customs took root, while a predominantly Norwegian influx from Ireland and the Hebrides left Norse traces in the north-west. Place-names ending in 'by' and 'thorpe' (originally 'torp') come from the Danish words for a town or village; 'toft' denotes a homestead, 'hulm' or 'holm' an islet. The makeshift shelters built on moors and hillsides for cattle were called 'booths' whence Bootham and Booth-by, among others. The Ridings of Yorkshire recall the Danish 'thrithings' or thirds. Names ending in 'gill' recall the Norse for a narrow ravine; 'breck' is a slope, or hillside.

South of the border, Alfred was busy building a fleet to guard his coasts, and forts to watch over his land. So that men would not be kept too long from their farms he altered the constitution of the fyrd and arranged a rota for periods of service. At the same time he took advantage of the peace, precarious as it might be, to encourage the spread of learning and fine craftsmanship. When he was almost forty he applied himself to learning Latin, and succeeded well enough to translate major Latin works into English as a basis for both religious and secular education.

In 892 a large force of wandering Vikings thrown out by the Franks attacked under the leadership of Haesten; as many as 330 ships were needed to transport them, and Haesten had no difficulty in securing a bridgehead on the south coast, later known as Hastings. Avaricious settlers in the Danelaw cheerfully broke their treaties and swarmed south to join him. But Alfred's navy and fortified towns proved their worth, and although intermittent fighting continued throughout his reign he managed to hold the balance.

Alfred the Great, 'England's darling', died in 899 and was buried in his capital of Winchester.

Alfred's legacy

Alfred left to his people the ideal of an England which, whatever its internal dissensions, must learn to become one nation. His immediate successors sought to bring the divisions and subdivisions of the country into harmony, and at the same time to cope not only with Vikings marauding from their own lands but also with attacks from Ireland, where the conversion of many Norsemen to Christianity had done little to quench their fighting ardour.

Matters were made worse by the endeavours of Harald Fairhair to achieve in Norway what Alfred had wished to do in England. Vowing not to cut or comb his hair until he had made himself king of a united Norway, Harald spent ten years driving out all the minor warlords and pirates from his land. When they came back to raid their own shores, he pursued them into their hideouts on Orkney and Shetland. Trounced by their own countrymen, they vented their spleen on England.

Nevertheless, Alfred's successors worked doggedly towards the strengthening and unification of the country, and gradually reconquered the Danelaw. Between 959 and 975 King Edgar 'the Peaceable' was accepted by Saxons and Danes as ruler of all England. In 973 Welsh and Scottish kings met to do homage to him at his long-deferred coronation at Chester. He encouraged the spread of learning, the revival of monastic life, and the ecclesiastical reforms of the saintly Dunstan, who had been made abbot of Glastonbury in 940 and whom Edgar appointed archbishop of Canterbury in 960.

After Edgar's death his son Edward reigned for only three years before being stabbed and replaced by his step-brother Ethelred, who was to be dubbed 'the Unready' or 'the Ill-advised'. He attempted to buy off renewed Danish invasions by imposing a tax on his people to provide bribes known as 'Danegeld'. Then, after inviting Danes into the service of his own household and paying Jómsborg Vikings to assist in the country's defence, in 1002 he capriciously gave orders for the massacre of all Danes in the land. One of the victims of this purge was the sister of Sven Forkbeard, king of Norway and Denmark, who swore revenge. Increasingly devastating raids took place almost yearly thereafter. In 1013 Sven drove Ethelred into abject flight to France, and had himself proclaimed king of England. Six weeks later he was killed in a fall from his horse.

Ethelred returned to England but was so ill that his son Edmund Ironside had to assume responsibility for defence of the country against the claims of Sven's son, Cnut or Canute. At a truce parley after Ethelred's death, Edmund and Cnut agreed to divide the kingdom between them. When Edmund died shortly after, Cnut became king of the entire country. He married Ethelred's widow, embraced Christianity, and when he died in 1035 was buried beside the Saxon kings at Winchester. The brief reigns of his two successors were undistinguished, and in 1042 Ethelred's son Edward was invited to return from Normandy as king.

Edward, known as 'the Confessor' because of his dedication to the Church and current notions of piety, had spent so many years abroad that he felt ill at ease with the powerful Saxon nobles responsible for his return. He married Edith, daughter of the most powerful of them, Earl Godwin of Wessex; but when a visiting friend from Norman days was rudely treated on Godwin's land, he banished the earl and promised to share out the earldom among other old friends. The promises did not get far towards fulfilment: Godwin, playing on the King's unpopularity, and with support from his son Harold, forced Edward to invite him back and restore his possessions.

Retreating from affairs of state, Edward became more and more

(1) Silver penny of Alfred the Great, c. A.D. 886.

(2) Lindisfarne Gospels: title-page for the gospel of St Mark.

imago leonis

OAGI
HAR
R

US
CUS

(1)

absorbed in the building of an abbey at Westminster. It was conse-crated in December 1065, but he was too ill to attend the ceremony and died a week later.

When the year 1066 opened there was some doubt as to who would succeed to the throne of England.

Dukes of Normandy

The English had not been the only ones to pray for deliverance from the fury of the Northmen. Friesland, in the Low Countries, and France had also suffered: Paris was sacked in 845 and on three later occasions. In 912 an attempt to appease one of the most ferocious of the plunderers was made by a grant of land. Rolf the Ganger (pro-perly translated not in the usual form of 'the Wanderer' but as 'the Walker' because he was 'of so stout a growth that no horse could carry him, and wheresoever he went he must go on foot') had been outlawed from Norway by Harald Fairhair because of his piratical activities against his own people. Now, settling down after years of looting along the French coast, he was given a duchy known there-after as Normandy, became a Christian, and changed his name to Rollo.

It was in this duchy that Edward the Confessor spent his time of exile, much of it in the company of his kinsman (though only by marriage through the female line), Duke William, who was a direct descendant of Rollo. After Edward was recalled to England, William visited him and let it be understood afterwards that he had been assured of the Confessor's wish that he should succeed to the throne in due course.

There have always been doubts about the truth of this claim. In any case, during the closing years of the Confessor's contemplative life, effective administration was in the hands of Harold, son of the late Earl Godwin, who was unlikely to slacken his grip any too readily. Between them, he and his three brothers had lordship over most of England apart from Mercia, and would have formed an unconquerable bloc had there not been a rebellion in 1065 against one of them, Tostig, earl of Northumbria. When the case came before the Witan Harold took the side of the new earl, brother of the earl of Mercia, thereby alienating his own brother and laying up trouble for himself later.

When King Edward died the members of the Witan were unani-mous in nominating Harold his successor. They ignored factors of which they must have heard rumour, and of which Harold God-winsson of all people certainly knew.

In 1064 Harold had met Duke William of Normandy. Caught in a storm in the Channel, his ship was wrecked on the Norman coast and he was taken to the court at Rouen. There he became a favoured prisoner, feasting and hunting with his host and even fighting beside William in a conflict with the king of France. Hospitably treated as he was, he nevertheless fretted to get back to England before power should fall into other ambitious hands. Playing on this, William offered him his liberty in exchange for an oath to support his own candidacy when the king of England should die. Harold swore allegiance; but later declared that he had not known at the time that

(2)

(1) King Canute and Queen Emma placing the altar cross of the new abbey at Winchester, early 11th century.

(2) Silver penny of Edward the Confessor, 1065, the founder of Westminster Abbey.

(1)

(2)

the boxes over which he had been tricked into taking the oath contained holy relics. Norse chroniclers also relate that Harold pledged himself to marry William's daughter, but conveniently forgot this once he was safely away from Rouen.

When the time came to honour his pledge, Harold accepted the kingship for himself instead. Well aware that this was inviting an invasion, he called men of the fyrd in from their fields and villages to add to his small professional fighting force of housecarls. He also, though in love with the beautiful Edith Swan-neck, prudently married the sister of the earls of Mercia and Northumbria.

The battle of Stamford Bridge

The previous, now deposed earl of Northumbria, Harold's brother Tostig, foresaw a conflict from which he might profit. Of his own accord he assembled a fleet and began a series of raids on the east coast. With foolhardy arrogance he made one deep thrust inland, and was so violently opposed that he and a few survivors had to flee in their remaining ships to Scotland and then on to Norway. Here King Harald Hardrada—'the Stern'—was all too willing to be persuaded that, as a descendant of Cnut, he was rightful king of England. Tostig offered to help him seize this inheritance.

Harold, with all his troops marshalled in the south awaiting an attack by the enraged Duke William, received the devastating news that Hardrada and Tostig had burned Scarborough, marched on York, and defeated the combined forces of Mercia and Northumberland.

Reluctant as he was to leave the south coast unprotected, Harold led his men northwards, collecting reinforcements as he went.

Saxons and Norsemen came face to face at Stamford Bridge. Lulled into a false sense of security by the ease of their first victories and by Tostig's cunning selection of hostages from among influential local families, whom of course he knew of old, Hardrada and his men had returned to their ships for a night's celebration before dictating their terms on the morrow. When they approached the meeting-place in a high good humour, it was to see a cloud of dust ahead as thousands of men moved into position across their path. King Harold's English army had arrived.

There was no time to summon the troops who had been left guarding the ships. Harald Hardrada set up his standard, the Land-Ravager. Harold Godwinsson set up his Fighting Man.

Before battle was joined, twenty horsemen rode out from the Saxon lines to parley. One called upon Tostig to yield, saying that his brother King Harold would allow him to rule again over Northumbria. Tostig asked what similar gift might be offered to his ally, King Harald Hardrada.

'Seven feet of English earth,' came the reply, 'or as much more as he may be taller than other men.'

Tostig chose for once to remain loyal; and, when the horsemen had ridden away, revealed to Hardrada that the spokesman had been none other than Harold himself.

'That was but a little man,' observed the Norwegian, 'yet he sat firmly in his stirrups.'

(1) Funeral procession of Edward the Confessor and (2) the coronation of Harold from the Bayeux Tapestry.

35

(1)

(2)

(3)

(1) The Alfred Jewel was probably owned by King Alfred for it bears the Anglo-Saxon inscription 'Alfred had me made', and it was found in 1693 near the Island of Athelney, where Alfred took refuge from the Danes.

(2) Clasp and (3) Gold fibula from the Sutton Hoo ship burial, 7th century.

OPPOSITE Page from the Benedictional of St. Aethelwold.

36

(1) Death of Harold from the Bayeux Tapestry. Traditionally Harold is supposed to have been killed by an arrow piercing his eye (*left-hand figure*); it is more likely that the falling figure on the right, receiving a death blow from the mounted knight, represents the stricken king.

(2) Four Kings: (top, l to r.) Henry II and Richard I; (bottom) John and Henry III.

The Saxons advanced and, after savage fighting, routed the Norsemen, whose disorganised remnants sailed away, leaving on the field the bodies of Tostig and Harald Hardrada himself, killed by an arrow through his windpipe. A year later the royal corpse was reclaimed and taken for burial in the church Harald had built in Trondheim.

Almost before Harold of England could draw breath, messengers rode in to tell him that the Normans had landed near Pevensey.

The battle of Hastings

William, to his surprise, met no opposition. He marched on Hastings and set the local inhabitants to strengthening the wooden fortifications of the castle. When word reached him of the battle of Stamford Bridge he decided to move on London in the hope of taking it before Harold arrived. He was too late. Harold had already left London—perhaps unwisely, since if he had remained entrenched there until reinforcements were gathered from those members of the fyrd who had earlier drifted back to their farms, William might well have been starved into retreat.

Instead, after another gruelling forced march, Harold reached Caldbec hill, a few miles from Hastings, and, seeing the Normans approaching, arrayed his men along the ridge of Senlac hill just below Caldbec.

The armies were fairly evenly matched, but Saxon strength increased as fyrdmen hurried to rejoin their leader. When the Normans attacked uphill they wasted their energies against an impenetrable shield wall and the murderous proficiency of the housecarls' axes. Again, if the defenders had simply stayed where they were, they would have had yet another chance of wearing out the invaders.

Collapse came when a contingent of the Norman army turned tail and ran. William's admirers later recorded this as a brilliant tactical manœuvre. Others say it was the result of sheer panic. Whatever the truth may have been, one thing is certain: the jubilant Saxons defied Harold's orders, broke the shield wall, and gave chase down the hill. This gave the Norman horsemen the opportunity they had so far been denied. Charging into the turmoil of foot soldiers, they hacked the Saxons to pieces and then rode up to break through the remnants of the shield wall.

Harold himself was killed in the closing hours of the battle, traditionally by an arrow in his eye, but more probably, if the Bayeux Tapestry is interpreted aright, by the sword of a Norman knight. After the carnage his beloved Edith Swan-neck came in search of his corpse, which by William's decree was allowed no grave other than a stone mound on the shore. Later, permission was given for the remains to be re-buried in the abbey which Harold had founded at Waltham in Essex, and at which he had prayed for victory on his way to meet the Normans.

Duke William now founded an abbey of his own around the altar which he had set up in thankfulness for his victory, at the place to be known henceforth as Battle.

Hen. secundus

The Middle Ages

Castles fit for a conqueror:
(1) the Tower of London and (2)
Dover castle, both built by order of
William I.

William the Conqueror was crowned king of England in Westminster Abbey on Christmas Day, 1066. Three months later he went back to Normandy, leaving his new possessions to be supervised by his half-brother Odo, the bellicose bishop of Bayeux, and William Fitz-Osbern. Estates and titles were distributed among Norman barons who had backed William's enterprise, but no man was given too great an expanse in one region: the estates were scattered all over the country so that they could not be combined into a possibly rebellious whole.

Dispossessed Saxon lords turned to the last member of the Confessor's royal line, Edgar the Atheling, in the hope of consolidating

(1)

resistance to the usurper; but Edgar came to terms with William, took his mother and sister to Scotland, and then during a prolonged exile in Flanders and France allied himself with those attacking William's continental territories.

The Conqueror may have contemplated residence in his dukedom rather than his kingdom. He soon found that it was not safe to stay long away from England. Glutted with their new riches, his barons grew quarrelsome among themselves and arrogant towards their underlings. Rapaciously they taxed and bullied the defeated Saxons until a rash of revolt broke out all over the country. William returned and, even though recognising the guilt of many of his own retainers, burned and slaughtered his way through all resistance. Those survivors still unwilling to bend the knee had to flee and seek service with King Malcolm of Scotland or with other monarchs beyond the Norman influence—even as far away as Constantinople.

One of the last of the old landowners to hold out was Hereward the Wake, who encamped with his followers in the Isle of Ely, at one stage using the monastery there as headquarters and feeding in the refectory. The treacherous, marshy fen was impassable to strangers.

(2)

(1) The nave of Durham cathedral, an outstanding example of Norman architecture.

(2) Great Seal of William the Conqueror.

William himself supervised a siege, but found a safe causeway for a direct attack only by threatening a monk with the seizure of all the monastery's lands if no assistance were rendered. Hereward himself escaped and continued guerrilla action against the Normans until finally captured. Unlike many of his kind he was pardoned, and apparently was taken into the admiring Conqueror's service.

The feudal system

With all major resistance crushed, William began to set up castles to guard all towns and important junctions, so that future rebellions could be contained before they gathered momentum. He allowed those barons he considered most trustworthy to build their own castles from their own resources.

All land now belonged officially to the Crown. A quarter of it was treated by William as personal property, the rest was leased out under certain stringent conditions. All landowners had to swear fealty to the king. The country was split up into 'manors' on which the majority of yeomen were mere tenants of an overlord. The new feudal system—so called from the Latin *feodum* for a fief or fee— exacted service on the royal Grand Council (which replaced the Witan), various dues, and above all military service from a baron and his attendant knights in return for the land bestowed on him. The baron kept as much of this demesne as he wished for his own use, and distributed the rest among knights who thereby bound themselves to meet his needs for fighting men when he or the king called for them. In their turn the knights allocated sections of their manorial demesnes to villeins who, at the bottom of the chain of command, had to provide free labour and seasonal dues in the way of food or service whenever, with or without warning, they might be demanded. A serf could not even allow his daughter to marry without his lord's permission; and for her to marry outside the manor was almost impossible, since it depleted the labour force.

Forest law subjected whole areas to the royal whim. King William created the New Forest as a private game reserve and declared other extensive woodlands sacrosanct. Not just the beasts of the chase were his, but the very leaves on the trees, so that it became a crime not only to kill an animal for food but also to gather sticks for a fire.

Domesday Book

In 1086 William decided to check and double-check his assets, comparing the population and possessions of the manorial estates with those at the time of his accession. This nation-wide inquisition was so searching that its victims spoke of the Day of Judgement, and the final assembly of documents as Domesday Book.

A record left by the then bishop of Hereford describes an operation worthy of the combined forces of our modern Inland Revenue and Customs and Excise:

'A survey was made of all England, that is of the lands of the several shires of England, and of the possession of each and of all tenants-in-chief. This was done concerning ploughlands and habitations, and of men both bond and free, both those who lived in cottages and those who had their homes and held lands in the fields;

(1)

(2)

(1) Orford castle, Suffolk. The 12th-century keep, 90ft. high with walls 10ft. thick, is all that remains of this masterpiece of medieval fortification.

(2) The 'grandest fortress ruin in England'; Kenilworth castle, Warwickshire.

OVERLEAF Caernarvon castle. Edward I built this formidable bastion 1283–1327 to master Welsh resistance.

and concerning ploughs, horses and other animals; and concerning services and payments due from all men in the whole country. Other commissioners followed the first; men were sent into areas they did not know and where they were unknown, in order that they might have an opportunity to check the first survey and, if necessary, denounce its authors as guilty to the king.'

The final analysis showed that since the Conquest the holdings of Saxon landowners had been so eroded that there were only two left as tenants-in-chief. Over a quarter of the country belonged directly to the king and his family, the barons shared about two-fifths, and the Church held the rest. In addition to other levies and service obligations, the populace had to pay tithes—one-tenth of annual increases in profit and productivity—for the upkeep of the Church: starting as supposedly voluntary offerings of food and other necessities to the parish priest or monastic communities, these were soon regulated as money payments.

William was a sternly religious man and a great benefactor of the Church. But he did not propose to let ecclesiastical authority interfere with his own. In Saxon times there had been a fairly free coming and going of churchmen and of correspondence between Rome and its English pastors. William would allow no bishop to visit Rome or to correspond with the Pope over his head. If the Pope issued any edict of excommunication within William's realm, it would not be enforced without William's express permission. He filled places in episcopal sees and abbeys as they fell vacant by death—or were vacated under his pressure—with Norman appointees, and approved the reforms of his archbishop, Lanfranc, to bring the somewhat untidy Celtic-Saxon Church more into line with Rome and European practice; but at the same time separated ecclesiastical courts from the lay courts, and brought many of the Church's everyday functions

(1)

(2)

under the authority of common law. As ultimate arbiter of the responsibilities of each, William kept this dual judiciary in reasonable equilibrium during his reign, though it must surely have occurred to him sometimes that he was presenting any less powerful successor with a number of potential problems.

He died in 1087 as the result of an injury sustained after the burning of Nantes, from which the French were pillaging the borders of Normandy. On his deathbed he wept and prayed, made many gifts to the Church, and gave Normandy into the care of his oldest son, Robert; but left his sword and the English crown and sceptre to his second son, William.

Sons of the Conqueror

When the red-haired William Rufus ascended the throne he at once set to work appropriating monastic revenues and extracting more taxes from the barons. It was said of him that he 'feared God but little, man not at all'. Anselm, made archbishop of Canterbury after Lanfranc's death, soon clashed with King William II and was exiled, later to be recalled by Henry I but very shortly exiled yet again. Hated by his barons, his priests and his people, William was mourned by none when he died while hunting in his father's New Forest in 1100. The arrow which killed him was 'accidentally' shot by Sir Walter Tyrell; but there was a great deal of contemporary speculation as to whether this was a knightly service rendered to a baron or group of barons who had grown weary of royal oppression.

It was even rumoured that William Rufus's younger brother Henry, who was taking part in the hunt, had a hand in the death. Henry, the Conqueror's youngest son, had been born in England two years after his father became king, and had the mystical conviction that this birth 'into the purple' gave him precedence over the sons who came into the world when their father was still merely a duke. Certainly he wasted no time after William Rufus fell, but commandeered the royal treasures and insignia and had himself crowned in Westminster Abbey three days later.

His elder brother Robert duly challenged this assumption, and they went to war. Henry defeated Robert at Tinchebrai in 1106 and imprisoned him for life. Having already brought about a liaison with his northern neighbours by marrying the king of Scotland's daughter, whose direct descent from Alfred the Great also added authority to his rule in England, Henry was now able to reunite England and Normandy.

(1) An October hawking scene from an 11th-century calendar.

(2) 'Uneasy lies the head that wears a crown': Henry I's sleep troubled by nightmares of threatening peasants and knights.

The White Ship with Henry I above.

The royal caravan still toured the country as in Saxon times, collecting dues and dispensing justice, but the time was ripe for the establishment of a central judiciary and financial clearing-house. Roger, bishop of Salisbury, a shrewd and worldly cleric who became Henry I's closest adviser and was given the title of justiciar, instituted a revenue counting system on a large chequered cloth like a chess-board, across which the royal treasurer and officials argued general policy and specific expenditure. This department soon came to be known as 'the Exchequer'.

In 1120 Henry's son Prince William, heir to the throne, died in the wreck of *The White Ship* while sailing home from Normandy. The king, a widower, married again but had no children by the union. Apart from a large number of illegitimate children towards whom he showed great affection without ever holding out any hope of the succession, he was left with only the daughter of his first marriage, Matilda. He made his barons swear to acknowledge her as queen, but when the time came in 1135 they jibbed. Matilda had lived too long abroad, having married first Henry V, the Holy Roman Emperor, and then Count Geoffrey of Anjou, and was known to be high-handed in her methods. In her stead they chose her cousin Stephen, who had taken the precaution of rewarding them with gifts and promising them new estates if they could persuade the archbishop of Canterbury that there were good patriotic reasons for getting round the oath which had been taken.

King Stephen

The country needed a strong man. Stephen proved not so much strong as wilful. He was charming and courageous, and in a lesser role could have been an admired soldier and agreeable companion. But, as Professor Christopher Brooke so aptly sums it up, 'his real weakness as king was that he could neither control his friends nor subdue his enemies'. He quarrelled with his predecessor's astute justiciar, antagonised the Church, and weakly allowed the barons to run their demesnes like petty self-contained kingdoms. Some of those who had once supported him decided they had backed the wrong horse, and called for Matilda to come and take her rightful place.

She arrived from France with her half-brother and landed unopposed. At Lincoln, Stephen was captured and thrown into a dungeon, while Matilda set herself up in state in London. Her arrogance made her so immediately unpopular that she was driven out of the city, and when her half-brother was captured she had to agree that in return for his release she would free Stephen.

Their strife continued for some years with no substantial gains to either side, but substantial losses for the common people of the country. The barons used the war as an excuse for settling old local scores, 'till the land was all undone and darkened with such deeds, and men said openly that Christ and his angels slept'. This state of anarchy did not last as long as some old chroniclers have reported; but even after Matilda had been finally driven out, Stephen's grip was never secure and there was continuing uneasiness throughout the country.

The battle of Crécy, 1346. The
French crossbowmen met their
match against the quicker-firing
English longbow. The difficulties of
reloading the crossbow are apparent
in this French manuscript
illustration.

The Plantagenets

When Matilda's son Henry was old enough he made several forays into England, winning the tacit support of many barons and churchmen. The death of Stephen's older son and heir, Eustace, prompted a move to reconcile the two men, and it was agreed that after Stephen's own death the Crown should pass to Henry. Stephen's second son, William, renounced all claim to the succession in return for rich grants of land.

King Henry II was crowned in 1154. As his father had been Count Geoffrey of Anjou, he and his descendants were referred to as the Angevin kings, but a commoner name was that of Plantagenet, from the broom flower *Planta genista* which Geoffrey wore as an emblem.

Knowing of his mother's experiences and having seen something of the turmoil of the country for himself, Henry made his first task that of bringing the barons to heel. Some, agreeing that firm discipline was needed, backed him; others had got out of the habit of revering a king, and fought back. Some changed sides. Earl Hugh Bigod, of the Norman family to which the Conqueror had gratefully awarded more than a hundred estates, first supported Stephen and then rebelled against him; now swore allegiance to Henry, then decided to defy him. An old ballad telling of his pursuit by one of the king's bailiffs recorded his boast:

> Now that I'm in my castle of Bungay
> Upon the river of Waveney
> I will ne care for the king of Cockney.

In addition to all this Henry had to contend with the administration of great territories in France, including those brought to him on his marriage to Eleanor of Aquitaine and which totalled about two-thirds of the area of modern France, and with the ever-troublesome Scots, Welsh and Irish.

Thomas Becket

The king's right-hand man in the taming of the barons, waging war, and restoring a proper legal system was a merchant's son who had studied law and taken holy orders. Thomas Becket and the king were not just master and servant but boon companions at the chase and at table. Becket rose to be lord chancellor in 1155 and served Henry's interests well and faithfully until 1162; then Henry, anxious to reduce the powers of the Church as he had reduced the powers of the barons, demanded his appointment as archbishop of Canterbury.

Becket had not sought the post, but once it was his he applied himself as earnestly to his duties as he had done in other fields. He resigned the office of lord chancellor and, instead of helping Henry, defied him.

The king accused the clergy of being too lenient in the punishment of wrongdoers within their own ranks, and proposed that after guilt had been established in an ecclesiastical court the cleric should be transferred to a civil court for sentence. Appeals direct to Rome, which had been resumed during Stephen's feeble administration, should cease. These and fourteen other points, which were in fact

(1) The Great Seal of Henry II showing the king on horseback.

(2) 13th-century stained glass, Canterbury cathedral.

(1)

(2)

(1) Canterbury cathedral; the nave, facing east.

(2) The murder of Thomas Becket, from a Latin Psalter miniature, *c.* 1200.

largely a restatement of old customs, were written down in the Constitution of Clarendon in 1164, including a bid to pre-empt all questions of patronage and preferment: 'If controversy shall arise between laymen, laymen and clerks, or clerks concerning the advowson and presentation of churches, the matter shall be discussed and terminated in the king's court.'

Becket and his bishops said no.

Trying to outflank his old friend, Henry accused him of withholding money which he had acquired while holding office as lord chancellor. Although Becket proudly refuted the charge, further splenetic accusations of treason were hurled at him and he thought it safer to flee the country.

After five years in exile he met Henry in Normandy and it was agreed that he should return. When he did so, he brought with him an authorisation from the Pope for the excommunication of all those bishops who had played him false in his absence, and all the barons who had been awarded pickings from his property. In a rage Henry cried out: 'Will no one rid me of this upstart priest?' He probably forgot his own words within an hour or two, and hardly expected them to be taken literally.

On 29th December 1170 four of Henry's knights strode into Canterbury Cathedral and murdered the archbishop on the altar steps.

Three years later Becket was canonised. A rich tomb was consecrated in his memory, and in 1174 Henry allowed monks to flog him through the streets towards it in penance. In that same year, sparks blown from burning houses near by set fire to the cathedral roof, melting the lead and destroying the choir. William of Sens, commissioned to rebuild, cleared the rubble and started all over again on a new choir and apse. The Becket shrine became one of the most revered in Christendom, and offerings accruing from devout pilgrims made possible the reconstruction of the cathedral on a lavish scale, including, some two centuries after the martyrdom, Henry Yevele's great Perpendicular nave. The faithful and their donations continued to flow in until the tomb was destroyed during the Reformation.

Enemies near and far

In spite of Hugh Bigod's self-confidence, Henry caught up with him in 1173, fined him a thousand marks, and ordered the demolition of his castles at both Bungay and Framlingham. But France was still troublesome, and in the west there was Ireland to contend with.

One of the Welsh barons, Richard Strongbow, second earl of Pembroke, had married the daughter of the king of Leinster and acquired more power than he could ever have aspired to at home. He duly inherited the kingdom. Other frustrated Welshmen went adventuring in Ireland and subdued most of the mixed Irish and Norse elements there. When they had thus cleared the ground, Henry decided it was time to assert himself. He won acknowledgment of his overlordship from Strongbow, who nevertheless continued to rule very much as he chose until his death in 1176, after which Henry appointed his own minister to tie the country as closely as possible to

(1) The tomb of Henry II at Fontevrault abbey.

(2) A Crusader doing homage.

(1)

(2)

the English Crown.

His strength began to fail when, one by one, his own sons turned against him. His wife not only did away with his mistress Rosamund, whom, according to Raphael Holinshed's *Chronicles*, he lovingly referred to as 'the rose of the world', but intrigued so maliciously for his downfall that he had to imprison her. This distressed their sons, who also had a number of individual grievances: the oldest, Henry, was angry at the youngest, John, having been given land in Anjou, and then envious of Richard's receiving Aquitaine; Richard was joined by Geoffrey, but would share nothing with John.

Henry II died in France in 1189, a few weeks after accepting a humiliating peace from King Philip of France and his own son Richard, and was buried in the abbey of Fontevrault. He lamented that his own flesh and blood had brought such shame on him, and wretchedly faced the prospect that his favourite son John would 'do more harm than the others in the end'—a prophecy which proved all too true for England.

Both Geoffrey and Henry, heir to the throne, had predeceased their father—the latter while making war against him. It was therefore his fourth son, the duke of Aquitaine, who succeeded to the throne (Henry's first son, William, had died early in Henry's reign).

The Crusades

Richard I was a handsome man more interested in tournaments, deeds of chivalry, and courage in the field than in the detailed administration of a country with which he was by now unfamiliar. Known as 'Cœur-de-Lion' because of his lionhearted valour, he had hardly been crowned before he was making plans to leave England for a dangerously long period. During the ten years of his reign, in fact, he spent less than a year in his own kingdom.

After William the Conqueror's death the French dukedoms under English suzerainty were in constant danger from other greedy claimants. The king of France, like so many Saxon kings of England, was ruler of only one state among many, and sought persistently to add to his dominions. A recurring theme in the story of England for centuries to come was to be that of claim and counter-claim on French territories, and of wars launched on the most complicated dynastic pretexts.

In 1095 many of the squabbling states of Europe had temporarily sunk their differences in a common cause which overrode all other antagonisms. Pilgrims returning from the Holy Land had brought appalling tales of cruelty shown by Turkish conquerors. Jerusalem

51

(1) Crusaders besieging Jerusalem from a 14th-century English manuscript.

(2) The round nave of Temple church, London, consecrated 1185.

(2)

was in the hands of the Muslims, many sacred places of the Christian religion were no longer accessible, and pious visitors were derided and persecuted. There was urgent need for what one might call an international rescue operation. The roads to the Holy Sepulchre must be made safe, and, if possible, all Palestine should come under Christian control.

The Pope gave his blessing to a Crusade, and a large but undisciplined force set out, exhorted and driven on by a French monk known as Peter the Hermit. It disintegrated on the way, but was followed by a more competent army which in 1099 liberated Jerusalem and set up a Christian kingdom. In spite of continual harassment from its neighbours it managed to survive until 1187, when Saladin, powerful sultan of Egypt, swept with his Saracens through the land and reclaimed Jerusalem for the Muslims.

A third Crusade was planned. Henry II of England and Philip Augustus of France ceased fighting each other for long enough to devise the raising of a Saladin tithe, a tax to be collected from their subjects and put to the freeing of the Holy Land. The king of Scots, owing loyalty to Henry, was also supposed to contribute but complained that he could not wrest a penny from his barons. Henry and Philip managed to raise the necessary sum between them; and then went to war with each other again.

Richard, on his accession, had no difficulty in coming to an arrangement with Philip—in whose cause he had, after all, served against his own father. They planned to set off together. The canny William of Scotland now offered a financial contribution if Richard would release him from his allegiance to the English Crown. Set on the splendours of the Crusade, Richard accepted.

In the struggle to restore light after the excesses of the Dark Ages, the Church of Rome had allied itself with warrior kings in the creation of a new Holy Roman Empire. The current Holy Roman Emperor, Frederick Barbarossa of Germany, started out with a huge force on the third Crusade, expecting to be joined by others. But Richard of England seemed to dawdle, and Philip of France was reluctant to move far from home until he was sure Richard had no intention of grabbing France in his absence. At last, after a number of irrelevant local skirmishes on the way, the allies reached Acre and laid siege to the port. Under Richard's skilful command they undermined the fortifications and so terrified the Saracens that Saladin called for a truce. At this stage the precarious alliance broke down. Some English soldiers insulted the Austrian flag, causing Duke Leopold to go home in a rage; and Richard quarrelled so irreparably with Philip over certain old scores that the French king also decided to go off and leave the English to it.

Richard fought on towards Jerusalem. He defeated the Saracens at Arsuf and then marched to Jaffa to consolidate it as a reliable supply port. Necessary as this was if his troops were to stay on in Palestine, it lost him valuable time. When he advanced through rain and mud on Jerusalem, Saladin had reinforced its defences and there was no hope of retaking the city. At a meeting with Saladin, when both men took an immediate liking to each other, Richard won assent to the unhindered admission of pilgrims to the Holy City. But the Muslims remained in charge, and the only people who really profited were merchants of both sides who had been quick to exploit the new possibilities of East–West trade.

The Lionheart's ransom

On his return journey in 1192 Richard fell into the hands of that same Duke Leopold whom his men had unwisely offended. He was handed over to the Emperor Henry VI, son of Barbarossa, who had been drowned while away crusading. There is a legend that Richard was tracked down to his prison in the castle of Dürnstein by a French troubadour, Blondel, but it is unlikely that he needed to be tracked down: the emperor made no secret of having the king in his keeping, and asked a ransom of 150,000 marks.

The sum was yet another burden on the taxpayers of England, already bled white by Richard's expenditure on equipping his crusaders, and there was at least one influential man in the land who would have been quite happy if it had never been paid, thereby condemning the Lionheart to rot in his cage.

Before leaving for Palestine, Richard had tried to iron out old grudges between his brother and himself by granting John control of Ireland and of six English counties free from all obligations to the central judiciary or exchequer. John worked assiduously in the king's absence to augment this power, and when he heard of Richard's incarceration tried to barter territory with the king of France in exchange for recognition of his own claim to the throne. His attempted treachery was unsuccessful: Richard's ransom was paid, and the king came home to a jubilant welcome.

Yet, though well aware by now of his brother's scheming nature,

Richard I as a prisoner of Leopold of Austria.

he still nominated John as his successor and was soon off on his travels again, this time taxing the country for a further war against King Philip of France. He died from an arrow wound in 1199, asking that he should be buried at Fontevrault beside the father he had once so resented—'perhaps as thinking they should meet the sooner, that he might ask him forgiveness in another world'.

Robin Hood

One of the great folk heroes of English legend is generally associated with this period of history, owing his misfortunes to John's misuse of power in the counties under his sway, and his rehabilitation to Richard. The first known mention of his name does not, however, occur for well over a hundred years from this time, when he appears in William Langland's allegorical poem, *The Vision of William Concerning Piers the Plowman*—unless one wishes to build a romance around the earlier reference to 'Robertus Hood, fugitivus' in a thirteenth-century pipe-roll, a parchment record of local sheriffs' accounts rolled and clipped at the end into the shape of a pipe.

Outlawed into the greenwood and living on game killed in defiance of the oppressive forest laws, Robin Hood represented a wistful ideal to set against the reality of bullying sheriffs, reeves, landlords and every kind of petty autocrat. He supposedly robbed the rich to feed the poor, an excuse which has made possible the glorification of many other law-breakers such as highwaymen, smugglers and footpads.

As with King Arthur, it might be said that if he did not exist it was emotionally necessary to invent him.

Magna Carta

As treacherous younger brother to the king, John had been unpopular with all save a few sycophants. As king, he was even more so. It was believed that he had connived at the murder of his nephew Arthur, son of the late Geoffrey, to remove any risk of another contender to the throne. He showed daring and great imagination in his pacification of the Scots, the Irish and the Welsh; did much to strengthen

The head of King John from the effigy in Worcester cathedral.

the fleet; and was respected by the common people as a fair judge when sitting in his own courts. But he managed in his wars against Philip of France to lose all the family possessions of Normandy, Anjou, Touraine and Maine, and at home antagonised the always restive barons by his arrogance and his habit of giving the most coveted jobs to foreign favourites.

He also, like many of his family before and after, contrived a head-on collision with the Pope. On the death of the archbishop of Canterbury, the monks selected one of their number as successor. John indignantly overrode this and nominated a reliable friend of his, John Grey, bishop of Norwich. Pope Innocent III denied the validity of either choice and ordered John to accept Stephen Langton, an English-born cardinal who had been educated in Paris and spent most of his life in France.

John refused. The Pope thereupon placed the whole of England under an interdict in 1208. Celebration of the Mass was prohibited, and the dead had to be buried in unconsecrated ground. John himself was excommunicated in 1209 but remained defiant until 1213, when the threat of a French invasion with the Pope's blessing forced him to capitulate, not only accepting Langton but offering the Pope temporal as well as spiritual sovereignty over England.

John's last contest against Philip Augustus to regain the lands north of the Loire ended in a crushing defeat at the battle of Bouvines in 1214, and he returned to England to face a situation scarcely less gloomy than the one he had left in France. A group of northern barons, joined by some from Essex and East Anglia, raised the standard of revolt against the king in support of baronial rights and liberties. Langton was called upon to mediate and, with a number of wise and able lords, persuaded John to accept the barons' demands and persuaded the barons to insert into their demands clauses that would benefit others than themselves. A document supporting purely baronial interests was thus transformed into the Great Charter, to which John affixed his seal at Runnymede, near Windsor, in June 1215.

Magna Carta guaranteed fewer freedoms for the ordinary citizen than we sentimentally imagine. The barons cared nothing for the man in the street or in the meadows: they merely wished to safeguard their own privileges. But in the framing of the various clauses, certain concepts were introduced which found their way into judicial thinking and eventually into the accepted principles of English life and legislation. First and foremost was that the king himself was not above the law of the land. And, more generally, the thirty-ninth article of the charter stated:

> No free man shall be arrested or imprisoned or dispossessed or outlawed or harmed in any way save by the lawful judgement of his equals under the law of the land. Justice will not be sold to any man nor will it be refused or delayed.

No sooner had he granted this than John sought ways of repudiating it, and soon persuaded the Pope, now his firm supporter, to annul it. When this happened the barons tried again to impose their will on him, but John now decided to use force, and plunged the country

The seal of King John from the Magna Carta.

(1)

into civil war. Some of the barons called for aid from Philip of France, offering the kingdom of England to his son, Louis. French troops were landing in England when John, his baggage-train laden with loot from the ransacked castles of defeated barons, tried to take a short cut from King's Lynn to Lincolnshire across the neck of the Wash at low tide. The tide came in and he lost all his treasures, dying soon after at Newark from a fever and dysentery probably aggravated by his excessive consumption of peaches and sweet ale.

The Barons' War

Some of the barons continued to support the French Prince Louis's campaign for the throne, but others rallied round John's nine-year-old son, Prince Henry, and made him King Henry III. It may well have been in their minds that, by acting as his council of regency until he came of age, they would build a firm foundation for future dominance. When Henry grew up, however, he proved to be a spendthrift and a political bungler, readier to listen to his mother's and his wife's hangers-on than to his senior advisers.

Simon de Montfort, earl of Leicester, came to the forefront of the barons' ranks when he married the king's sister Eleanor in 1238, and

(2)

(1) The seal of Simon de Montfort, earl of Leicester, 1258.

(2) The west front of York Minster is a fine example of the decorated architecture of the early 14th century. Most of the cathedral is built in the plainer style of the 13th century.

(3) Fan-vaulting at the West Walk of Canterbury cloisters.

(3)

(1)

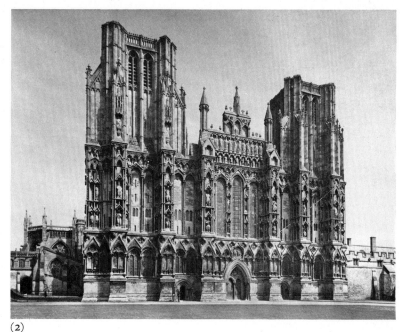

(2)

(3)

(1) Lincoln cathedral; the Angel choir.

(2) Wells cathedral; the west front.

(3) Salisbury cathedral; the 404ft. spire, a 14th-century addition, is the tallest in England.

for a while was one of the royal favourites. He acted several times as a trusted ambassador and between 1248 and 1252 governed the province of Gascony efficiently if harshly. But he was resolute in urging on Henry that the principles embodied in Magna Carta, increasingly showing signs of neglect, should be implemented.

Other elements were slowly making themselves felt in the effective government of the country. The lords met in small groups more frequently, not just when summoned by the king but when they felt matters of state warranted discussion. County and city representatives were invited to represent local interests at meetings with the barons or with the king. Although it must be admitted that these gatherings were usually convened in order to find ways of raising taxes, they fostered the idea of a nationally representative assembly and may be regarded as the first steps towards a true Parliament.

Strained relations between the headstrong king and his nobles snapped when he demanded financial support, first in order to accept the crown of Sicily for his son Edmund, which had been granted him by the Pope in 1254, and then to meet the expenses of the election of his brother, Richard of Cornwall, as king of the Romans in 1257. A council summoned at Oxford in 1258 imposed upon Henry a committee whose advice he agreed henceforth to follow; but with the Pope's approval he soon decided to defy this and rule as he chose. A number of barons thereupon went to war against him under the leadership of Simon de Montfort.

At the battle of Lewes in 1264 both the king and his son, Edward, were captured. De Montfort, far ahead of his time and displaying even traces of democratic ideas, called a Parliament (from the old French *parlement*, parleying or speaking), including a number of commoners, to administer the country, probably the first time townsmen were summoned in parliamentary history. His fellow barons were none too happy about the composition of this, or about the hooliganism and brutality of many of his supporters towards royalists in various parts of the country. Also they were beginning to find the earl himself too dictatorial. As quarrels broke out among them, Edward escaped from prison, raised a loyal army, and defeated and killed Simon at the battle of Evesham in 1265. The earl's head was stuck on a pike, and his limbs torn off and distributed among towns which had favoured his cause.

Released, Henry was content to allow his son to run the realm, which Edward calmed so effectively that he was able to go on a Crusade and not return for his own coronation until 1274, two years after his father's death.

Henry's worthiest legacy was the flowering of ecclesiastical architecture under his patronage. During his reign Westminster Abbey was rebuilt, and the great Early English Gothic style came to fruition (at Salisbury Cathedral, for example) and developed into the Decorated Gothic of the Choir of Lincoln Cathedral and the west front of York Minster.

Princes of Wales

King Edward I was determined to suppress dissident elements in Wales and Ireland, and in due course to make himself master of Scotland. For all this he needed money. He set out to win the loyalty of the barons by agreeing unequivocally to honour the terms of Magna Carta. He also summoned a Model Parliament which, meeting for the first time in 1295, represented all three estates of the realm—clergy, nobles, and commons—and continued to experiment with the constitution of such councils throughout his reign. Appointments of knights and burgesses to these was no markedly democratic procedure: only certain wealthy, influential men in each borough were allowed to nominate or vote for them. Like so many of his forebears, Edward was primarily interested in the ability of local worthies —by now including a merchant class grown rich on the wool trade— to raise taxes for his continuing wars.

In addition he speeded up legal reform, created conservators of the peace (precursors of justices of the peace), established the independence of judges and clerks in courts of law and, through a Court of Equity or Chancery, provided for royal intervention in disputes not covered by civil or canon law and for appeals against unduly rigorous decisions made by other courts.

A supporter of Simon de Montfort during the Barons' War against Henry III had been Llewelyn ap Griffith, who styled himself Prince of Wales. The Celtic lords, who retained from one generation to another their old language and their hatred of English and Norman usurpers, had for some time seen the advantage of pooling their resources. By Edward's time they had accepted the leadership of the princes of Gwynedd, an area covering the modern counties of Caernarvon, Anglesey, Merioneth and part of Denbigh. Their support gave Llewelyn the confidence to refuse the oath of homage he owed to the new English king.

Edward seized Eleanor, daughter of Simon de Montfort, as she was on her way to join Llewelyn, to whom she had been married by proxy. A year later, in 1276, he launched an invasion of the Principality.

Edward I in Parliament.

Conway castle, Caernarvonshire, one of Edward I's impregnable network of defences in Wales.

The Welsh forces were driven back into the mountains, and Llewelyn was hunted through Snowdonia. He might well have held out in his native fastness if it had not been for hunger. The English captured Anglesey, from which came most of the produce for the Welsh contingents in the region, and the last rebels were starved out. Llewelyn was allowed to retain the title of prince but had to do homage to Edward at Westminster in 1278.

The peace was an unstable one. The semi-independent Marcher lords who had been granted almost untrammelled power and privilege by William the Conqueror in return for the protection of his western borders continued their depredations. Edward's own functionaries dodged their obligation to observe old Welsh law and custom. Llewelyn and his brother David revolted once more. Both were killed—Llewelyn in a skirmish near Builth in December 1282, David executed as a traitor.

Although the Marcher lords were to present a continuing problem until well into the sixteenth century about half the present area of Wales had now been brought under English control. Edward divided this into five shires and built a chain of castles to watch over them. At one of the most imposing, Caernarvon, his son Edward was born and later proclaimed Prince of Wales.

Hammer of the Scots

When Edward first turned his attention to the Scots, he hoped for a peaceable union of the two countries. Scotland had preserved a sturdy independence under a succession of kings skilled in controlling the rivalries of local chieftains, until in 1286 Alexander III was thrown over a cliff by his horse. His heiress was his granddaughter Margaret, the 'Maid of Norway', and although she was only a child Edward won approval for her marriage to his son. She set sail from Norway in 1290 but died on reaching Orkney, and Edward's dream of a personal union between the two Crowns vanished. Edward was then asked by the Scots to be the impartial judge between a dozen claimants to their throne.

He chose John Balliol on condition that Balliol paid homage to him. The new ruler obeyed, but his people were less eager to submit. Edward's insistence upon being the final judge in Scottish legal cases alienated the Scots, who forced Balliol to rebel and gave Edward the excuse for a full-scale invasion to assert his overlordship. From Wales he imported the new, devastating long-bow. About six feet in length, made of supple ash or especially of yew, its force could drive arrows even through armour. The time would soon come when yew forests would be royally protected to ensure an adequate supply of these weapons. Thus equipped, the vanguard of the English army defeated Balliol at Dunbar in 1296. Edward appointed regents to rule Scotland on his behalf, and removed to London the coronation stone of Scone, or Stone of Destiny.

The following year Sir William Wallace took advantage of the fact that Edward was now absorbed in plans for a war against France, and raised forces to eject the English officials. A hurried attempt to check his advance was defeated at Stirling. Wallace declared himself guardian of Scotland, but Edward, 'the Hammer of the Scots', dropped everything and came marching north again. Wallace's men were routed at Falkirk in 1298, and the Guardian himself fled abroad in search of foreign aid. Denied it everywhere, he returned to operate as a guerrilla leader until captured. He was hanged, drawn and quartered, and his head was exposed on London Bridge.

Among Wallace's followers had been Robert Bruce, grandson of one of the would-be monarchs whom Edward had passed over in favour of Balliol. He had not been consistently a rebel: at times he sided with Edward in the hope that his father and in due course himself might be recognised as more suitable rulers of Scotland. After Wallace's death, however, his resolve hardened and he began to gather the still-contentious elements in the country about him. In 1306 he made dangerous enemies by murdering Balliol's nephew, the Red Comyn, in church at Dumfries after a quarrel. When, two months later, Bruce was crowned king by the bishop of St Andrews at Scone, he had not only the English against him but the Comyns. They soon scattered his forces and drove Bruce himself into hiding, after which his possessions were confiscated and he was written off as dead.

The story is told that during his wanderings, when he himself was almost ready to believe that he was finished, the persistence of a spider gamely spinning a web persuaded him that he must try and try again.

Longbowmen at practice. Parliament repeatedly passed laws forbidding the playing of village games like football so that more time would be spent in archery.

(1)

(2)

In 1307 he reappeared to inflict a set-back on the English, severe enough to bring Edward himself back into the struggle. But by now Edward was dying. One of his last injunctions to his son was to continue the fight until Scotland was subdued once and for all.

A king's favourites

Edward II was a man of very different mettle. Even where there was goodwill he managed to lose it. His father had held a Parliament in Ireland at which a cry familiar throughout Irish history was raised— the question of profiteering absentee landlords. The fairness of Edward's rulings had won him great respect, and with remarkably little strife Ireland's economy began to improve. Now, both there and in Wales, the new king's feebleness opened the way for further disorder.

He married, but showed less affection to his French wife, Isabella, than to his belligerent, acquisitive foster-brother, Piers Gaveston. Edward I had banished the insolent Gaveston from the country, and his return as Edward II's favourite, in what was probably a homosexual relationship, did not please the barons. Claiming to be acting only in the best interests of the king and his realm, they drew up a number of reforming ordinances, kept Edward under the strictest surveillance, and in May 1312 pounced on Gaveston and summarily executed him at Kenilworth.

The injunction to press on with the campaign against Scotland had never greatly appealed to the effeminate Edward, and it was not until Bruce had firmly re-established himself that he trod reluctantly north in his father's footsteps. His large army, with which Edward I would surely have triumphed, was so badly led that it allowed itself to be trapped in a bog at Bannockburn in June 1314 and was cut to shreds. Scotland was free and seemed likely to remain so. It also remained troublesome: after its recent experiences with the English, it tended wherever practicable to ally itself with the French rather than with its nearer neighbours, and lost no opportunity of discomfiting England.

With his new favourites, Hugh le Despenser and his son, Edward blundered from one error to another until his wife left him and took their son to France. In 1326 she returned with her lover, Roger Mortimer, earl of March, and forced the king to abdicate in favour of his

(1) The effigy of Edward II in Gloucester cathedral, portrays him in a pose of saintly majesty and not as the weak man he seems to have been.

(2) The coronation chair at Westminster Abbey.

(1)

(1) A gold medal of Edward III, 1360–69.

(2) The Hundred Years War: the siege of Ribodane.

son. The Despensers were executed and Edward was imprisoned in Berkeley Castle in Gloucestershire, there to be hideously killed by a red-hot spit thrust into his entrails.

The Hundred Years War

More courageous than his father, Edward III made another attempt to conquer Scotland after the death of Robert Bruce. He scored a victory at Halidon Hill in 1333 but was unable to follow it up. The Scots' allies in France opened a second front by attacking the English possession of Gascony, and Edward decided to concentrate now on these old traditional enemies.

In 1330, three years after his accession, he turned against the immoral Mortimer and had him hanged at Tyburn. He then sent his mother to the lonely fortress of Castle Rising in Norfolk, but her banishment was not too uncomfortable: she was allowed to travel in state from one country-house to another, and Edward did not hesitate to use her name as justification for his claim to the French throne

(2)

Flemish dyers and weavers at work in the 15th century.

after the death of her brother, Charles IV.

The French, disapproving both of descent on the distaff side and of the English in general, chose a French successor, Philip of Valois. To the two contenders, almost as important as the Crown itself were the control of Gascony and the Bordeaux wine trade, and the wool trade with Flanders.

The Hundred Years War which now gathered momentum was really a series of recurrent conflicts rather than a sustained campaign. By the time it ended the ordinary people in both camps were exhausted and had little to show for their sacrifices. At the start, however, Edward had not merely his family pride to fortify him but the enthusiasm of the nation and of a rebellious faction within the French domains.

In his attacks on the Scots, Edward had experimented with a new weapon of war—the cannon. Its most skilled artificers and operators were Flemings, hired from the Netherlands and frequently opting for continued service in England rather than a return home. Others among their fellow countrymen also had strong ties with England. The craft of cloth manufacture in Flanders had for some time gone hand in hand with the expansion of sheep-farming in England. When the French imposed restrictions on imports of raw material to Flanders, weavers were coaxed to practise and teach the art of cloth production in England itself with the promise that, once settled, 'they should feed on fat beef and mutton till nothing but their fulness should stint their stomachs'. But Flanders still needed a steady flow of best-quality wool, and a Ghent clothier, Jan van Artevelde, promised that he and his fellows would recognise Edward as king of France if he would break the present stranglehold and establish staple towns in places such as Ghent or Bruges. These centres were a sort of bonded warehouse through which all exports of a country's staple commodity had to be channelled, so that duties could be calculated exactly and collected by the government.

Through his wife, Queen Philippa of Hainault, Edward was connected with the Emperor Lewis of Germany who, for a long time embattled with the Pope and with France, also added encouragement by declaring an alliance with England and allowing Edward a free hand in France.

In 1340 things got off to a fine start with the utter destruction of a French fleet off Sluys, which gave England mastery of the Channel for the next thirty years. On land Edward showed himself at first an able commander, but then began to lose his grip. In his anxiety to fight a colourful patriotic fight, full of ceremony and all the chivalrous paraphernalia to which he was even more romantically devoted than Richard Cœur-de-Lion had been, he squandered money, muddled his French and Flemish operations, and had to face both the loss of his German ally, now bent on peace, and the anger of townsfolk at home when the south coast was attacked by French pirates taking advantage of the absence of the country's fighting men. With no money left and no likelihood of Parliament supplying any, Edward had to make a truce.

By 1346 he had reawakened enthusiasm for his cause, and led an army of some twenty thousand into France, making straight for

(1)

(2)

Paris until blocked by a vastly superior host. He made a quick diversion, only to be halted again on the river Somme.

Crécy and Calais

The English troops formed up on a hillside near Crécy with their archers in the forefront, and waited. The French, too, would have been well advised to wait; but their mounted knights, sure of numerical and tactical superiority, charged so recklessly that they ran down many of their own archers. They were met by a hail of arrows from the long-bows of England. Behind the archers, the knights on foot had simply to wait for the already over-taxed foe to come within reach.

One young man who distinguished himself in the hand-to-hand mêlée was the king's son Edward, known from the colour of his armour as the 'Black Prince'. Watching the ebb and flow of the battle from the vantage point of a windmill, King Edward brushed aside the fears of his attendants with the injunction, 'Let the boy win his spurs.' The prince did indeed win them, being knighted on the battlefield, and taking for his own the emblem and motto—*Ich dien* (I serve)—he found on the fallen standard of John, the blind king of Bohemia.

Edward's next objective was Calais. It could be made an excellent staple town for the English wool trade, and a thoroughfare for many other commodities. Command of Calais would also mean command of the Channel and dispersal of the raiders who had been harrying the Kent and Sussex coasts and attacking English wine shipments from Bordeaux.

The town proved less easy to take than he had expected. It endured a year's siege, by the end of which the English had built their own town of huts and tents outside its walls, and Queen Philippa and her retainers had come to keep Edward company. When hunger had sapped all resistance and surrender was offered, Edward vengefully laid down the humiliating proviso that the keys of the town should be brought to him by six leading burghers with halters round their necks, ready to be hanged. Philippa pleaded with him on her knees until he relented and spared their lives.

Calais came into English hands and was to remain in them until 1558.

(3)

(1) Edward III in his garter robes. In his foundation of the Order of the Garter he tried to re-create the chivalrous days of King Arthur.

(2) Burghers of Calais surrender the town keys to Edward III. On the pleading of his wife, Queen Philippa, he treated them with mercy despite their long resistance.

(3) Burying plague victims 1349. The Black Death wiped out perhaps a third of the population of Europe.

The Black Death

There was a break in hostilities when a more terrible enemy arrived from the East. Travelling in the fleas which rats carried from merchant ship to shore, bubonic plague reached Melcombe Regis (now Weymouth) in 1348. The characteristic hard black spots and tumours in armpit and groin made it known as the Black Death. Once it had taken hold it could develop a pneumonic form which needed no rats or fleas to transport it: infection came simply from the tainted breath of those already stricken.

Doctors, still practising alchemy and astrology rather than medicine, knew of no antidote. The rich fled the centres of population and remained in the country in the hope that the terror would not pursue them. Some were fortunate; others carried the disease with them and passed it on.

The poor had less hope of escape. The crowded, insanitary conditions in which they lived were an ideal forcing-ground for the pestilence. When at last it died away, it was estimated that more than a third of the population had perished.

For the survivors there was one unexpected benefit. Over half the villages in England decayed during the ensuing century, when there were a couple more spasmodic outbreaks, but in those that remained, labour was scarce and the lords and landowners could no longer bully peasants into service with threats of starvation. Workers on the land now wanted not only food and a roof over their heads, but a reasonable wage. Finding it easier to get holdings for themselves, they preferred not to do the drudgery of the hitherto obligatory work-days for the lord of the manor, but to commute these into cash payments. If a man decided to leave one master and offer his services to another, retribution was no longer inevitable: with labour so hard to come by, few landlords felt any scruples about poaching from another man's work force. Gradually a new kind of farmer emerged—a man free to work how and where it suited him, renting land from a lord unable to manage estates any longer on the old feudal system, guaranteeing a certain proportion of meat and produce to the manor but otherwise buying and selling much as he chose.

The horror ravaging his kingdom did not distract Edward altogether from his delight in tournaments, war and chivalrous gestures. At a court reception in 1344 he is said to have picked up the countess of Salisbury's garter when it fell and, in defiance of his courtiers' suppressed grins, fastened it on his own leg and said: 'Honi soit qui mal y pense.' ('Shame on him who thinks evil of it.') This, in conjunction with his wish to establish for himself and a chosen few a new knightly order in the Arthurian tradition, led to the creation of the Order of the Garter in 1348, with its noble hall in the Round Tower of Windsor Castle.

In 1355 the war with France was resumed when the Black Prince went raiding and pillaging through the country as far as the Mediterranean. In the following year King John of France trapped him at Poitiers with such a huge array that the prince offered, in return for the freedom of his men and himself, to surrender his accumulated spoils and not fight on French soil again for at least seven years. King John preferred to settle the matter by a spectacular defeat, and battle

A 14th-century tournament: knights in combat provided amusement for king and court.

was joined. The defeat was spectacular, but not as he had planned it: the French, fighting uphill in heavy armour, were no match for the desperate English, and London was soon treated to the astonishing spectacle of the captured French king being paraded through its streets.

The Peace of Bretigny in 1360 brought a huge ransom for King John, together with agreement to recognise English sovereignty over Aquitaine, Calais and Ponthieu, in return for which Edward renounced his claims to the French throne. The Black Prince and his wife Joan, the Fair Maid of Kent, set up a brilliant court in Aquitaine, and Edward himself was at the height of his popularity at home.

This popularity soon waned. Entanglements in Spain stirred up war again, and England lost most of the territory won in France. The Black Prince, after his savage destruction of Limoges in 1370, had to return to England, where he died of dropsy in 1376 and was buried in a massive tomb in Canterbury Cathedral.

Barons and commoners turned against Edward for his maladministration. His own fourth son, John of Gaunt (Ghent), whom he had created duke of Lancaster, intrigued against him. And at the last, on his deathbed, only a year after the death of the Black Prince, he was stripped of all his jewellery, including the rings wrenched from his fingers, by his mistress Alice Perrers.

Geoffrey Chaucer

The ideal of courtly love which appealed so greatly to Edward III was also to form the theme of many works written by a poet born in the twelfth or thirteenth year of his reign.

Geoffrey Chaucer was the son of a vintner, prosperous enough to bring him up comfortably, give him a sound education, and introduce him into the service of the countess of Ulster. At the age of nineteen Chaucer went with her husband to fight in France, where he was taken prisoner and ransomed. In 1366 he married one of the queen's ladies-in-waiting, and on the death of his patron two years later attached himself to John of Gaunt.

Many profitable appointments came his way. He served at various times as customs controller in London, as a justice of the peace, and as supervisor of building operations at Windsor Castle. Most im-

(2)

(1) Soldiers looting a house during the Hundred Years War. It was the French peasants who suffered most as both sides ravaged the land.

(2) The gilt-copper effigy of Edward the Black Prince. Canterbury cathedral, c. 1380.

portant of all were his travels abroad on commercial missions for the king, for from these he returned with a love of French and Italian poetry, and the urge to create an English equivalent.

The first of his poems which can be accurately dated is *The Boke of the Duchesse*, an elegy on the death of John of Gaunt's first wife in 1369. It showed strong French influence, and in the same vein he contributed to the translation of *Roman de la Rose* into *Romaunt of the Rose*. His visits to Italy gave him new themes and metres; but, although he readily adapted these forms and stories and rarely invented any of his own, he brought a powerful originality and vigour to his handling of them. His work culminated in the robust, magnificently characterised *Canterbury Tales*, in which pilgrims travelling from London to the shrine of Thomas Becket are not merely vivid creations in their own right but give, in their individual stories, a detailed picture of religious and social life in the fourteenth century.

When he died in October 1400, Chaucer was buried in Westminster Abbey, the first and perhaps the greatest occupant of what was to become Poets' Corner.

The Peasants' Revolt

Chaucer's use of the vernacular was austerely echoed in the work of John Wyclif, a theologian and Master of Balliol College, Oxford, who asserted the right of every man to read the Bible in his own language and to interpret it according to his own convictions. He translated a large part of the Bible into English, preached the doctrine that all authority must be founded on grace and that therefore no homage was owed to wicked kings, popes and prelates, and denied the Church's right to lavish possessions or to any concern in temporal affairs.

John of Gaunt took advantage of a growing tendency towards anti-clericalism during his struggle for power, and used many of Wyclif's arguments against autocratic bishops in government. Though probably not much interested in these puritanical teachings save for their manipulation in his own cause, he stood by Wyclif when the reformer was in danger from a charge of heresy as a result of his denial of actual transubstantiation at celebration of Mass.

Wyclif's disciples, known as Lollards from a Dutch word meaning 'mumbler' (of prayers), could not preach his doctrines from church pulpits, so went out on to the roads, into towns and villages, spreading a new mood of rebelliousness among those who had for so long been told they must remain meek and obedient in the social order to which God had appointed them.

There were many ready to listen. Although the old hierarchy had been broken up sufficiently for the new breed of farmers to become, as it were, a middle class in the rural scene, most of the more gruelling and unrewarding work was still done by a disorganised, exploited mass of labourers. In an attempt to control the prices which peasants had been demanding for their services the Statute of Labourers passed in 1351 had imposed a 'wage freeze', with severe financial penalties for employers who tried to reach private agreements against the national interest. Prices, however, rose unchecked. The peasantry were soon, relatively, in as bad a situation as they had been

(1)

(2)

(1) Geoffrey Chaucer reading to a company at court.

(2) A pilgrim badge of St Thomas Becket.

(1)

(2)

before the Black Death.

The thunderings of John Ball, a travelling priest whose oratory was devoted as much to secular as to religious matters, told them what they had perhaps sullenly thought but never dared to cry aloud:

At the beginning we were all created equal; it is the tyranny of perverse men which has caused servitude to arise, in spite of God's law; if God had willed that there should be serfs He would have said at the beginning of the world who should be serf and who should be lord.

Ball was in prison in Maidstone when, in 1381, the harangues of himself and his fellow itinerants kindled a blaze. The first outbreak, at Brentwood in Essex, soon spread into a general rising of the Essex peasants against the tax-collectors. Hitherto all taxes had been levied on land, but in an attempt to raise funds quickly for the fruitless war in France the Council acting for fourteen-year-old Richard II, son of the Black Prince, imposed a poll-tax on every adult in the country. This included rich and poor alike, with gradations most unfavourable to the poor. Angry peasants in Essex chased the collectors away and began to march on London, led by Jack Straw. Kentish protesters gathered round Wat Tyler and, on their way to the capital, freed John Ball from gaol. His sardonic verse became their maxim:

When Adam delved and Eve span,
Who was then the gentleman?

It was enthusiastically decided that when the objectors had won their demands—which grew in extent with every exuberant mile they trod—the priest would be made bishop and chancellor.

The two mobs converged. It ought to have been a simple matter to keep them from joining up: London Bridge was the only way by which the Kent contingent could cross the Thames, and of its twenty

(1) John Ball and the Peasants' Revolt.

(2) The Great Hall at Penshurst Place, Kent. England's finest 14th-century domestic hall. Chestnut timbers support the roof.

(1)

(2)

(1) The Tower of London in the early 15th century.

(2) Richard II, son of the Black Prince and successor to Edward III.

arches one carried a drawbridge which could be raised to allow boats through—or, at a time like this, to bar the approach to the city. Whether through negligence or through the surreptitious help of a local sympathiser, the bridge was left open and the mob was free to rampage through London.

If Tyler had been able to maintain discipline over his followers so far, it was gone now. The rabble, drunk with the realisation of their own strength, went on an orgy of destruction; and among the buildings burnt out was, ironically, the Savoy, the palace of the pro-Lollard John of Gaunt. One group stormed the Tower of London and murdered the lord treasurer and the archbishop of Canterbury, who had taken refuge there.

In the teeth of dissuasion from his advisers, young King Richard now showed remarkable courage. He rode out to meet the assembled rebels at Smithfield and expressed his willingness to hear their complaints. Tyler shook him by the hand, but grew more and more blustering until an exasperated squire from his own county shouted abuse at him. There was some confusion immediately after this, and eyewitness accounts vary. Some say that the lord mayor of London stabbed Tyler to death; others that Tyler drew a dagger on the mayor and was then run through by a knight with a sword. Nobody was in any doubt about the sequel. The enraged peasants milled forward, but Richard's nerve did not fail him. 'I am your captain and your king,' he assured them. They must disperse to their homes while he made himself personally responsible for righting the wrongs they had voiced.

As soon as the rebels were safely disbanded, the king's emissaries pounced. Known or supposed ringleaders were hanged and left to rot in key towns and villages. John Ball was hanged, drawn and quartered, and his remains taken from one place to another as a fearful lesson to would-be agitators. Royal promises to abolish serfdom were retracted. For a time repression was worse than ever. Yet seeds of caution had been planted. Villeins might still be beasts of burden, but they were strong beasts and thinking beasts, and might run wild again if goaded too cruelly. The poll-tax was dropped. Even the most deep-dyed autocrat needed men to work his land, and to work assiduously rather than grudgingly.

The sign of the White Hart

Having betrayed his lowliest subjects, Richard when he came of age proceeded to antagonise his nobles. His influential counsellor, John of Gaunt, was preoccupied in contesting a rival's claim to the throne of Castile, which Gaunt felt was rightly his through his second wife. Unfettered, Richard ran up debts, heaped titles on his intimates, and made a mockery of his grandfather's Garter ceremonial by inviting sycophants and their not always respectable womenfolk. Parliament and the judiciary were packed with his placemen.

Lords and bishops combined and threatened possible deposition unless he accepted the guidance of a regulatory council. Richard gave in, but then dismissed Parliament, won a ruling from his judges that the council infringed his royal prerogative, and began to raise troops in the Midlands. The royal army was scattered at Radcot Bridge in

Oxfordshire, and the lords summoned the 'Merciless Parliament' of 1388, which brought charges of treason against the most notable members of Richard's personal clique, executed some, and sent his corrupt judges into exile.

For a number of years Richard made a pretence of submission and governed along the lines required of him. Secretly, however, he planned revenge. Once again he endeavoured to insinuate his place-men into government, and allowed his favourites to raid the estates of others. At the same time he slyly encouraged the formation of militant groups all over the country, ready to combine into a large private army when needed. Their loyalty was sealed with the grant of his personal emblem, the badge of the White Hart. In the last two years of his reign he took the offensive against the lords appellant who had humbled him in 1388, and something approaching a reign of terror ensued.

In 1398 John of Gaunt's son, Henry Bolingbroke, openly quarrelled with the duke of Norfolk on the subject of the king's duplicity, and it was decided to resolve the matter in a duel. Richard allowed preparations to go ahead, but at the last moment forbade the contest and exiled both men.

On the death of John of Gaunt himself in the following year, he was rash enough to seize all the Lancastrian estates and distribute them among his favourites. Richard's disregard of the rights of inheritance, his perversions of justice in obtaining the conviction of people who had spoken against him ten or more years previously, his growing megalomania, and his dependence on favourites and hangers-on all combined to unite the opposition of lords, commons and clergy against him.

Lancastrian King

While Richard was away trying to pacify a newly resurgent Ireland, Henry Bolingbroke landed at Ravenspur in Yorkshire in July 1399 and gained the support of many nobles, including the Percy family, by vowing that he had no personal ambitions other than the restitution of his own good name and estates. In the cause of a reformed government he and his allies arrested Richard upon his return from Ireland, forced him to abdicate, and then imprisoned him in Pontefract Castle.

Henry was now less ready to settle for being merely duke of Lancaster. He claimed the throne and was duly crowned in September 1399 as King Henry IV. Word was spread about that Richard was alive and comfortable in Pontefract, but by February of the next year there were two other rumours: one that he had died as the result of what today we would call a hunger strike; the other, more plausible, that Henry had had him murdered.

The king of France, whose daughter had married Richard and who for a spell had been on unusually good terms with England, was appalled by this regicide. Henry saw that war between the two countries was bound to flare up again, but decided first to tackle the Scots so that they would be deterred from making mischief on behalf of their French friends. He was disconcerted when his supporters, the Percies of Northumberland, showed themselves more

(1) Detail of an English needlework cope with coloured silks and silver-gilt thread in split stitch, c. 1330–50.

(2) Detail from the Wilton diptych, c. 1395 showing Richard II kneeling before his patron saints Edmund, Edward the Confessor and John the Baptist.

(1) A bronze jug bearing the arms and white hart badge of Richard III, found in Ghana.

(2) An anonymous contemporary portrait of Henry V.

adept at fighting the Scots than he was; and even more disturbed when the earl and his son Harry Hotspur, their appetite growing by what it fed upon, decided to join forces with the rebellious Welsh.

Owen Glendower, a Welsh gentleman claiming descent from the great Llywelyn of Gwynedd, had lived peaceably enough and kept up amicable relations with the English during Richard's reign, but grew restive under Henry's increasingly centralised administration. When his English neighbour, Lord Grey of Ruthin, annexed a slice of his estate, he protested formally to Henry, but received a dusty answer. Still balanced somewhat precariously on his new throne, Henry preferred to antagonise Glendower rather than a noble as powerful as Grey.

Proclaiming himself independent king of Wales, Glendower gathered troops, sacked Ruthin, and ravaged the border Marches. He seized castles and estates, and must have been especially pleased to make Lord Grey his prisoner. Henry sent hasty expeditions against the rebellion, but when hard pressed the Welshmen simply vanished into the shelter of their mountains, sallying forth again when it suited them. Glendower began to make plans for a free Welsh Parliament and a university, and wrote to the kings of Scotland and France as one reigning monarch to another.

When the Percies threw in their lot with Wales, and the threat of French assistance grew stronger, Henry realised he could afford no more failures. He led a stronger army to meet the Welsh and Northumbrian allies at Shrewsbury in 1403 and, with his son Prince Henry beside him, scattered them and killed Hotspur; the earl of Northumberland maintained his opposition to the régime until his defeat and death at the battle of Bramham Moor in 1408. Glendower escaped and appealed to other countries for aid, but was gradually worn down by the steady attrition and skill of Prince Henry, and finished his days as a wanderer in the remote corners of the land.

Fair stood the wind for France
The young King Henry V succeeded his father in 1413 and almost immediately decided to renew the neglected war against France. The time seemed propitious. The king of France was half mad, and his nobles were engrossed in the old sport of bickering among themselves. It was also advisable that Henry's own nobles should not be allowed the leisure in which to dream up plots against the Lancastrian monarchy: better to keep them fully occupied in foreign fields.

In 1415 Henry took the key port of Harfleur, but the siege had been carried out in the hot days of August and September and disease had wrought havoc among the English forces. The king sent his sick and wounded back to England by sea while he and the few thousand able-bodied men left to him made their way towards Calais. Before they could reach it, a French army about three times the size of Henry's confronted them at Agincourt.

It was 25th October, St Crispin's Day. Henry prepared a make-shift stockade of sharpened stakes and then made some provocative sorties to tempt the French across a field between two patches of woodland. When the mounted knights were lured into charging, they had little room to swing their weapons and, floundering in the damp

The battle of Agincourt, 25th October 1415. English cavalry charge supported by archers and infantry.

ground, provided a closely packed target for arrows from the deadly long-bows. A thousand prisoners were taken, including many of the nobility of France—those who had not perished on the field. Ransoms swelled the English coffers.

Further funds were readily forthcoming from a jubilant Commons. Henry rebuilt his army, rushed through a programme of ship-building, and in 1417 set out again. His supply system was highly organised, his troops well disciplined, well fed, and well cared for. In three years Normandy was reconquered, Brittany chose neutrality, and the Burgundians defected, leaving the French no option but to sue for peace. By the treaty of Troyes in 1420 it was agreed that Charles VI should nominally retain the Crown during his lifetime but with Henry as regent and eventual heir. Henry married Charles's daughter Catherine, who presented him with a son soon after their return to England.

In 1422 both Charles VI and Henry V died. His son, heir to the thrones of England and France, was only an infant. Henry's two brothers, the dukes of Bedford and of Gloucester, acted as regents, with Bedford taking on the supervision of France. If the French had resented their subservience to a royal English regent, they liked even less the idea of having to obey a mere English nobleman. Bedford met at best with passive resistance and at worst with armed outbreaks. He was a good soldier and a humane administrator, but whatever laws he laid down were evaded or ignored as soon as his officials had moved on a few miles. Large parts of southern France still openly declared their allegiance to their own royal prince, Charles the Dauphin.

The Maid of Orléans

In March 1429 a girl who called herself Jeanne d'Arc arrived at the Dauphin's castle at Chinon and told him that since the age of thirteen she had been guided by angelic voices, which had now commanded her to leave her village of Domrémy and save France from its oppressors.

Because the Dauphin, like the rest of his countrymen, was longing for a miracle, he was readier to listen than he might otherwise have been. Joan of Arc was supplied with troops, dressed herself like a

boy, and in white armour led the way to Orléans, besieged by the
English and in imminent danger of collapse. She raised the siege in
May and, hailed as the Maid of Orléans, went on to further victories,
culminating in the coronation of the Dauphin as King Charles VII at
Rheims in July.

The English and their French time-servers were sure that only a
witch could have accomplished such marvels in such a short space of
time. When the Burgundians captured her after she had made a vain
attempt to relieve Compiègne, they were quick to hand her over to
the English. After a typical ecclesiastical trial, in many ways fair by
the standards of the day, she was burned to death as a heretic in the
market-place of Rouen.

The French, however, roused from their apathy, came to regard
her as a saint. Bedford tried to nullify the effect of Charles's coronation by having the nine-year-old Henry crowned king of France in
Paris, but this evoked only scorn from his supposed subjects. The
spirit of resistance had been kindled, and even Burgundy decided to
change sides. Years of warfare followed, with England's hold being

gradually, relentlessly prised open. By 1453 England's sole remaining possession in France was Calais.

In August of that same year King Henry VI went mad.

The Wars of the Roses

Henry's domestic policy had been feeble at the best of times. His nobles shared out and intrigued for commercial privileges among themselves, did what they could to sabotage the wasteful war effort, and neglected their lands and people. One, the duke of Suffolk, was impeached in 1450 for having made contact with the French enemy, and Henry did little to increase his own popularity by helping the duke to flee the country. On board ship, an indignant crew took matters into their own hands and beheaded Suffolk.

In 1450 there had been another popular rising, not this time of peasants but of Kent and Sussex yeomen under the leadership of Jack Cade, himself a man of some substance. They objected to the profiteers with whom the king had surrounded himself, and to oppressive taxation. This time royal troops were despatched to meet them before they got too close, but were defeated at Sevenoaks. The rebels pressed on to London. The townsfolk found them as unwelcome as did the government, and after three days of unco-ordinated looting and a few killings, the rebels themselves seemed hazy about their own motives. A parley was offered, and after remedies had been promised for some abuses most of them drifted back home. Cade himself wanted to continue the revolt but, without support, had to go into hiding. He was finally tracked down and killed in Sussex.

Among the nobles jockeying for position were two descendants of the Plantagenet line. The duke of Somerset belonged, like the king, to the Lancastrian strand; his rival, and heir presumptive to the throne in the absence of any child of Henry VI, was Richard, duke of York. To be friendly with one was axiomatically to be the enemy of the other. In the absence of firm royal control, the country began to split into two armed camps.

At the onset of the king's insanity, the duke of York made a bid for the regency. Somerset was out of favour with Parliament as a result of his mishandling of the last stages of the French war, and was sent to the Tower while York became protector.

Then, disconcertingly, the queen gave birth to a son. Richard of York had to acknowledge the boy as rightful heir to the throne, but with a bad grace. When, equally disconcertingly, the king recovered his sanity, Margaret urged him to reinstate Somerset and get rid of Richard.

That was to be the pattern of the next thirty years: thrust and counter-thrust, advantage to one side and then to the other, a grotesque and destructive weather-house with first one figure and then another popping out—red rose and white rose, as we think of it. In fact, the emblems which have given the Wars of the Roses their name were not in general use during the struggle: the white rose of York was adopted only in the second decade of the wars, and the red rose of Lancaster only when they were over.

The wretched Henry was imprisoned, released, and again imprisoned. Parliament pleaded with the opposing factions, suggesting

Edward IV. In youth he was renowned for his good looks and manly figure but he grew fat in middle age.

that Henry should live out his reign and then be succeeded by Richard. Queen Margaret urged the Lancastrians to repudiate such a compromise, and herself raised an army which triumphed at Wakefield in 1460 in a battle during which Richard of York was killed. A paper crown was set on his severed head, which was then placed over one of the gateways of York. Again Henry was released from prison, and again showed himself insane and unfit to rule. The Yorkists set up another clamour, this time in favour of Richard's son Edward, the earl of March.

After the battle of Towton in 1461 Edward was acclaimed king as Edward IV and Henry fled, only to be recaptured in 1465 and taken by the earl of Warwick to the Tower of London. Warwick, whose propensity for juggling with royal claimants earned him the nickname 'the King-maker', was anxious to ensure that the French did not give too much help to Margaret of Anjou, Henry's queen, now back in their midst. He hastily arranged a betrothal between King Edward and a French princess, only to learn that Edward had

Opening page from Chaucer's *Canterbury Tales* published by Caxton.

(1) Caxton's device from his edition of the *Canterbury Tales*.

(2) Chaucer's pilgrims at dinner, from the Prologue to the *Canterbury Tales*.

already contracted a secret marriage with Elizabeth Woodville, from a family of no great consequence and, what was worse, widow of a Lancastrian killed at the battle of St Albans during the recent conflict. Once established as queen, Elizabeth made sure of advancement for the members not only of her own family but also of her dead husband's.

Warwick, a congenital schemer, was dismayed to find power slipping through his fingers and to be told that the increasingly self-assertive king would not allow the marriage of his brother to the earl's daughter. Warwick persisted with the marriage arrangements and took the king captive; then, forced to release him, added further complexities by defecting to the Lancastrians.

He and Queen Margaret settled their differences and drove Edward out in 1470. They released the mad Henry from the Tower to act as a figurehead. Edward returned, killed Warwick at the battle of Barnet, and in May 1471 captured Queen Margaret at Tewkesbury and killed her son. This left the Yorkists at last with no counter-claimants. The Lancastrian heir dead, Henry returned for the last time to the Tower, where it was said by some that he pined away, by others that he was murdered on the night of Edward's triumphal entry into London.

William Caxton

One of the most momentous transitions in the middle of the fifteenth century was that from the limited production and circulation of handwritten and hand-illustrated manuscripts to the potentially unlimited production of printed texts.

The earliest 'block books' had been constructed by binding together sheets duplicated from woodcuts painstakingly chipped out—words as well as pictures—by hand. Movable type was invented somewhere between 1451 and 1456, by Johannes Gutenberg of Mainz. At first wooden characters were used, but the advantages of longer-lasting metal type were soon realised.

William Caxton, an Englishman who had gone to Bruges at the age of about sixteen to complete his apprenticeship in the silk trade,

(1)   (2)

Richard III was not the twisted hunchback of Shakespeare's play; his deformity was invented by the Tudors to blacken his memory.

is thought to have made his first contact with the new art of printing in Cologne. He set up his own press in Bruges, and then returned to England and began printing in Westminster in 1476. He not only printed books but made his own translations of French romances and legends. Great works of literature and learning could now be brought within the reach of anyone who could read; and, by a natural sequence, this encouraged the wider spread of reading itself.

Caxton's two most famous publications were his versions of Chaucer's *Canterbury Tales* and Malory's *Morte d'Arthur*.

Princes in the Tower

When Edward IV died in 1483 his brother Richard, duke of Gloucester, was appointed protector of the thirteen-year-old Edward V. Richard had acquired great wealth and estates in the north of England when he married a daughter of the earl of Warwick, and was eventually made the king's lieutenant-general of the north. He proved a scrupulous and popular administrator.

When he assumed responsibility for the young king's welfare he had good reason to fear the influence of the boy's maternal relations, the acquisitive Woodvilles. On the grounds that it was for the children's safety, he removed both Edward and his younger brother, the duke of York, from their mother's custody and incarcerated them in the Tower. Then he set himself to scour every vestige of Woodville influence from the court.

Once started on such a path, he must have realised there could be no turning back. In his own interest and, he was doubtless able to persuade himself, the best interests of the country, he declared himself rightful king of England. To justify such a step he had to denounce the two boys as illegitimate, and drive the supposedly adulterous Queen Elizabeth into the seclusion of an abbey.

The fate of the two princes in the Tower gives rise to the most heated controversy to this day. It was widely believed at the time that Richard himself had done them to death, and Richard himself never troubled to deny it. Later scholars, however, had doubts, pointing out that the generally accepted testimony of the saintly Thomas More was suspect, coming as it did from a supporter of Richard's sworn enemies.

Certainly the boys died, and certainly two youthful skeletons were found in the Tower in the seventeenth century. It was also true that the austere-looking Richard, nicknamed 'Crouchback' because of a slight deformity rather less marked than his detractors would have us believe, behaved sternly towards some nobles and time-servers in his endeavour to suppress disorder and corruption in the realm. But there was a need for a firm hand. Richard came down severely on corruption in the legal system, promoted a drive for foreign trade, and promised to cut down on royal demands for money. He was a brilliant and courageous soldier, and in all his personal dealings was conceded to be meticulous and even generous: many a humble suppliant was grateful for his kindness, and his popularity in the north remained unquestioned.

But he had brazened his way to power, the dark hints about his

Jousting knights displaying coats of arms, painted in 1430 for Sir Thomas Holme, Clarenceux King of Arms.

Relic of a vital battle: processional cross from Bosworth.

deeds would not be stilled, and when his son died there was no heir to carry on any tradition he might try to establish.

The way was open for the only surviving Lancastrian with the strength to take and keep the throne. Henry Tudor was a descendant of John of Gaunt through that duke's illicit marriage to his mistress. He had spent half his life in Wales, the rest on the Continent. Urged to intervene, he found Welsh forces eager to join him when he landed at Milford Haven, and led them on into England. Richard met them outside Market Bosworth, near Leicester, on 22nd August 1485.

The royal army was larger but fought with less conviction. Many nobles on whom Richard was relying had already decided to defect. Richard himself fought bravely, but was accorded little respect for this after his death. The crown of England, found in a bush, was placed on Henry Tudor's head, and the corpse of the dead king was stripped naked, tossed across a horse, and carried unceremoniously to Leicester.

After his coronation King Henry VII made haste to unite the country's two quarrelsome factions by marrying the Yorkist Elizabeth, daughter of Edward IV. At first he was on excellent terms with his mother-in-law, the dowager queen, but soon found her liking for intrigue so irrepressible that he ordered her into the seclusion of Bermondsey Abbey and handed over all her property to his own queen.

The last of the Plantagenets was gone. The stage was set for the Tudors.

OPPOSITE Henry VIII with Jane Seymour and their son Prince Edward. This idealisation of the Tudor succession was not painted from life, for Edward's birth killed Jane Seymour.

The Tudors

The Tudors

When the reign of Henry VII began few of his fellow monarchs in Europe rated his chances of survival very highly. Quite unashamedly they gave sanctuary and even encouragement to pretenders and conspirators eager to turn the tables. But during the century ahead the Tudor dynasty was to prove capable of defying all threats from Europe or from within; the slow increase of population since the end of the Black Death began to speed up, until by the end of Henry's most famous granddaughter's reign there were some four million people in England; trade expanded vigorously; and the

(1)

(1) Henry VII by Michael Sittow, 1505. A masterly depiction of the despotic but shrewd administrator.

(2) Cambridge: King's College Chapel, begun in 1446, the supreme achievement of Gothic architecture.

country felt a new sense of nationhood and confidence in its destiny.

Henry lost no time in making sweeping reforms in the dilatory legal system, which in its clumsiness and corruption was far from honouring the Magna Carta pledge that 'Justice will not be sold to any man nor will it be refused or delayed.' He revived the central royal judiciary, called the Court of Star Chamber from the ceiling decoration of the Westminster room in which it was held. In spite of later misuse, suppressing not merely sedition but any controversial speech whatsoever by arbitrary judgements, torture and mutilation, the court sorted out many problems more effectively than common law courts were capable of doing, and halted the lawlessness rife after the Wars of the Roses.

Those thirty years of fighting had taken their toll of the nobility. No great harm had been done to the countryside, whose workers toiled on little affected by the squabbles of their betters. The growing class of successful merchants had, if anything, profited, and many a commercial upstart had become 'respectable' and swollen the ranks of the newly emergent gentry—a class whose separate existence was never formally acknowledged, but whose capabilities and pretensions were to be most skilfully used by Henry and, in due course, his son.

A number of the great old families had lost fathers and sons, and often lost their lands as fortunes swayed to and fro. Some manors were split up among smaller-scale property-owners. As if the attrition of these parochial wars had not been enough, the king now clamped down on the remaining barons. The overweening ambitions of many of them had always been a threat to the Crown and the stability of the country. Henry and those who came after him, though never denying the social supremacy of the aristocracy, found that royal patronage of the ambitious gentry brought better returns in the way of loyalty and grateful service than could be guaranteed from the hereditary, often vainglorious lords.

Two puppets

Henry dealt with various spasmodic rebellions and with the claims of other aspirants to the throne. A carpenter's son, Lambert Simnel, was groomed as the supposed son of that duke of Clarence who had been brother to Edward IV and Richard III, and crowned as King Edward VI in Dublin. The real son was in fact in the Tower, from which he was brought to be shown to the London public. Simnel's invasion of England in 1487 was soon put down, and the rather absurd puppet was sent to work in the king's kitchens.

Another pretender, Perkin Warbeck, denied the story that Richard III had killed the princes in the Tower and asserted that he was the younger of the two, the duke of York. He received great encouragement from the French and Scottish kings, and between 1488 and 1498 tried to ferment insurrection a number of times; he was finally captured after failing to take Exeter in 1497, and though he escaped the following year he was soon recaptured, sent to the Tower, and eventually executed at Tyburn in 1499.

Henry had no real taste for wars, at home or abroad. He wanted a peaceful, prosperous England. His financial expertise set the

(1) The court of the exchequer in the 15th century. Money being counted before a presiding judge and barons.

(2) Elizabeth of York, queen consort of Henry VII.

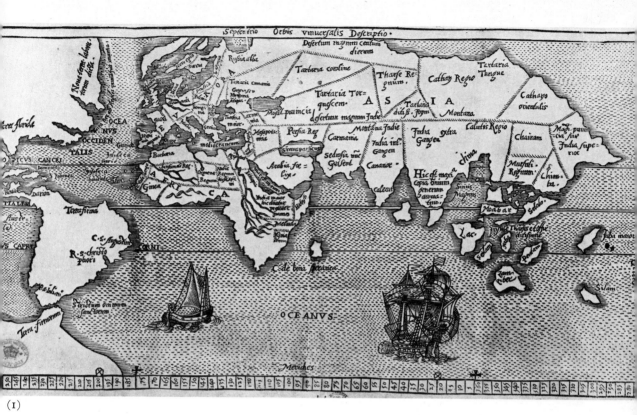

Septentrio · Orbis vniuersalis Descriptio ·

(1)

(2)

(1) A map of the world drawn in
the early years of the 16th century.
(2) A 15th Century mariner's
astrolabe

OVERLEAF
Henry VIII, school of Holbein.

Catherine of Aragon by Michael
Sittow.

country's economy on a firm footing. He cut down on wasteful
expenditure, checked all the Exchequer's dealings himself, administered his own estates profitably, and encouraged others to do likewise.
He also realised that England must look outward if she were to
prosper as other maritime nations were prospering. He encouraged
exports while protecting home industries; and he sought new markets
and new riches by backing the ventures of John Cabot, though perhaps not quite fervently enough.

New frontiers

In 1492 an adventurous sailor from Genoa, Christopher Columbus,
having failed to arouse Henry's interest by letters setting out his
beliefs in the roundness of the world and the possibility of reaching
the Indies by a westward route, won support from Queen Isabella of
Spain for an exploratory voyage. After ninety days, during which
there was serious danger of mutiny and of his being forced to turn
back, Columbus reached land, named it San Salvador, and claimed
it for Spain. Further voyages made it clear that a whole new world
had been discovered, and in 1494 Spain and Portugal agreed by the
Treaty of Tordesillas to divide it between them.

A Genoese pilot, Giovanni Caboto, who had settled in Bristol as
John Cabot, merchant, had long shared Columbus's views. He
persuaded Henry to provide him with a ship so that he could set out
on England's behalf. In 1497 he discovered a bleak, inhospitable
'new-found-land' which he took to be part of Asia. Returning home
to report the disappointment, he pressed for a larger vessel so that
he might explore further and perhaps find a north-west passage to

85

The Tudor kitchen at Hampton Court Palace.

the riches of the East. Bristol merchants hopefully contributed to this venture, but Cabot's further study of the North American mainland did not inspire him, and he abandoned it to the more determined Spaniards.

If he failed to pursue that colonial possibility strongly enough, Henry was not lax in strengthening the country in relation to its powerful neighbours; but where possible he avoided any violent trial of that strength. Threatened by war with France, he won a large grant of money from Parliament, and then presented such an alarming challenge that he was able to demand a large indemnity from the French in return for not going to war with them. This was a method of settling disputes much to Henry's taste.

He married his son Arthur to Catherine of Aragon, and his daughter Margaret to James IV of Scotland. The name of the heir to the throne carried deeply romantic British resonances. It is interesting to speculate how the mystique surrounding the very name of a King Arthur might have affected the country when Henry VII died. It can never be more than speculation. Arthur, truly a Prince of Wales, married for political reasons at the age of fifteen, died in his sixteenth year. The question of whether or not the marriage was ever consummated became a question of some importance to the flamboyant, pleasure-loving younger brother who took his place—and his widow—and was crowned King Henry VIII in April 1509.

Anne Boleyn.

Bluff King Hal

Towards the end of his life, Henry VII had exhorted his successor to maintain the Spanish alliance by marrying Catherine. The Church's prohibition against a man marrying his dead brother's wife had to be overcome, and it suited the young king at this stage to avow his belief that there had been no true marriage between Arthur and Catherine. The Pope gave his blessing, and Henry was wed.

The new ruler had inherited a solvent, going concern. All he needed to make him happy was an heir to whom the running of the business could be entrusted in due course: England could not be handed on to a Board of Directors or—so thought Henry, not dreaming of what was to come—to a woman.

Queen Catherine produced a son on New Year's Day, 1511. Seven weeks later he died. Each year for the next four years she was delivered of a child. They all died in infancy. At last there was a sixth who survived; and this was a girl, Princess Mary. Catherine continued to produce, and the children continued to die.

Henry sought his pleasure elsewhere, and fathered a bastard son, Henry Fitzroy, whom he created duke of Richmond at the age of six. But he was growing desperate for a legitimate heir.

His lust and his hopes fastened together upon dark-eyed Anne Boleyn, who had been a maid of honour to his sister Mary when for a brief spell she was wife of the king of France. Back in England, Anne became the focus of the king of England's attentions. He showered presents on her, which she flaunted before the queen, and profitable appointments upon her family. The liaison scandalised the court and visiting ambassadors, but they consoled themselves with the thought that the king would soon tire of this mistress as he had tired of others, and then brusquely discard her.

But Anne Boleyn was not a mistress like others. She kept Henry at arm's length for years, refusing to let him bed her unless they were married. His appetite grew; she refused to satisfy it. Utterly obsessed by her, Henry managed to persuade himself that he had been wrong to marry his dead brother's widow. His failure to father a son was proof of God's wrath, and it would clearly be best for his kingdom and for himself if Catherine could be set aside. It was not, however, going to be so easy to persuade the Pope of this and obtain an annulment of the marriage, especially as Catherine's nephew Charles was the Holy Roman Emperor and held the Pope virtually a prisoner.

The task of dealing with this awkward situation was entrusted to a man who had been Henry VII's chaplain, and whom Henry VIII had raised to the heights of lord chancellor and archbishop of York. He was Thomas Wolsey, son of an Ipswich grazier, who became Cardinal Wolsey in 1515. Like his master, Wolsey was a great one for pomp and circumstance, and his extravagances in dress and ceremonial made some mutter that it was he 'who rules the king and the whole kingdom'.

Wolsey helped Henry make a fine display during his first military campaigns in France—the ritual wars which Henry VII had avoided, but which his son felt it almost a matter of honour to resume. When it was obvious that no far-reaching conquest could be made, it was Wolsey who connived at the marriage of the king's sister Mary to

CARDINAL WOOLSE

the ageing king of France. When that monarch shortly died, to be succeeded by the aggressive young Francis I, it was Wolsey who brought the two kings together in 1520 on the sumptuous Field of the Cloth of Gold near Ardres in France, putting on a glittering display with which to dazzle the onlookers.

Now it was Wolsey who must perform a much trickier service for his master.

Defender of the Faith

During Henry's absence on one of his self-glorifying campaigns, James IV of Scotland decided to invade England as a gesture of solidarity with the French. Queen Catherine took charge and sent an army under the earl of Surrey to halt the Scots. There was a battle at Flodden Field in Northumberland in 1513, where modern weapons began to take over from the old: long-bows and cannon worked side by side to annihilate the raiders, and by the end of the day James was dead, along with most of his earls and lesser nobles.

Henry VIII arriving at the Field of the Cloth of Gold for his historic meeting with Francis I of France in June 1520.

(1)

(2)

(1) Henry VIII jousting before Catherine of Aragon.

(2) The suit of armour worn by Henry VIII.

OVERLEAF

(1) Elizabeth I by Nicholas Hilliard.

(2) Robert Dudley, earl of Leicester by an unknown artist.

Whatever gratitude Henry may have felt to his resourceful queen was forgotten by the time he decided she must give way to Anne Boleyn. And whatever he owed to Wolsey was forgotten when the cardinal failed to talk the Pope or his emissaries in England into facilitating a quick divorce and remarriage. The tempestuous Anne was even more vehement in her denunciations. Wolsey called her 'the night crow'; she, for her part, was set on disgracing him.

Denuded of belongings and appointments, Wolsey was banished from court in 1529; pardoned in 1530; and then recalled to be tried for treason, largely on Anne's insistence. He died on his way from York to London, murmuring, 'Had I but served my God as diligently as I have served my king, he would not have given me over in my grey hairs.' Henry took over the rich palace which Wolsey had built at Hampton Court. Of the college which the grazier's son had longed to build in his birthplace, Ipswich, all that remains is a gateway with an eroded coat of arms.

Wolsey's secretary, Thomas Cromwell, had come from humble beginnings like his master. With the cardinal disgraced and dead, Cromwell won Henry's ear by suggesting that the Pope's views were not necessarily binding in England. Like Anne, he allowed himself a leaning towards Lutheran doctrines when they suited him, although they were proscribed as heretical. And Anne herself had paved the way for this new approach by persuading Henry to read Tyndale's *Obedience of a Christian Man*, in which the argument that kings must be ultimately responsible for the spiritual as well as physical well-being of their subjects gave Henry a philosophical basis for defiance of the Pope. It was not only politic but morally right that the king of England should declare himself also head of the Church of England—a logical conclusion to his predecessor's steps in bringing Church authority more rigorously under the control of secular law.

It was never Henry's intention to renounce the Roman Catholic Church. He was staunchly anti-Protestant, assiduous in the prosecu-

(1)

tion and burning of heretics, and as a result of a pamphlet he had written against the perils of Lutheranism had been declared 'Defender of the Faith' by Pope Leo X—a sobriquet which remains in the form of *Fid :Def :* or *F.D.* (*Fidei Defensor*) on coins of the realm to this day. But he thought he could get away with flouting Pope Clement VII, doubtless assuring himself that Clement was acting under duress and would come round once he was out of Charles of Spain's clutches, and he was in any case so infatuated with Anne that he was prepared to risk anything.

With the aid of an obedient Parliament, the co-operative Archbishop Cranmer, and a terrorised clergy still stunned by the fall of Wolsey, he had himself declared 'Protector and supreme head of the Church and clergy in England'. He allowed the addition of a proviso, 'as far as the law of Christ allows', confident that no rigid interpretation could ever be put on this clause.

Now was the time for an English convocation to prove its independence from Rome and grant him the ruling he had waited for so long.

Henry and Anne were actually wed before the divorce was ratified. With the achievement of her highest ambitions in sight, Anne must have thought it wise to reward the king, or perhaps to spur him on, by allowing him intercourse at last. Some time in January 1533 she told him she was pregnant: this, too, may have been part of her plan, to ensure that for Henry there could be no turning back. On 25th January they married in secret. Henry, anxious that their child should be publicly recognised as his legitimate heir, urged the archbishop's tribunal to get on quickly with its business. In May, Cranmer declared the king's marriage to Catherine null and void, and on 1st June Anne was crowned queen of England.

The child was born in September. It was a daughter, Elizabeth.

(2)

(3)

ue my spirit.

er Iohn.

(4)

(1) Thomas Cromwell by Holbein.
A brilliant representation of
Cromwell's icy power.

(2) Sir Thomas More and his
family. More, one of Europe's
foremost scholars, died for his
principles.

(3) Thomas Cranmer, archbishop
of Canterbury under Henry VIII,
was burned by Mary.

(4) The burning of Cranmer at
Oxford, 1556.

Five more queens

Henry's lord chancellor, Sir Thomas More, resigned office rather
than agree that the king had the right to challenge papal supremacy
or set Catherine aside. When ordered to take an oath, as everyone in
the land had to do, acknowledging the vesting of the succession in
children of the second and not the first marriage, he refused this also.
A Supremacy Act and a Treasons Act were pushed through Parliament and employed to bring charges against More and the similarly
stubborn bishop of Rochester. Both were executed.

The Pope pronounced excommunication upon Henry until such
time as he left Anne Boleyn and returned to his lawful wife.

Those who had once predicted that the king would soon weary of
Mistress Boleyn when she had become truly his mistress were
belatedly proved right. Her physical charms lost their power; she
failed to present him with the male heir he craved for; and she was
proving to be a scold, mocking him in front of his courtiers, sneering
at his taste in clothes and music and poetry, and gossiping maliciously with her favourites about his sexual inadequacy.

(1)

Having disposed of one queen, why should he scruple to dispose of another? His roving eye had already alighted on the demure but shrewd Jane Seymour, maid of honour to Catherine and Anne in turn. Anne had the humiliation of seeing the girl wearing the king's gifts as she herself had once worn them. On more than one occasion she found the two of them closeted together, and several times threw herself on Jane, biting and scratching.

The flirtatiousness which had first endeared Anne to Henry was now turned against her. The king contrasted her shrewishness and flighty indiscretions unfavourably with the gentleness of his new love. At a May Day tournament at Greenwich Palace in 1536, Henry publicly accused a courtier of having committed adultery with the queen, and then commanded that the queen be brought to trial.

Anne appealed to him to 'let me have a lawful trial, and let not my sworn enemies sit as my accusers and my judges'; but her husband was interested in speed rather than in legal niceties. She was charged with 'following daily her fickle and carnal appetite and wishing that several familiar and daily servants of our lord the King should become her adulterers and concubines' and procuring and inciting 'by sweet words, kissing, touchings and other illicit means' a number of courtiers, including her own brother. The proceedings were rushed through, and Anne was beheaded on Tower Green.

Two days before her execution, Cranmer presided over a court which solemnly ruled that the king's admitted earlier adultery with Anne's older sister Mary had invalidated the marriage right from the start. This meant that Anne's daughter Elizabeth was now, like Catherine's daughter Mary, technically illegitimate.

(2)

Four brides of Henry VIII:

(1) Anne of Cleves

(2) Jane Seymour

(3) Catherine Howard

(4) Catherine Parr

98

(3)

KATHARINE PARRE

(4)

Jane Seymour gave Henry his heart's desire. Their son Edward was born in October 1537. The queen herself died within a few days. Henry heaped honours on her family, and at his own death left instructions that it was beside Jane he wished to be buried.

Her successor was chosen by Thomas Cromwell. Seeking a strong link with Protestant Germany, he recommended to the king the charms of Anne of Cleves. When they met, and it was too late to retract his offer of marriage, Henry was horrified by the ugliness of 'this Flanders mare'. At the wedding he said wretchedly to Cromwell: 'If it were not to satisfy the world and my realm, I would not do that I must do this day for none earthly thing.'

The marriage was not consummated. The couple lived together only a short time. Henry found the lady as dull as she was plain: whatever his many faults, Henry was a great lover of the arts and especially of music, which aroused no flicker of response in Anne. There was no question of executing this queen. Her European relations were too powerful. But Thomas Cromwell's rivals, anxious for his downfall, had already suggested to Henry a possible replacement for his unattractive wife. Her name was Catherine Howard, daughter of the scheming duke of Norfolk, and soon the king was impatient to acquire her. Parliament was easily persuaded to annul the unfortunate marriage, and in return for the gift of two houses and an income of £500 a year Anne of Cleves proved quite docile.

As though to make up for having allowed the dismal queen to retain her head, Henry turned on Cromwell, had him charged with treason and heresy, and sent him to the block. It was doubly ironical that Henry, setting himself up as supreme ruler of the English Church, should in time have grown disenchanted with Cromwell's encouragement of Protestant elements; and that Cromwell, who with Cranmer had ordered the introduction of the Bible in English into

all churches and instigated the suppression of the monasteries, should in the hour of his death affirm that he remained a Catholic.

Henry and Catherine married on the day of Cromwell's execution. She was presented with most of the destroyed minister's estates, and much more besides, by her doting husband.

Catherine had been reckless before marriage, and went on being so after. Henry bored her. She flirted more shamelessly than Anne Boleyn had ever done, and did little to conceal a succession of adulteries. It was suggested to Henry that she was continuing a relationship with the man she had originally intended to wed. Archbishop Cranmer, alarmed by the rise of the Norfolks and their Catholic adherents, made it his business to report as damagingly as possible to Henry on Catherine's past and present. Like Anne, she was beheaded on Tower Green.

Her successor, Henry's sixth and last consort, was the twice-widowed Catherine Parr, a Protestant. She was a good-natured woman who showed the greatest kindness to his children by previous marriages, and won their affection. She outlived Henry and married Thomas Seymour, brother of the king's revered Jane.

Dissolution of the Monasteries

During the reign of Henry VIII even the most agile religious trimmer must have found it hard to express his opinions safely. Cranmer worked on an English prayer book and believed that Henry's Church should move towards Protestantism. Henry clung to orthodoxy—provided he was the one who said what was orthodox and what was not. He broke with Rome yet had heretics burnt at the stake. In the statute of Six Articles, forced through a far from happy Parliament in 1539, he laid down six cardinal doctrines of Catholic belief which he intended to preserve in the English Church, with severe penalties for those who transgressed; yet at the same time he was fervently occupied in the dissolution of the monasteries.

Ever since the time of William the Conqueror monks had been

(1) Liquor in monasteries was distributed by a monk cellarer who held cellar keys and enjoyed special privileges.

(2) The world we have lost: the rack, prime instrument of Tudor interrogation, in use on Cuthbert Simson in 1556.

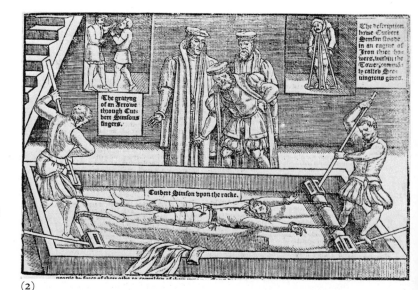

(2)

Title-page of the Bible in English, 1539.

coming into England from the Continent and establishing religious houses, often with funds supplied by grateful nobles who had come with William. For many of them this new—indeed, alien—country was a challenge: a place in which they could lead a simple, austere life in a still largely wild countryside.

Over the years the austerity had given way to a more relaxed and even luxurious way of life. The monasteries owned and exploited vast acres. Devout patrons loaded them with treasures, and the involvement of many clerics in political matters gave them an appetite for both power and pleasure. When Cromwell put into Henry's head the idea of disciplining those who were reluctant to accept his ecclesiastical authority, at the same time filling a depleted Treasury, it was not difficult to find plausible excuses.

They started with the smaller foundations, on the grounds that 'manifest sin, vicious carnal and abominable living is daily used and committed amongst the little and small abbeys'. Royal inspectors were sent to prepare reports on these houses. It was clear what kind of report was expected of them. The Suppression Act of 1536 trans-

Rievaulx abbey, Yorkshire; founded in the 12th century, dissolved in 1539.

ferred all buildings and possessions to the Crown, but made allowance for pensions to be paid to displaced abbots and abbesses, and for humbler monks and nuns to take up residence in larger surviving houses or, if they wished, to renounce their vows and come out into the world.

Whatever the vices of some establishments, and they were many, their closure was a loss to many ordinary folk. They had provided food, shelter, and often a rudimentary education to their lay employees and the faithful in the neighbourhood. No needy traveller was ever turned away. A protest march, the Pilgrimage of Grace, began in the north in 1536, provoked not only by the hardship brought to certain areas by the abandonment of the monasteries but by other grievances over taxation and arbitrary land enclosures.

Robert Aske, a gentleman of Yorkshire, led the pilgrimage to York and on to Doncaster, where the marchers were promised full consideration of their problems by the king. They dispersed, while Aske himself went to London at Henry's request for further discussions. While he was away, others who suspected that Henry's promises had been merely a play for time while he prepared savage reprisals, broke out in renewed disorder. They were right: Henry, ready for them this time, struck mercilessly. Many of the leaders, Aske among them, were accused of treason and executed.

In the same year that he demanded obedience to the Six Articles, Henry turned his attention to demolition of the larger monasteries. He had dealt mercilessly with the heads of any communities which had given shelter or approval to the Pilgrimage of Grace or any of its known supporters, and continued to be ruthless. The abbot of Glastonbury, protesting against the invasion of the king's officers, was summarily hanged. Instead of being allowed the option of transfer to another foundation, more and more monks were driven out—some on pension, some to seek solace in continental houses.

Henry took the monastic treasures for himself. Lead from the roofs was melted down to make cannon shot. Left unoccupied and all too often stripped of roofs and doors, abbeys and priories and their chapels soon decayed.

Despot under the law

If he despoiled many magnificent buildings, Henry created or developed many others. He added much to Hampton Court Palace, including the ornate vaulted roof of the Chapel Royal; was also responsible for the choir roof of St George's Chapel at Windsor, and for the main gateway and the north terrace; and did not neglect the strengthening of the vulnerable south-east coast by a number of castles.

Henry was described as a 'despot under the law'; but he was at least concerned with the forms of the law, and while much of his despotism might be due to personal arrogance, he also personified the growing sense of nationhood, and shared with his subjects their mistrust of all foreigners. With his Welsh ancestry he found it possible between 1534 and 1536 to achieve greater harmony between Wales and England than had ever existed before. By 1543 the freedoms of the Marcher lords had been abolished, and a legal and administrative system was instituted which gave Wales more peace and better order than she had enjoyed for years. The Scots proved less amenable: adhering strictly to Rome, King James V went to war against Henry, but was deserted by many of his jealous lairds and ignominiously defeated at Solway Moss in 1532. He died soon after, learning on his deathbed that his wife had just given birth to a daughter, who was to become Mary Queen of Scots.

It was almost obligatory for Henry to make another assault on France late in his reign. He made a great show of it in 1544, but achieved nothing more remarkable than the capture of Boulogne. In reprisal the French assembled an invasion fleet, which was driven off.

Here is to be found one of Henry's greatest achievements. He founded Trinity House and the forerunner of our modern Admiralty. He extended the royal dockyards and encouraged the construction of faster ships with superior fire-power. He laid, as it were, the keels of that future navy which was to thwart the ambitions of one greedy enemy after another. It was still a motley force, its professionals hastily reinforced by a crowd of conscripts in time of emergency: the Cinque Ports and the increasingly important West Country ports, for instance, had certain obligations to supply ships and the men to work them, for invasion transport or urgent defence needs, but once a crisis was over these auxiliaries would go back to their usual jobs. Nevertheless the courage and imagination were there, the breaking down of national insularity and the growth of an adventurousness that would enable the poet Edmund Waller to boast in the following century that

Others may use the ocean as their road,
Only the English make it their abode.

(1) Sir Thomas Wyatt, courtier and poet, by Holbein.

(2) The *Henry Grace à Dieu*, flagship of Henry VIII's navy.

(1) Succession and true religion: the dying Henry VIII points to his successor Edward VI. In the foreground the Pope is crushed by the new prayer book.

(2) The timber-framed guildhall at Lavenham, Suffolk, pride of the Tudor cloth industry.

(1)

(2)

Prince and protector

When Henry died in 1547 his son Edward was only nine years old. Henry had given strict instructions on the future administration of the realm to a council of ministers, but most of these decrees were flouted by the Lord Protector, the duke of Somerset. Somerset, a member of the Seymour family whose interests Henry had done so much to promote, was a staunch Protestant and proceeded to undo some of his late master's work and to push other features of it to extremes. The statute of the Six Articles was repealed. The Act for the suppression of chantries, passed in Henry's day as a follow-up to the dissolution of the monasteries but so far left in abeyance, was put into operation. There was greater freedom of debate, especially on economic matters, but in religion Somerset was in his own way as dogmatic as Henry: he forced the Book of Common Prayer upon the populace by an Act of Uniformity in 1549, destroyed shrines and images, and shared out vast quantities of Church spoils between himself and friends of the right persuasion.

Henry might have been wryly amused by the chaos brought about by these revisions, all in defiance of his own wishes. The coinage was debased, prices and rents rose, there were riots and demonstrations. Country folk lamented their lost shrines and lost mentors, and were to face further hardships: their arable land and the little patches from which they wrested the food they needed were all being swallowed up in the enclosures which rich landowners needed for pasture. Somerset, genuinely opposed to the ruthlessness of the profiteers, sent commissioners out to assess the facts and deal with the unrest; but they served only to provoke it further.

Sheep and men

'The sheep do eat up the men.' It became a common cry. Whether tied to a master or renting an acre or two from him, the cottager had always relied for subsistence on his patch of allotment and had grazed his cattle or geese on common land. When England's prosperity, and so the profit of the landowners, came to rely mainly on the soaring demand for English wool, old customs were swept aside. Common land was purchased in defiance of the peasants' flimsy rights or, in areas where a lord's writ ran large, taken by brute force. There was money in sheep, and money to be saved by the elimination of men. One shepherd and a dog paid bigger dividends than any number of tillers of the soil.

Thomas Spring, 'the Rich Clothier', who provided the funds for Lavenham's magnificent Late Perpendicular church, was only one among many with surplus riches to spare for investment in a sort of heavenly insurance policy. Raw material and finished cloth were major exports, and much in demand at home. Workers in that trade prospered. Farm-workers and unskilled labourers did not.

In 1549 there was an uprising in Cornwall against the use of the new Book of Common Prayer, and a much more serious one in Norfolk which was not religious but economic in origin. Robert Ket, a landowner of some standing in Wymondham, led a considerable body of protesters towards Norwich. They camped outside the city on Mousehold Heath, offering no violence but settling into what was in effect a sit-down strike. Ket drew up a list of demands for presentation to the Lord Protector, including a provision that he and some of his associates should serve on whatever committee was appointed to tackle these reforms.

Somerset, already sympathetic towards the rebels' grievances, was reluctant to take firm measures against them. His vacillation allowed his rival, the earl of Warwick, to take charge; and Warwick had no intention of negotiating. When Ket decided it was advisable to occupy Norwich itself, Warwick's army met and destroyed his forces there. Robert Ket and his brother were hanged.

Somerset, too, was destroyed. Warwick sent him to the Tower and in 1551 had him tried on a flimsy charge of treason and executed. Also in 1551, Warwick became duke of Northumberland.

A clash of queens

The young King Edward VI was completely dominated by Northumberland. All the duke's plans for the spread of Protestantism and the demotion of his Catholic opponents were readily acceded to. Protestant refugees from earlier persecutions came flooding back into the country.

But if Edward should not survive, Northumberland's lofty position could become a dangerous one. The boy had been sickly from birth, and by the age of fifteen it was clear that he had not long to live. His successor would be Mary Tudor, daughter of Catherine of Aragon, a devout Catholic who would have no compunction in dealing with a Protestant *éminence grise* such as the duke.

Relying on the support he might expect from those many lords and commoners unwilling to see a rebirth of Catholic power in the land, Northumberland staked everything on a supposed succession through Henry VIII's younger sister Mary, who had become duchess of Suffolk after the death of her first husband, the king of France. He forced through the marriage of his son Guildford Dudley to the reluctant Lady Jane Grey, the duchess's granddaughter, persuaded

Lady Jane Grey, queen for nine days.

(1)

Edward on his deathbed in 1553 to nominate Lady Jane his successor, and talked the Privy Council into accepting this and proclaiming her queen.

Dismayed by the responsibility thrust upon her, Jane was a shy and unhappy nine-day queen. From Framlingham Castle, which had been given to her by her young brother, Mary Tudor sent an order to the Council asserting her own royal claim. Northumberland marshalled troops and marched out of London to deal with her. She unfurled her standard, a rising in the Midlands intercepted the duke, and Mary marched unopposed on London.

Northumberland was arrested, sent to the Tower, and executed after a cowardly recantation of his Protestant faith. His son and Lady Jane were also sent to the Tower. Mary would probably have spared the life of the girl who had so obviously been only a tool in the hands of unscrupulous exploiters; but Jane's father allied himself with Sir Thomas Wyatt in a rebellion against the queen's avowed intention of marrying the Catholic Philip of Spain, and Mary was persuaded to authorise the execution of the young couple.

Mary's marriage to Philip II of Spain was a clear warning to the English that they were to be steered back towards Rome. The excommunication was lifted. An attempt was made to restore the monasteries, but the rich lords who had shared out monastic lands between them fought manfully against this. Mary pursued heretics with such zeal that even her husband, though approving the ultimate goal, urged caution. Archbishop Cranmer was imprisoned along with bishops Latimer and Ridley, who refused to abjure their faith and were burnt at the stake in Oxford. As the flames were kindled, Latimer declared: 'We shall this day light such a candle as I trust shall never be put out.' The ageing Cranmer was cajoled and bullied into signing a recantation; but at the last moment reasserted his Protestant beliefs and was also rushed to the stake, where he thrust 'this unworthy right hand', which had signed the document, first into the fire.

(2)

(1) Mary Tudor with Philip of Spain. She was utterly devoted to her much younger husband and was heartbroken when he left England.

(2) Spaniards attacking a Netherlands town.

(3) Ships at the Calais roads.

(4) Elizabeth carried by her courtiers, c. 1600.

Philip was little seen in England, being fully occupied with the expanding Spanish empire and his continental entanglements, especially the rebellious Netherlands. He was distrusted by the English, whose lords had managed to ensure that the marriage treaty contained a clause stipulating that he should retain no royal prerogatives in this country if Mary died without producing an heir. After little more than a year he left her to rule virtually alone, disillusioned by her inability to bear a child. His anger was aroused by the forays of privateers from England circumventing his monopoly in the New World and playing at piracy; but Mary could do little to stop them. He inveigled her into his war against France, but offered little help when the English troops were hard pressed. The last ignominy was the loss of England's final French possession, Calais, in 1558.

'Bloody Mary' died in November 1558. Bonfires were lit in London —fires of thankfulness, not of persecution.

The Elizabethan Age

'I have the body of a weak and feeble woman, but I have the heart and stomach of a king, and of a king of England too.'

So said the daughter of Henry VIII and Anne Boleyn, addressing her troops at one of the most crucial moments of her reign. From the very opening of that reign she set herself to win her subjects' devotion as no other monarch had deigned to do. Long before there were any

(3)

(4)

mass media to 'project an image' she travelled throughout the country and established her flesh-and-blood reality in people's minds.

In the eyes of Catholics and even of many Protestants, Elizabeth Tudor was illegitimate. The king of France openly avowed his support for the claims of his daughter-in-law, Mary Stuart, to the throne of England as well as her own Scotland. Philip II of Spain, widower of the late Queen Mary, might have done the same if he had not been opposed to the spread of French influence. For a while he maintained a cautious courtesy towards Elizabeth, and even debated the possibility of marrying her and winning her back to the true faith.

Elizabeth played him along, but knew better than to commit herself. The Anglo-Spanish alliance had never pleased Englishmen. The Franco-Scottish predominance which would result from the accession of Mary Stuart was equally mistrusted. Elizabeth's independent spirit was perfectly in tune with what her people wanted. It was a time of exploration—of the outside world, of science, and of the arts—and the symbol of this material and intellectual expansion was not a statesman, not a bold soldier or sailor, however heroic, but this red-haired young woman with all the pride, patriotism and temper of her father, and far more skill in deploying them.

The men of her realm were a formidable lot. William Cecil, Lord Burghley, the wise minister whose family was to exercise a powerful influence over many centuries still to come; the flamboyant Robert Dudley, who flattered and tantalised her and whom she undoubtedly loved, though never so recklessly as to make a fool of herself; Walsingham, ruthlessly competent founder of the earliest

(1) William Cecil, Lord Burghley, Elizabeth's most trusted minister.

(2) The Ambassadors by Holbein. Jean de Dinteville (left) and George de Salve, bishop of Louvain, were French ambassadors at Henry VIII's court.

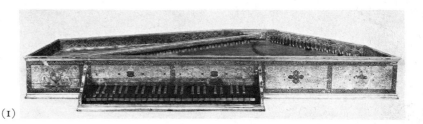

(1)

secret police system: all men of high ambition and wide education, but none of them with a surer grasp of practical politics than the queen herself.

Elizabeth could match most of them in the scope of her education. She had been well looked after by the amiable Catherine Parr, and later had been a pupil of the brilliant scholar Roger Ascham, whom she appointed to her court as secretary and tutor when she became queen. During the five years of Mary's reign, when there had several times been threats against her life, she had kept clear of intrigue and continued her studies. She was an accomplished musician and enjoyed having distinguished composers and executants close to her: during one period Thomas Tallis and William Byrd shared the duties of organist in her Chapel Royal, and were allowed a monopoly in printing and selling music. She spoke French, Spanish and Italian, and could write well in Greek and Latin. She composed verse, and was surrounded by courtiers and men of action who combined practical skills with a more than dilettante taste for poetry and philosophy.

During the reign of this talented Good Queen Bess, the beauty and accomplishment of English verse and prose rivalled their continental counterparts, as they had not done since the days of Chaucer. Spenser dedicated his great poetic fantasy, the *Faerie Queene*, to her. Sir Walter Ralegh found time during his many ventures abroad to write sonnets and inspired histories of his expeditions. Thomas Nashe virtually created the English picaresque novel. In this fertile plot, six years after Elizabeth's accession, were born two playwrights who grew up to work with troupes of travelling players and to transform the English theatre: Christopher Marlowe and William Shakespeare.

Perhaps the epitome of the Elizabethan Age, next to the queen herself, was Philip Sidney. His beautiful sonnets were an inspiration to other poets of his own and later ages; he raised literary criticism to rare heights in his *Defence of Poesy*, and merited Spenser's dedication of the *Shepheard's Calendar* to him. Lord Burghley and the earl of Essex were among his influential friends and admirers; he married Walsingham's daughter; and although, like so many courtiers, he suffered a spell of the queen's displeasure, he was soon taken back into favour, knighted, and sent to fight bravely against Spain in the Netherlands. Dying at Zutphen in 1586, he chivalrously passed a cup of water to a dying soldier, saying, 'Thy need is greater than mine.'

2)

Navigators and buccaneers

Some adventurers managed to combine patriotism with profit. A Plymouth mariner, John Hawkins, carried Negro slaves from

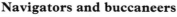

(1)

(2)

Africa to the Americas in defiance of Spanish and Portuguese monopolies. His sailors acquired the habit of tobacco smoking from their contacts with Philip of Spain's American subjects, though it was left for Ralegh to make it a fashionable pastime among the nobility. Neither Hawkins nor his fellow captains were too scrupulous about the observation of such little niceties as the fact that England and Spain were nominally at peace with each other. The Spaniards protested about English buccaneers raiding their settlements and intercepting their treasure ships. Elizabeth expressed her displeasure; and collected her share of the booty. English merchants put up the capital for further privateering ventures.

Every year from 1554 onwards Martin Frobisher, a Yorkshireman, went on expeditions to Africa and the Levant, and then in 1576 made his first attempt to find a north-west passage through the complex waterways of what is now northern Canada, but was frustrated by 'mountains of ice'. Later John Davis continued the search, and found his way through the strait now bearing his name to Baffin Bay. Sir Humphrey Gilbert also sought a way through, and while in the region formally annexed Newfoundland to the Crown, but died in 1583 when his frigate capsized at the start of the homeward journey.

Among John Hawkins's officers on one venture which went badly wrong, when the Spaniards hit back hard at San Juan de Ulua, had been another west-countryman, Francis Drake. When Hawkins was appointed treasurer of the Navy and applied himself to rooting out corruption and incompetence, Drake set up on his own and harried the West Indies, returning each time with shiploads of plunder. At the end of 1577 he set out in his *Golden Hind* to find a south-west route to Asia, sailing through the Magellan Strait between the South American mainland and Tierra del Fuego. He supplied his crew and himself with food and loot from the Pacific coast and, after a journey which took in California, the Spice Islands, the Indian Ocean and the Cape of Good Hope, reappeared in England three years later, having become the first Englishman to circumnavigate the globe. Queen Elizabeth came aboard his ship some months later to bestow a knighthood on him.

This was tantamount to a slap in King Philip's face. It made nonsense of all Elizabeth's denials of complicity in the privateering trade of which Drake was known to be the most relentless exponent. The Spanish ruler began to prepare for an inevitable war.

Mary Queen of Scots

Mary Stuart, daughter of that Scottish king who was said to have died of a broken heart after his defeat at Solway Moss, had married the Dauphin of France in 1558. He became King Francis II of France in 1559, but died the following year, when Mary returned to Scotland. Her behaviour there shocked the mass of her own people. She remarried, but made such a favourite of her secretary, Rizzio, that her husband, Lord Darnley, murdered him. Soon Darnley himself died when his house was blown up, and the scapegrace earl of Bothwell was charged with the crime but acquitted, whereupon Mary married him.

The fanatical Calvinist preacher, John Knox, who had sounded

(1) Francis Drake aged 42, a miniature by Hilliard.

(2) Drake capturing the Spanish treasure ship *Cacafuego* 'Spitfire' in 1579.

(3) Mary Stuart, Queen of Scots, by François Clouet, 1559.

(1)

(2)

his *First Blast of the Trumpet against the Monstrous Regiment of Women* while a refugee in Geneva from the Catholic Queen Mary, now inveighed even more furiously against this other Catholic Mary and her rumoured immorality. She was deposed in 1567 in favour of her infant son James, and imprisoned in Lochleven Castle. From there a loyal servant helped her to escape and she tried to raise an army, but was defeated and forced to flee to England, where she appealed to Elizabeth for aid.

Elizabeth provided shelter but no support. Mary was a dangerous guest: as a direct descendant of Henry VII through a line untainted by charges of illegitimacy, she was in Catholic eyes the rightful queen of England as well as of Scotland. A large minority of Catholics also looked to her as the person most likely to restore the old faith. Even if she genuinely wished at the start to be no embarrassment to Elizabeth, Mary's desire to recapture her Scottish throne involved her in many interchanges of secret and often ambiguous letters. Walsingham's spies brought details of so many Papist plots that Elizabeth had to order a string of executions. Jesuit priests were smuggled into England to preach regicide to those Catholics who had too meekly accepted the Protestant régime. A mixed force of Spaniards and Italians was sent to Ireland to stir up rebellion there. Burghley urged the queen not merely to provide military aid to the Protestant resistance movement in the Spanish Netherlands but also to safeguard herself and her own country by removing the centre-piece of Catholic trouble-making, the Queen of Scots.

Elizabeth procrastinated, even when presented with evidence that Mary had condoned a plot to assassinate her, but at last signed the death warrant—typically denying, later, that she had meant it to be carried out so briskly.

The Spanish Armada

Mary's execution in Fotheringhay Castle was, to Philip of Spain, the last straw. Plans went ahead for the assembly of a vast armada which should wipe the English from the seas and allow Spanish troops to invade their country. All Catholic Europe was agog. The Pope gave his blessing to the venture, and England was once again excommunicated until such time as its transgressions should be expiated.

It was impracticable to transport a complete invasion force with all its arms and stores the whole way from Spain. The Armada's main function would be to provide cover for the duke of Parma as he moved a large section of his Netherlands-based troops from Dunkirk across the narrow Channel and on to English soil.

The operation was delayed when Drake impudently sailed into Cadiz in 1587 and 'singed the king of Spain's beard' by burning many of the galleons assembled there and then escaped unscathed. By May 1588 all seemed auspicious, but again there was a delay, this time of two weeks, because of unfavourable winds, followed by an outbreak of dysentery and then the need to replace supplies. Not until 15th July did the mighty Armada, under the command of the duke of Medina Sidonia, reach the western approaches to the English Channel.

The defending fleet was commanded by Lord Howard of Effing-

(1) Mary Queen of Scots with her son James VI later to be James I of England.

(2) The trial of Mary Queen of Scots. The queen is seated at top right.

(1) Ships of the Spanish Armada in battle formation.

(2) Lord Howard of Effingham, admiral of the fleet against the Armada.

ham. Drake and Frobisher served under him, and the treasurer of the Navy himself was back aboard ship. It was to Hawkins more than anyone that the fleet owed its present strength. With Drake's backing he had urged upon the queen the increased production of those faster, more easily manœuvrable ships which her father had favoured, in place of clumsy galleons which were little more than troop transporters. Longer-range guns were installed on continuous gun-decks. The knighthood bestowed on Hawkins by Lord Howard at the end of this engagement was well merited, if a trifle overdue.

Instead of concentrating all his resources in the narrows off Dunkirk, the lord admiral stationed a large contingent at Plymouth to shield the south coast from a direct landing by the Spaniards. The tale is told that Drake was playing a game of bowls on Plymouth Hoe when the enemy hove in sight, and insisted on completing it before taking up his position. Many of the Armada's captains did in fact favour a direct assault, but Medina Sidonia's orders from Philip strictly forbade this, and the fleet sailed on from the Lizard to Calais, sniped at and chivvied by the nimble English ships but suffering no major damage.

The news at Calais, however, was disquieting. Parma was nowhere near Dunkirk and there was no sign of any invasion force ready for embarkation.

Worse was to come for the Spaniards. At midnight on 28th July, Howard sent eight fireships into their congested ranks. Many captains cut their cables in their haste to get away from the flames, fouled other cables and rudders, and blundered out under the guns of the waiting English. At point-blank range, the gunners could hardly fail. The fast ships dodged in and out between the ungainly galleons. The Spaniards had always been used to the formal tactics of grappling and then fighting hand to hand: but here they were faced not by seaborne soldiers but by fighting sailors.

A change in the wind seemed at first to favour the scattered, harassed Armada. Blown northwards out of range, Medina Sidonia's ships had a chance to regroup and assess the damage while planning a renewed attack. But the wind became a gale, and even if they had had the courage to face the English guns they could not have struggled back against it. Further and further north they were driven, some sinking, some going aground. The survivors made their desperate way round the Orkneys and down the coast of Ireland. If they had expected succour from the Catholic Irish, they were disappointed: unless rich enough to be worth ransoming, anyone thrown ashore was liable to be killed and stripped of clothes and valuables, or at best handed over to the English authorities.

The remnants of the proud Armada limped home. It has been estimated that about sixty-three ships and about twenty thousand men had been lost. England lost not a single vessel, and only about a hundred men. Another invasion was planned, but wiser counsels prevailed: the Spaniards decided to concentrate on keeping their sea lanes to the New World open rather than risk another head-on conflict.

The fruits of victory

Elizabeth, who had so resoundingly addressed her troops at Tilbury before the battle, now had a commemorative medal struck with the inscription *Deus flavit, et dissipati sunt* (God blew, and they were scattered), but proved reluctant to spend any more money on the navy which had protected her. While Philip rebuilt his fleet, Elizabeth made stringent economies. Many a courageous sailor was left to starve in the streets. Drake's plans for a blockade of Spain and an attack on Portugal received inadequate support and were dismal failures, for which he was blamed. Even a renewal of the old piratical attacks on Spanish treasure ships was less successful than of old: the vanquished, learning from the victors, had built faster ships to show their pursuers a clean pair of heels.

Howard, Essex and Ralegh carried out one daring raid on Cadiz and burned ships there as Drake had done years before. But by this time Drake himself, along with Hawkins, Grenville and Frobisher, had died—the first three of them at sea, far from home.

Yet the glory could never be altogether dimmed. A spark had been kindled in the hearts and minds of the different peoples who made up the population of England and Wales: they had a sense of identity, of mutual achievement and, even in the confusion of poverty and unemployment which marred the closing years of the queen's reign, of a new prosperity just over the horizon. In 1600 the establishment of the East India Company opened up a sphere of influence which did much to counterbalance the exclusion of any substantial English interest from the western El Dorado. And soon, somehow, it would surely be possible to arrange a more substantial toehold on those western shores as well.

Silver medal of Elizabeth commemorating the defeat of the Spanish Armada

Mr. WILLIAM
SHAKESPEARES
COMEDIES,
HISTORIES, &
TRAGEDIES.
Published according to the True Originall Copies.

LONDON
Printed by Isaac Iaggard, and Ed. Blount. 1623.

1) Title-page of the first folio edition of Shakespeare's plays, 1623. This is the only authentic portrait of Shakespeare. The likeness is confirmed by Ben Jonson's prefatory verse to the folio edition.

2) Macbeth and the three witches, from Holinshed's *Chronicles*, 1577, Shakespeare's source for his play.

Elizabeth's life drew to a close in March 1603. The favourites of her youth were dead; the favourite of her old age, the earl of Essex, had tried to rouse a mob against her most trusted advisers, and wretchedly she had condemned him to death. In the early years her ministers had been perturbed by her lack of a husband and an heir. But she had survived all plots and perils, and given forty-five of her seventy years to her country. Now, with neither son nor daughter to follow her, she was implored to designate her successor. Bereft of speech, she made a sign which was interpreted as signifying assent to the nomination of the son of that Catholic Mary of Scotland who had once seemed such a menace to her life and realm.

The bard of Avon

A giant figure straddles the last years of the Tudors and the first of the Stuarts. Born in Stratford-on-Avon in 1564, William Shakespeare went to London in his early twenties and soon became a member of the lord chamberlain's company of players, which in James I's time became the king's company. By 1592 he was also writing plays. He learned the playwright's craft the hard, practical way, and although he gradually withdrew from acting he never lost touch with the players or the environment in which they had to perform. He had a share in the syndicate of the Globe theatre on the south bank of the Thames, and although he bought the largest house in Stratford and many other properties in the town, he continued to spend a great deal of his time in London.

Shakespeare's earliest play was probably *Henry VI*, written in three parts between 1589 and 1592, followed by *Richard III* and *The Comedy of Errors*. His last play, *The Tempest*, was written between

(1) Shakespeare's daughter Susanna married a Dr John Hall: their house, Hall's Croft, is probably the only authentic building in Stratford associated with the playwright.

(2) The Globe Theatre: watercolour based on Visscher's *Long View of London*, 1618.

(3) Barrington Court, Somerset, a fine Ham-stone house in the 'Elizabethan' style, *c.* 1520.

(4) The Long Gallery, Hardwick Hall, Derbyshire built by Bess of Hardwick, 1591–97.

OVERLEAF

(1) The wedding feast of Sir Henry Unton.

(2) James I, whose succession to Elizabeth's throne united the crowns of England and Scotland.

(1)

(2)

1611 and 1612, though he contributed some scenes to *Henry VIII*, a play whose production at the Globe in 1613 had unfortunate consequences: cannon fired at the end of the first act ignited the thatch, and the theatre burned down.

Few of Shakespeare's themes were original. He took much of his history from Holinshed's *Chronicles*, other tragedies and comedies from classical legend or foreign sources; but once he had chosen his story, he made it his own. On plots as absurdly melodramatic or convoluted as those of grand opera in later centuries he imposed the music of the English language, and made masterpieces of them. 'The stream of time,' wrote Dr Samuel Johnson in the eighteenth century, 'which is continually washing the dissoluble fabricks of other poets, passes without injury by the adamant of Shakespeare.' His poetry, his wit and his sentiment appealed to Queen Elizabeth and King James; his dramatic flourishes and knockabout comedy to 'the groundlings' in the audience. And, responsive as every great writer must be to the spirit of his age, he spoke for all England and England's burgeoning self-assurance:

Come the three corners of the world in arms,
And we shall shock them.

Kings and Commonwealth

The succession of the Scottish dynasty of the Stuarts to the Welsh Tudors, when James VI of Scotland became James I of England, was achieved without bloodshed—though not without some mutterings of opposition.

Reformation and Counter-Reformation had fragmented the Continent into opposed religious factions, some in uneasy alliance, others forming pockets of dissension within the majority at present in power. James had been brought up to eschew his mother's Catholicism. He believed in the divine right of kings, with himself answerable to God alone, and the Church of England answerable to him as its divinely chosen head. There could be no varying interpretations of doctrine, and no backsliding. Sunday churchgoing was compulsory. No Catholic might celebrate the Roman Mass. No Puritan might choose to worship God in his own austere way. Any hopes that James might slacken the regulations were rudely dashed at the Hampton Court Conference in the year after his accession. There he made it clear that, so far from initiating any reform within the Church of England, he proposed to make all would-be defectors conform.

The finest product of this conference was the commissioning of an 'authorised version' of the Bible to be prepared by eminent scholars and divines, closely following the translations of the once-reviled heretics, Tyndale and Wyclif.

The Gunpowder Plotters dragged to execution, 31st January 1606.

Gunpowder Plot

A small group of Catholics under the leadership of Robert Catesby and Thomas Percy decided to stage a truly dramatic protest by blowing up the king at the state opening of Parliament on 5th November 1605. They managed to place a number of barrels of gunpowder in the cellars under the House of Lords, supervised by one of their number, Guido or Guy Fawkes, who had served with the Spanish army in the Netherlands and knew a great deal about explosives.

As the time drew near, one of the conspirators began to worry about Catholic friends among the lords who would suffer along with the guilty. He sent a letter to warn one of them not to attend Parliament on the fateful day. The recipient passed the warning on, and late on the night of 4th November a search of the cellars led to the arrest of Guy Fawkes, standing guard over his barrels. He was tortured until he revealed the names of his accomplices. They were all tried, hanged, drawn and quartered. 'Gunpowder treason and plot' is commemorated not only in the fireworks and bonfires of 5th November each year but in the ritual search of the cellars before the opening of Parliament.

As for the Puritans, they had many supporters among the squire-

archy and in Parliament itself. It was this very anti-episcopal element which most infuriated the king, starving him of money and making insolently clear its disapproval of his Church, its panoply, and his own claim of divine right. In spite of the Gunpowder Plot he was harsher on Nonconformists than on Catholics—but then, he wanted to keep well in with Spain so that in due course his son Charles might make an advantageous marriage to a Spanish princess and cement an alliance between the two countries. The Puritans had no such bait to offer: indeed, in Scotland, where they were most powerful, they had made his childhood and adolescence a misery, and here in England were a constant nuisance.

A good many Catholics had been driven out to European states where they could live with folk of their own persuasion. Far more Puritans were driven by persecution in quite the opposite direction.

Outward bound

The skimpy English settlements in North America were so insecure as to attract only the most hardy, or those willing to make any sacrifice for the sake of freedom of worship. In Elizabeth's time Ralegh had tried to found a colony which he named Virginia in honour of the Virgin Queen, but had been forced to abandon it. In 1607 another expedition landed and established a village which they named Jamestown, after the king. Although they developed their trading and tobacco-growing on a largely communal basis, a natural leader soon emerged. He was Captain John Smith, who had already led an adventurous life in the East when sold into slavery by the Turks, from whom he escaped only by killing his master. Smith tried to barter with suspicious local Indians, but was captured when out one day with an exploring party. His companions were killed, and he would have shared their fate but for the intervention of the Indian

(1) The Gunpowder Plotters including Fawkes, Catesby, Percy and Wright.

(2) Execution of the Plotters; official butchery of this hideous nature was a popular spectacle with the English public of the day.

(1)

(2) John Smith

(3)

chief's young daughter, the Princess Pocahontas. She grew up to marry one of the settlers, John Rolfe, who brought her back to England with him. She died at the age of twenty-two and is buried at Gravesend, leaving one son from whom many modern Virginian families proudly claim descent.

The quest for the north-west passage continued. Between 1607 and 1611 Henry Hudson explored the land, water and ice which had been tackled so often before, and discovered the bay which bears his name. He died in its southern offshoot, James Bay, abandoned by a mutinous crew.

The Virginian tobacco trade was proving a profitable one, though King James himself disapproved of the smoking habit as 'loathsome to the eye, hateful to the nose, harmful to the brain, dangerous to the lungs, and in the black stinking fume thereof, nearest resembling the horrible Stygian smoke of the pit that is bottomless'.

Ralegh's introduction of the habit into genteel society may have been another of the things which James held against him. Accused of plotting to prevent James reaching the throne and then of plotting to unseat him, Sir Walter had been tried and condemned to death in 1603. His estates were seized, but instead of being executed he spent the next thirteen years in the Tower on scientific research and writing his *History of the World*. He was released in 1616 because of his assurances that he knew how to find and exploit fabulous gold-mines in Guiana. James consented to his fitting out an expedition on the stringent condition that he avoided any clash with the Spaniards. During their fruitless explorations Ralegh's men attacked a Spanish settlement, and on their return to England found the Spanish ambassador demanding revenge. If Ralegh had come home laden with treasure, James might have emulated Elizabeth and fobbed the Spaniards off. But the expedition had found nothing. On 29th October 1618 Sir Walter Ralegh was beheaded in Old Palace Yard, Westminster.

Two years later another expedition set out for his now healthy colony, Virginia. Puritans from Nottinghamshire and Lincolnshire

(1) Pocahontas the Indian princess who saved the life of the colonist Captain John Smith (2).

(3) Departure of the Puritans from Delft Haven to join the *Mayflower*.

who had sought freedom of worship at Leyden in Holland decided to join with merchants in England to establish a self-sufficient community in the New World. They set sail from Plymouth in the *Mayflower*, but instead of reaching Virginia were blown off course and ultimately set foot on firm ground at Cape Cod, naming the disembarkation point Plymouth Rock. These Pilgrim Fathers founded what became the New England colonies, and were followed ten years later by so many others from the Fen country that the capital of Massachusetts came to be called after their home town, Boston.

Parliament and divine right

In the days when barons had held land mainly as a gift from the king, there were certain tributes he could expect from them in the way of military assistance and taxes. Many proved ungrateful and rebellious; but at least the basic formula was accepted by both sides. By the early seventeenth century the social pattern had changed considerably, and not to the benefit of the king. Many members of the House of Lords had far less effective power than merchants and smaller but more prosperous landowners in the House of Commons. If James wanted money, he had to prove that it was for the benefit of the country as a whole—by which the merchants, farmers and industrialists meant themselves–rather than just to satisfy some whim of his own.

(2)

(1) Illustration from a 17th-century pamphlet condemning the evils of coffee and smoking.

(2) George Villiers, duke of Buckingham.

Elizabeth of Bohemia, daughter of James I.

If he wanted an alliance between his son and Catholic Spain, they wanted to know why.

Yet, if Parliament was zealously building up a code of its rights, the king still retained some of his own. Tired of financial frustration, he dissolved Parliament, and paid for his extravagances by selling peerages and baronetcies to the highest bidders. He was also promised a huge annual payment from a London group anxious to break the Merchant Adventurers' monopoly in the export of undressed cloth and to go into the business of finished, dyed cloth. Bribery was the order of the day. Licences and patents were liberally granted to royal favourites, especially to George Villiers, duke of Buckingham, and his associates. The result was economic confusion, starvation wages throughout the land, and protests from further afield: prophetic of much that was to come, the Virginians protested against all their trade being controlled by the Crown.

James's daughter Elizabeth had been married as a child to Frederick, elector of the Rhenish area of Germany known as the Palatinate. Shakespeare's *Winter's Tale* was performed at the wedding. Elizabeth was only sixteen when the Bohemians, in revolt against Austrian domination, offered her husband the throne of their country in 1619. This independent monarchy was so short-lived that Elizabeth was referred to afterwards as 'the Winter Queen'. Hard pressed by the Austrian Habsburgs and their Catholic League, she and Frederick appealed for support from the Protestant nations and in particular from her own father. James, however, described by Henry IV of France as 'the wisest fool in Christendom', shied away from such a dangerous coalition. Instead he devoted himself to persuading Spain not to support Austria.

His appeal went unheeded. Spain occupied the Palatinate, and Bohemian resistance was crushed at the battle of the White Mountain outside Prague. An Anglo-Scottish regiment which fought for the Bohemians was more representative of the mood of the country than were James's nervous dabblings. When news of the flight into exile of his daughter and son-in-law reached London, there were noisy demonstrations in the streets. James had to recall Parliament, which immediately urged that his son should contract a Protestant marriage and that preparations should be made for war against Spain. The king denied the rights of Lords or Commons to meddle in foreign policy—he still regarded Parliament as basically a fund-raising organisation—and when they asserted their right to free debate he petulantly announced another dissolution.

Henry IV's view of James as a wise fool was not shared by Macaulay, who, assessing him more objectively from the safe distance of the nineteenth century, summed him up as 'two men—a witty, well-read scholar who wrote, disputed and harangued, and a nervous, drivelling idiot who acted'.

James continued to act in the cause of the Anglo-Spanish marriage. So that it might be contracted with a minimum of unfavourable publicity, he agreed to a proposal that the duke of Buckingham should accompany the heir to the throne, Prince Charles, incognito to Spain and there win the hand of the Infanta in return for secret promises that Charles would consider becoming a Catholic and would in any case allow children of the marriage to be raised in his wife's religion. James also secretly guaranteed that Catholic worship would be allowed in private throughout his kingdom until such time as he could have the penal laws repealed. In view of all this, would Spain please be kind enough to vacate the Palatinate?

The 'Spanish Marriage Venture' fell through. Charles and Buckingham behaved with such arrogance in Spain that they were sternly rebuffed, and Buckingham became militantly at one with those who favoured war. A recalled Parliament now raised no objections about raising money.

James, tired and dejected, died in 1625, leaving the whole chaotic situation to his son.

King Charles I

Buckingham lost no time in urging upon the new king a marriage to Henrietta Maria, daughter of Henry IV of France. This appealed little more to Parliament than a Spanish alliance would have done: here was another Catholic who as a matter of religious duty must press upon her husband the need to bring up their children in the Roman faith. But at least it kept France friendly while war with Spain went ahead.

The war did not in fact progress very far. Troops sent to the Netherlands were struck down by disease. An attempt to repeat Drake's exploit at Cadiz went awry, and on the harrowing return

Charles I and Henrietta Maria.

(1)

(2)

voyage the crews were decimated by starvation and thirst. When Charles asked Parliament for more money so that Buckingham might carry on with the war, he was faced instead by a demand for the duke's impeachment. As fervent a believer in divine right as his father had been, Charles promptly dissolved Parliament.

France had avoided offering help on the grounds that it was having its own internal troubles with rebellious Protestants, who established a Huguenot stronghold in the seaport of La Rochelle. To free his hands for dealing with this, the powerful French minister, Cardinal Richelieu, made peace with Spain. This was enough in Buckingham's eyes to make him England's enemy. Money for a campaign against France was raised without Parliament's sanction: those who refused to contribute found themselves rushed before the royal courts and sentenced to imprisonment, or forced to endure the billeting of troops in their households.

Buckingham's French expedition of 1627 was another fiasco, causing a contemporary to remark that the expedition returned to England 'with no little dishonour to our nation, excessive charge to our treasury, and great slaughter of our men'. The Exchequer was now empty; there remained many outstanding bills to be paid; and more money would have to be raised if another army was to be sent to France. Charles faced a hostile Parliament which he had humbly had to recall. Before they would consider any further contributions, the Commons formed a Committee of Grievances and presented the king with a Petition of Right in 1628, designed to protect the subject from any future taxation unauthorised by Parliament and from imprisonment without due process of law. Charles signed reluctantly. Buckingham, once more boasting of victories to come, nevertheless failed to set out with his new forces. At Portsmouth he was stabbed by a naval officer who considered he had been cheated of promotion. Charles was distraught at the death of his favourite, but public and Parliament were delighted.

There were wild outbursts in the Commons in 1629 over detailed interpretation of the Petition of Right, ending in the doors being locked against the royal guards while religious and economic matters were thrashed out. Charles took this as calculated defiance, and yet again dissolved Parliament.

It was not recalled for eleven years.

The Muses

In his play *The Bondman*, Philip Massinger made a thinly veiled attack on Buckingham. The theatre was often outspoken in its dealings with current affairs: sometimes satirical, sometimes crude. Webster's savage melancholy was inherited by John Ford. Dekker, who worked on occasion with both Massinger and Ford, had a sunnier disposition, and there was in general much lighter entertainment to be had. A taste for the pastoral mingled with the mannered, lightly romantic: Herrick poured out sylvan lyrics from his Devon vicarage, while Sir John Suckling versified with gallantry and grace, swaggered and gambled at court—and, while he was at it, invented cribbage. Michael Drayton, who had lauded the beauties of his native land in the long poem *Polyolbion*, worked on for almost seven productive

(1) Two cavaliers smoking in a tavern.

(2) Costume design by Inigo Jones for the Lord's Masque, 1613.

(3) Printed music for virginals by Orlando Gibbons, William Byrd and John Bull.

(4) Charles I dining at Whitehall Palace.

years into Charles's reign and was rightly accorded burial in Westminster Abbey.

Ben Jonson was still at the height of his creative powers, in essence the first Poet Laureate, though the title had not been specifically conferred on him when James I granted him a pension. He continued to produce masques for the Court, including one which gave young John Milton the inspiration for his masque *Comus*, presented at Ludlow Castle in 1634 with music by Henry Lawes.

At Court and in country mansions it was taken for granted that anyone with any pretensions to good breeding would be able to perform reasonably well upon at least one musical instrument and would be able to sight-read the parts of elaborate madrigals. Solo songs with keyboard accompaniment were increasing in popularity, and instrumental music from the time of Orlando Gibbons (1583–1625) onwards grew more ambitious. Neglected in his own country until late in life, John Dowland was at last appointed lutenist to King James, and succeeded by his son.

Even in churches there was elaborate music on fine organs, much frowned on by the Puritan element because of its floridity and Italianate style. There was also the vocal magic of great preachers: the poet John Donne became dean of St Paul's, and delivered some of his finest sermons before the king.

(1)

In 1629 the Flemish painter Peter Paul Rubens, who had known Charles as Prince of Wales and referred to him then as 'the greatest amateur of painting among the princes of the world', came to London as envoy from Spain to negotiate the preliminaries to a peace treaty. 'This island', he wrote, 'seems to me to be a spectacle worthy of the interest of every gentleman, not only for the beauty of the countryside and the charm of the nation . . . but also for the incredible quantity of excellent pictures, statues and ancient inscriptions which are to be found in this Court.' The successful conclusion of his mission won him a knighthood from Charles, for whom he then prepared the great ceiling paintings of Inigo Jones's Banqueting Hall in Whitehall.

Another Fleming to be knighted was Anthony van Dyck, who had been given commissions by James I and was appointed court painter by Charles in 1632.

As well as his father's artistic tastes, Charles shared his love of sport, especially of horse-racing. He sought refuge from cares of state by protracted visits to Newmarket. There he founded the Autumn and Spring meetings, and a Gold Cup race, and for his comfort added substantially to the small palace which James had built.

Black Tom Tyrant

One of those instrumental in drafting the Petition of Right had been Sir Thomas Wentworth, but its final version was too extreme for his liking. After the death of Buckingham he sided with the king and served him so effectively during the years when Charles governed without a Parliament that he came to be known as 'Thorough' Wentworth—or, by those who suffered under his yoke, as 'Black Tom Tyrant'. As lord deputy of Ireland in 1632 he sorted out abuses and imposed the firmest administration the country had yet experienced, though in doing so he alienated the planters of Ulster and antagonised the landowners of Connaught and elsewhere.

Charles created him earl of Strafford and recalled him in 1639 to prepare for action against the Scots. William Laud, archbishop of Canterbury, had decided after the suppression, imprisonment and mutilation of Puritans in England to carry his tactics on into Scotland. All Scottish churches were ordered to use the English Prayer Book from a certain Sunday in July 1637. The English were already suspicious of Laud's supposedly Papist leanings. The Scots, much more ascetically Calvinist, pelted and threw from their pulpits the clergymen who attempted to implement the new rulings. Bishops were first denounced and then abolished: the Presbyterian temper of the country recognised no episcopal authority. Thousands signed a Covenant to maintain what they regarded as the true religion, and offered support to the English Parliament in return for acknowledgment of their doctrine throughout England, Scotland, Wales and Ireland.

In this crisis, Strafford's first demand came as a shock to the king. A scratch English army had already been trounced on the Border, resulting in the signing of an equivocal and obviously temporary truce at Berwick in 1639. If it was to be replaced by a stauncher fighting force with proper arms and supplies, money was essential.

(2)

(1) Inigo Jones, the great architect of the first half of the 17th century.

(2) Sir Thomas Wentworth, first earl of Strafford.

The five eldest children of Charles I, from left to right: Princess Mary (who married William of Orange), Prince James (James II); Prince Charles (Charles II), Princess Elizabeth and Princess Anne (who died as children). From the painting by Van Dyck.

The king must recall Parliament.

During the 'eleven years' tyranny', Charles had resorted to many shifts to raise money. Among them was ship-money, a levy on towns and landowners ostensibly to support his fleet but which, as the divine embodiment of the law, he was in no way obliged to account for. He applied fines and customs dues based on old and dubious precedents, and enforced obedience with a sterner Star Chamber. One who re-refused to pay what he considered to be an illegal levy was John Hampden, gentleman of Buckinghamshire and member of Parliament. He remained adamant before the Exchequer court, and although judgement went against him by the votes of seven judges to five, Parliament was later to quash the conviction. There were others who stood firm, but it is Hampden who is remembered as having established that among an Englishman's cherished freedoms must be

Parliament assembled at Westminster, 1640.

the freedom to disobey an unlawful order, even the order of a monarch or his officials. The king, in short, was not above the law.

Charles thought otherwise. But since ship-money and similar expedients would not meet Strafford's needs, he summoned Parliament. Strafford, autocratic in the extreme, hoped to use it as masterfully as he had used officials in Ireland, and tidy everything up briskly. Instead, led by his erstwhile friend Pym and by that Hampden who had already defied the king's tax-gatherers, Parliament refused even to discuss any vote of financial aid until its accumulated grievances were satisfied. Strafford impatiently told the king that such recalcitrance absolved him from any duty to honour concessions he had made in the past, and in 1640 set off to drive out the Scots with another ill-assorted rabble. They mutinied, looted the northern countryside, and gave the Scots every chance to consolidate their positions and seize further territory, for which they demanded in the treaty of Ripon a daily fee until a satisfactory treaty could be made with them.

These obligations made inevitable the calling of another Parliament, but Parliament's demands had to be met. And now the first of these was that Strafford should be impeached. It was impossible to prove a charge of treason, so a Bill of Attainder was brought in, superseding all common law procedure and arbitrarily demanding the death of the accused. Charles refused to sign until the clamour of a pro-Commons mob in Whitehall and the near-hysteria of his queen, Henrietta Maria, broke his nerve. When the incredulous Strafford heard that Charles had set his name to the death warrant, he com-

A. Doctor Vther Lord Prim
te of Ireland.
B the Sherifes of London
C the Earle of Strafford
D. his kindred and Friends

Execution of the earl of Strafford.

mented, 'Put not your trust in princes', and went scornfully to his death on Tower Hill in May 1641.

The Long Parliament

The new assembly survived for so many years that it came to be known as the Long Parliament. The king was soon of the opinion that it had already sat too long. His remaining friend and adviser, Archbishop Laud, was imprisoned; his Star Chamber was abolished and his supposedly dutiful Commons asserted their power over all customs dues and other taxes; plans for undermining the Church of England and his own spiritual supremacy took ominous shape.

The Scots were paid off and withdrew. But now the Irish, taking advantage of Black Tom Tyrant's removal and the political confusion in England, rose against English and Scottish exploiters of their land. Catholics killed their Protestant neighbours indiscriminately, or stripped them naked and threw them out to die in the winter cold. One Ulster leader announced that he held a written commission

OVERLEAF

(1) Oliver Cromwell by Van Dyck.

(2) Charles I by Van Dyck.

A PROGNOSTICATION Vpon W. LAVI late bishop of Canterbury written Año: Dom: 1641: which accordingly is come to passe

(1)

(2)

from Charles himself to take possession of any property in Protestant hands.

This accorded all too well with what the Commons and the public already knew of Charles. Had he not allowed Spanish money to pass through England on its way to pay soldiers fighting in the Netherlands—and, more recently, allowed the transit of actual troops? The so-called commission to Ulster Catholics was a forgery; but many were ready to believe otherwise. If an army went to Ireland to crush the rebellion, it could hardly be entrusted to royal control: indeed, might not the king turn such an army immediately against Parliament to crush the freedoms so precariously won?

The two factions, 'Court' and 'Country', had been driven too far apart ever to meet amicably again.

Charles decided to reassert himself. Both his favourites had been threatened with impeachment and now were both dead. Archbishop Laud was to be impeached. It was a weapon which the king, too, could use. In 1642 he instructed the attorney-general to issue an impeachment against one peer and five members of the Commons, among them Pym and Hampden. When the Commons failed to react, Charles led a troop of horsemen to the House and demanded the surrender of the five members. But they had been warned of his impending arrival, and were gone.

The autocratic gesture did not go down well with the watching crowds, or with the rest of the country when the news spread. Armed bands in London declared themselves for Parliament and against Popery. Alarmed by Charles's despatch of Henrietta Maria to the Continent in search of aid from foreign Catholic powers, the Commons demanded control of the trained bands of citizen militia, and of forts and arsenals. The king removed his household and courts from tumultuous London to York, and insisted that control of the militia was vested in him and would remain so.

(1) Execution of Archbishop Laud, 10th January 1645. Gifted and loyal servant to Charles I, Laud was the fifth archbishop of Canterbury to die violently.

(2) Declaration of Parliament Medal on the eve of the Civil War. Its policy: 'the safety of the King's person'.

Parliament issued Nineteen Propositions in the hope of reaching, even at this late stage, a settlement. They called for a new constitution recognising their own supremacy. Ministers and judges must be appointed not by the king but by Parliament, they must be consulted on the choice of tutors for the royal children, and all Church and military matters must come under their control.

Charles gathered his faithful lords and officers about him, together with some dissentient members of the Commons. The remaining Lords and Commons set up a Committee of Safety and conscripted an army under the command of the earl of Essex. Squires and yeomen of the shires began to drill forces of their own, including such horsemen as they could muster.

The Civil War

On 22nd August 1642 Charles set up his standard at Nottingham, and on 23rd October it was carried into battle at Edgehill by Sir Edmund Verney in the first major clash of the Civil War. There had been uncertainty and vacillation leading up to this confrontation, and a great deal of uncertainty remained. Neither faction had really meant to become embroiled in out-and-out war. On either side were men whose sympathies could often be swayed towards the other. Many Parliamentarians were horrified by the idea of fighting their own king; and on the Royalist side, Verney had more sympathy for the Puritans than for the king, but remained faithful to Charles because, as he said, he had eaten of his bread for so long that he could not desert him now. In the fighting Verney was killed, but his grip remained so tight in death that the standard could be taken from him only by cutting his hand off.

In many parts of the country, landlords and the minor gentry

Charles I dictating despatches to Sir Edward Walker during the Civil War (artist unknown).

James I attains the status of a
god, surrounded by cherubs;
Rubens's magnificent ceiling,
Whitehall banqueting hall, painted
for Charles I.

Dutch ships in the Medway,
20th June 1667. English ships on
fire. Painting by Jan Peters.

The Thames frozen, 1677. View
from below old London Bridge by
Abraham Hondius.

The King's Baggage

Broad Moor

Cavaliers

The King's Regt. of Foot or Lift Guards

Prince Ruperts Regt. of Foot

Prince Rupert

Prince Maurice

Sr. Barnard Astley

Coll. Howards Horse

Coll. Howards Horse

Sulby Hedges lined with Dragoons

Lift Wing Commanded by Commiss. General Ireton

His Tertia

K: Charles I.

Lord Bards Tertia

Sr. George Tertia

Coll. Butlers Regt.

Coll. Normans Regt. commanded by Major Huntingdon

Regt. Commiss: Gen: Ireton

Forlorn Hope

Musquettiers

Major Gen:

Sr. Hardres Waller.

Coll. Pickerees

Coll. Riches Regt.

Coll. Fleetwoods Regt.

Troops of

Coll. Pride Reserve

Montagues

Rutnutt Hill

Penny Hill

ne Lease ll

The Train Guarded by Fire-Locks

Mill Hill

L: Coll. Pride Rear Guard.

Coll. Hammond Reserve

Coll. Rainsbro's

The Village of NASEBY Situated on the N.West Side of

The opposing armies in line of battle at Naseby. Charles's army at top.

wavered, hoping to stave off the need to commit themselves irrevocably one way or the other. But the pattern of allegiances gradually clarified. The north, with the exception of some areas in Yorkshire and the cloth-making centres of Lancashire, was for the king, as were much of Wales and the Midlands, and the extreme south-west. Parliament's strongest backing came from the south and south-east. A member of Parliament turned soldier, Oliver Cromwell of Huntingdon, grouped the county recruiting and supply committees of East Anglia and its neighbours into the Eastern Association. Bristol and Gloucester formed the nucleus of a Western Association under

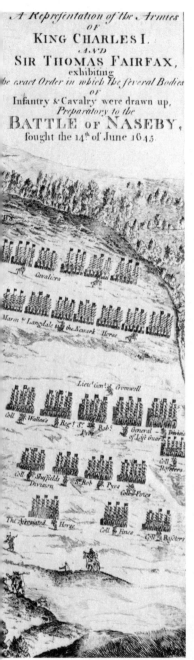

Sir William Waller.

In the long run Charles was bound to lose. Parliament controlled London, the customs, and the key ports—which meant money. During the ensuing struggle, many of the king's supporters changed sides because they found that Parliamentary soldiers got paid more regularly.

The encounter at Edgehill, however, was not an auspicious beginning for the Parliamentarians. Their amateurish foot soldiers had little chance against the skilled Royalist cavalry under a leader with such panache as Prince Rupert, nephew of Charles and son of the Winter Queen. Yet it was the impetuous Rupert who perhaps threw away the one great chance of ending the war in its early stages: having got so many of the enemy on the run, he gave chase instead of using his superior forces to finish off the main battle. The result was that the Parliamentary foot soldiers defeated the Royalist foot, which counterbalanced the Royalists' superiority in cavalry. Edgehill was thus a drawn battle, though Charles needed a decisive victory in that first autumn of the war.

Thousands of fleeing survivors deserted and went home. The troops with which the earl of Essex fell back on London were insufficient to protect the capital if Charles pressed home his advantage. Prince Rupert and the king's commander-in-chief, the earl of Forth, wanted to do this. Charles wavered. By the time he was ready to march on London, the city was ready to repulse him.

The lesson of Edgehill was learnt. Because of their superior cavalry the Royalists came to be known as Cavaliers. The Parliamentarians were dubbed Roundheads, reputedly from a comment once made by the queen on the Puritan Samuel Barnardiston's short-cropped hair: 'What a handsome roundhead is there.' But the Roundheads now concentrated on assembling a cavalry force of their own. Other setbacks in the West Riding and Cornwall, and the loss of John Hampden in a brief battle at Chalgrove Field, reinforced the lesson.

Oliver Cromwell, by now Colonel Cromwell, made a great showing with his horsemen in Lincolnshire, and though driven out of the county began to build from his nucleus of 'godly men' a disciplined regiment of 'Ironsides'. By 1645, realising that the war could never be won by the unco-ordinated activities of semi-independent fighting groups, an ordinance was passed for the formation of a New Model Army under the command of Sir Thomas Fairfax but built upon Cromwell's ideas.

Scottish Covenanters and Cromwell's horse had turned the tide of battle at Marston Moor the year before. Now, within a few months of the formation of the New Model Army, came the decisive engagement at Naseby, a village in Northamptonshire; and once more it was Cromwell who struck the vital blow. Prince Rupert started off in fine style with a devastating cavalry charge, and Fairfax was in danger of collapse when Cromwell routed one wing of the Royalists and threw all his weight against their centre. Rupert repeated his Edgehill mistake by allowing his men to pursue the Roundheads as they scattered, and then found he could not round them up in time to stave off defeat.

(1)

(1) Charles II, 'the merry monarch'.

(2) Nell Gwyn, the most famous
of the many mistresses of Charles II.

(1)

(2)

The road to the scaffold

Charles fled with a few horsemen to Ashby-de-la-Zouch. His baggage-train was captured intact—the stern Cromwell had promised death to any soldier indulging in looting—and provided an unexpected prize; copies of all the letters passing between the king and queen during the last few years, which showed that, in spite of the supposed attempts Charles had made to reach an armistice with Parliament at one time and another, he had all along been trying to bring Irish rebels and foreign mercenaries into the country, and had never had any intention of reaching a compromise. The correspondence was gleefully published so that all might see what kind of man it was who set himself up as God's chosen ruler of the English people.

Unable to reassemble an army capable of giving battle anywhere in his own country, Charles surrendered himself to the Scots in the hope of their support. As he would not agree to further the spread of their Presbyterian religion throughout his kingdom, they handed him over to Parliament in return for a large ransom.

The king was imprisoned in reasonable comfort, and set to work writing more letters. Encouraged by squabbles breaking out between the Covenanters and the English Puritans, he promised the Scots to accept their religious demands if they would come to his aid.

Cromwell moved in ruthlessly. So far he and others had maintained that they wished merely to bring the king to his senses, certainly not to depose him. Now, however, Cromwell was convinced that patience and negotiation were useless. He smashed the Scots, put down a few other Royalist uprisings, and associated himself with the demand for a republic. When members of the Long Parliament showed themselves hesitant, Colonel Thomas Pride was sent by the Council of the Army to deal with them. As a result of 'Pride's Purge' in December 1648 ninety-six Presbyterian members were forcibly ejected from Parliament, and the sixty or so members who were left were henceforth known collectively as the Rump Parliament.

King Charles I was put on trial as a 'tyrant, traitor, murderer, and public enemy of the Commonwealth' on a resolution of the Rump and without the concurrence of the Lords.

Throughout the trial he conducted himself with the greatest dignity. Whatever despicable stratagems he may have resorted to in endeavouring to preserve his Crown, he never wavered in his belief

(1) Illustration from Captain Nathaniel Burt's *Military Instructions* (1644), showing mounted musketeers.

(2) Charles I at the time of his trial.

(1)

(2)

that the authority of the Crown overruled, by divine right, the pretensions of any other would-be authority in the land.

'I would know by what authority I am called hither,' he said proudly. 'Remember I am your king, your lawful king, and what sins you bring upon your heads, and the judgement of God upon this land—think well upon it—I say, think well upon it, before you go further from one sin to a greater.'

Steadfastly he refused to recognise the validity of the court which tried him. Many of Parliament's supporters, including Fairfax who had fought so bravely in its cause, were uneasy on that score and utterly opposed to the death sentence passed upon their king.

But the sentence was carried out. On the afternoon of Sunday, 30th January 1649, Charles stepped on to a scaffold before the Banqueting Hall windows of his Whitehall palace, and was beheaded. His body was taken in the darkness of a snowy morning to be buried in a lead wrapping at Windsor Castle without any religious service, the Prayer Book having by now been proscribed.

England was no longer a monarchy.

The Commonwealth

Now that Cromwell's army was in effect the governing power, the House of Lords was abolished and a Commonwealth declared.

It was not to everybody's taste. There were sporadic outbreaks of

(1) Cromwell's dismissal of the Rump Parliament, 1653.

(2) Execution of Charles I, 1649.

143

protest, and although the Irish had not shown themselves favourable towards the monarchy during the days of Charles's legate, Wentworth, they now staged a major rebellion. Cromwell, glad of the excuse to avenge the massacres of Protestants in Ireland, took personal charge of its suppression. He raged through the country slaughtering Royalist cliques and Catholic peasants alike, massacring the garrisons of Drogheda and Wexford as he went. He left a bloody trail through the ranks of those he denounced as 'barbarous wretches who have imbrued their hands in so much innocent blood', and bequeathed the Irish question a new and violent bitterness of which we are still reaping the legacy.

Acts of Settlement and Indemnity in 1652 handed over two-thirds of the land to Cromwellians and merchants who had financed the Parliamentary cause. However, the native Irish were not transplanted, as the new landlords wanted them as labourers, with the result that the landlords remained Protestant and became divided from the small landowners and peasants, who remained Catholic. Reduced to the status of a military-occupied province, Ireland was allowed to send members to the English Parliament, but they were Puritan soldiers and no Catholic was allowed to stand for election or to vote. In many respects Cromwell treated Ireland in an enlightened fashion far in advance of his time, but his ruthlessness and the land settlement coloured all future relations.

Cromwell himself was not there to finish off the campaign or enforce the terms of settlement: he had hurried home to face another threat.

The Scots had decided to back the young Prince Charles, who renounced his father's adherence to the Church of England and swore to adopt the Covenant if he were set upon the throne. Fairfax, still shaken by Cromwell's forcing through of Charles I's execution, would not lead troops for the Commonwealth against the Scots; so Cromwell took command of this operation also, and won a resounding victory at Dunbar in 1650. King Charles II was crowned at Scone, however, and decided to strike into England itself, getting as far as Worcester in 1651 before Cromwell sprang his trap. Charles managed to escape as his followers were cut to pieces, and hid in many places to avoid capture—in a Shropshire oak tree, according to the most popular story, and then during six perilous weeks in the homes of faithful friends. He was over six feet tall, with a distinctive, dark complexion, and by no means easy to conceal. Yet, although there was a price of £1000 on his head, even those who recognised him never gave him away. Gradually he was moved down through Hampshire towards Brighton and, through the careful negotiations of a loyal Colonel Gunter, smuggled out to France.

The Rump Parliament's slipshod administration soon irritated Cromwell, who had for some time associated himself with the victorious army rather than with the representatives of merchants and landowners. Pym and Hampden were dead; there were few left with the courage to stand up to him. He would have no nonsense with would-be democrats: John Lilburne, who with his Levellers believed in the freedom and equality of all men, soon found himself in prison. Like the king whose downfall he had so implacably engi-

(1) Contemporary painting of the fire of London.

(2) Charles II as a boy, by Dobson.

neered, Cromwell believed that he had a personal mandate from God. To facilitate the spread of his beliefs, on 20th April 1653 he took a picked body of soldiers with him to the House of Commons and, leaving them outside, marched in and told the assembled members of the Rump to begone: 'Depart, I say, and let us have done with you—in the name of God, go!' He then called in his troops and, pointing to the Mace, symbolic authority of the House when in session, cried: 'Take away this bauble!'

The Lord Protector

Having ejected one Parliament, Cromwell set up another of his own nomination under a dour Puritan named Praise-God Barebones. Fearful of making any move in any direction, it proved even more inept than its predecessor, and finally Cromwell had himself proclaimed supreme ruler under the title of Lord Protector. Though disdaining regal affectations and furiously dismissing a sycophantic attempt to have him crowned king, he was not reluctant to occupy Hampton Court Palace during his term of office and to have his daughter married from the Chapel Royal.

His was a severe administration. Theatres were closed, dancing and other pastimes banned, and the strictest religious observances were demanded of the entire population, especially on Sundays. All 'graven images' which could possibly be associated with Catholicism were destroyed. The dreaded Parliamentary Visitor, William Dowsing, went from church to church smashing fonts and statues, shooting bullets into the exquisite woodwork of angel roofs, and devoutly recording the cleansing process: '24 superstitious pictures; one crucifix and picture of Christ; and twelve angels on the roof; and divers Jesus' in capital letters: and the steps to the rood-loft

(2)

(1) Prince Rupert, the dashing and gallant leader of Charles's cavalry in the Civil War.

(2) Destruction of religious images under Cromwell.

Admiral Blake.

to be levelled.' Worthy asceticism became arrogant iconoclasm. The loving craftsmanship of centuries was battered to fragments. Not an echo of music lingered in the bleak churches.

Yet Cromwell, like many a dictator, had a vision of a better world. He preached, and put into practice, religious toleration—save for Catholics. Liberty of conscience was his watchword—though his own conscience would not let him suffer a whisper of Popery in the land or allow ex-Royalist 'delinquents' to hold office or vote.

He longed to bring peace and prosperity to England; but when faced by war with the Dutch, a Protestant country with which he hated to be at odds, he was as efficient as ever in his prosecution of the battle. A Navigation Act forbidding transport of goods into England in any save British ships or those from the country of origin had infuriated the Dutch, who had cornered most of the merchant shipping trade. Cromwell strengthened the navy, abolished many of its abuses, and thus was able to give a worthy weapon to Robert Blake, whose military career was as remarkable as the Lord Protector's own—member of Parliament, soldier, and then sailor.

Blake had scattered a fleet assembled by Prince Rupert in Prince Charles's cause, and captured three of the last Royalist strongholds— the Scilly Isles, Jersey, and Guernsey. Now he was matched with the resourceful Admiral Tromp, who with a broom at the masthead promised to sweep the English from the seas. In their first encounter off Dover in 1652, Blake's smaller fleet defeated the Dutch, though later in the year he suffered a reverse off Dungeness. The fleet was strengthened, and at the battle of Portland in February 1653 a decisive victory was won. Blake was seriously injured, but lived on to prepare with his colleague Monck new tactical instructions for line-ahead formation in sea warfare. Then, when the Commonwealth went to war with the old enemy, Spain, he carried off a brilliant coup at Santa Cruz, destroying sixteen ships as well as the town for the loss of only fifty men. Cromwell sent a portrait of himself set in gold and diamonds, and the country waited to welcome the hero home. But Blake, never fully recovered from his wounds and racked by illness, died at sea in August 1657 as he approached Plymouth.

Monck, both admiral and general, commanded the army in Scotland towards the end of the Commonwealth. After Oliver Cromwell's death in September 1658 his son Richard Cromwell became Lord Protector, but within nine months was ousted by a military junta and returned gladly enough to his farm. The army soon expelled Parliament, and the Committee of Safety which it appointed to rule the country in October 1659 was both oppressive and incompetent. Courts of justice ceased to function, there was lawlessness throughout the country. Monck, though a military man, had no taste for army dictatorship. He decided to march from Scotland to London and insist on the restoration of Parliament. Before he could reach the Tweed, an army from the south was on its way to stop him.

Fairfax came out of semi-retirement to join him, and all resistance collapsed. The Long Parliament was re-established, including the still-living members excluded by Pride's Purge, and no one could be in any doubt about its wishes or the wishes of the people. Early in

Charles's departure from
Scheveningen in Holland to regain
the throne.

May 1660 Fairfax headed a mission to the Hague asking King
Charles II to return; and at the end of the month, escorted by a
shouting and cheering army, Charles rode through the crowded
streets of London to the palace of Whitehall where his father had
met his end.

The Restoration

Creative energies and appetites repressed during the austere years
of the Commonwealth burst out exuberantly now that the cultured,
hedonistic king was home. There were some shocks at first—the
Church of England was re-established, Nonconformists were harried, and Charles's earlier promises to respect the Covenanters were
broken without compunction—but the public on the whole sought
opportunities for singing and laughing again rather than continuing
the religious debates which had led to so much strife.

Theatres reopened, the bawdy extravagances of Restoration
drama filled the stage. William Wycherley rose to favour after the
duchess of Cleveland, one of the king's mistresses, drew royal attention to his work. John Dryden, who had written *Heroic Stanzas*
on the death of Cromwell, hastened to greet the new monarch with
Astraea Redux, and went on to write both tragedy and comedy,
Marriage à la Mode being perhaps the gayest and best. He was the
first poet to be given the actual title of Poet Laureate.

Horse-racing came back to Newmarket. Though no great gambler

(1)

himself, Charles loved the sport and allowed his numerous mistresses to bet and run up debts which he in the end had to pay. His taste for amorous sport was also responsible for his nickname of 'Old Rowley', after a stallion of the time renowned for its prowess at stud. Nell Gwyn, the Covent Garden orange-seller and actress who remained his favourite despite other liaisons, stayed often in Newmarket when he was in residence, reputedly in a house linked to the little palace by a subterranean passage.

Puritans might frown at the new licentiousness, but if they spoke out too frankly they risked being sent to prison. One such was John Bunyan, an assiduous reader of the Bible and an eloquent Nonconformist preacher. In the November after the king's return he was arrested for preaching without a licence and, refusing to acknowledge the new regulations against Dissenters, was sent to gaol and remained there for twelve years. After a short spell at liberty he was imprisoned again, when he wrote the first part of *The Pilgrim's Progress*, an allegory of the tribulations of Christian and his wife on their journey from the City of Destruction to the Celestial City.

Music came back to churches, to the stage, and to the Court. John Blow and Pelham Humfrey were both choristers in the Chapel Royal immediately after the Restoration. Blow became organist at Westminster Abbey in 1668 and composed many anthems and other choral works. Humfrey was sent by Charles to study under Lully in Paris, and returned to compose and teach. Among his pupils was a

(2)

(1) Frontispiece to *The Pilgrim's Progress*, showing John Bunyan's dream.

(2) Henry Purcell, the greatest English composer of the age.

young chorister who was also assistant to the keeper of instruments at the Chapel Royal: Henry Purcell. In 1682 Purcell became organist at the Chapel Royal, and in the following year was appointed 'composer in ordinary' to the king, for whom he composed the dramatic, almost operatic anthems with organ and orchestra which especially appealed to Charles. The greatest of English composers, unmatched to this day, he created the first true operas in this country, assimilating Italian and French styles but speaking always with a quite individual voice in *Dido and Aeneas* (composed for a boarding-school for gentlewomen), *King Arthur* and *The Fairy Queen*. He died at the age of thirty-seven in the reign of William III, and was fittingly buried beneath the organ in Westminster Abbey.

The Plague

In 1665 a dreaded old enemy came back to London. Bubonic plague was rampant again. It spread so fast through the insanitary warrens of the city that soon there was no time for decent burials, nor could coffins be made fast enough. At night carts would go through the streets, and to the mournful cry of 'bring out your dead' bereaved families would toss a corpse—often more than one—into the grisly pile, to be taken for communal interment in great pits on the outskirts. In an attempt to prevent the spread of the disease the authorities ordained that any house with a plague victim in it must be closed up, with a red cross on the door and the words 'Lord have mercy upon us'. Some families tried to hide any member who fell

London during the Plague.

(1) The disease scrofula or King's evil was supposed to be curable by royal touch. From the time of Edward the Confessor until its discontinuance after 1714 ceremonial touchings were commonly arranged in which diseased subjects were brought before the king. Charles II is here seen administering the cure.

(2) Ligatures and circulation of the blood, from William Harvey's *Anatomica*.

(1)

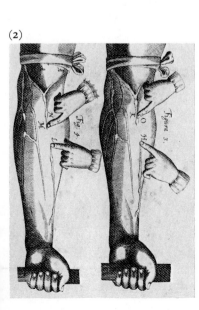

sick, or to bribe the women 'Searchers of the Dead' not to report the truth to the authorities. By August, Samuel Pepys, conscientiously remaining in London at his work as surveyor-general of the naval victualling office, was reporting in his diary deaths of three to four thousand a week. And still they increased:

> The people die so, that now it seems they are fain to carry the dead to be buried by day-light, the nights not sufficing to do it in. And my Lord Mayor commands people to be within at nine at night all, as they say, that the sick may have liberty to go abroad for ayre.

Having moved out to the more rural area of Woolwich, from which he commuted to the city, the always dandified Pepys relaxed slightly and decided to risk wearing the fine new periwig he had so far left unused, 'because the plague was in Westminster when I bought it; and it is a wonder what will be the fashion after the plague is done, as to periwigs, for nobody will dare to buy any hair, for fear of the infection, that it had been cut off the heads of people dead of the plague'.

As in the days of the Black Death, anyone who could flee to the country did so. The king and his court went. Not until the New Year, after winter had frozen the plague germs out, did a wary drift back to the towns begin.

Medicine and magic

Methods of counteracting such pestilence were crude and ineffective. It was believed that fires burning in the streets would decontaminate the air. Everyone had his favourite cure: hot toddies, fumigation of the house with strange fuels, sniffing of vinegar-soaked sponges, the application of newly killed pigeons to the buboes, and innumerable salves and potions owing more to necromancy than to science.

The College of Physicians had been founded in 1518, issuing licences to medical practitioners, and in 1540 a charter was granted to the Fellowship of Surgeons. But progress in medicine and surgery was slow, and old remedies such as herbal potions and the blood of mice and bats gave many patients more confidence than the ministrations of doctors. It was generally accepted that blood-letting was good for one, either by surgical instruments or the use of blood-sucking leeches. Barbers still practised as unqualified surgeons, and even after more rigid codes of conduct were drawn up they were still allowed to draw teeth and carry out bleedings. For major operations there were no antiseptics and no anaesthetics—other than large doses of raw spirit to numb the patient into drunkenness. It was usual to tie the victim down so that he could not struggle under the knife.

Right through the reigns of the Stuarts the common ailment of scrofula—'the King's Evil'—was thought to be curable by a touch from the royal hand; and many thousands of sufferers paraded before Charles II.

Yet in the middle of superstition and fatal blundering, light was dawning. A physician of St Bartholomew's Hospital, who had already stimulated his students with his anatomical lectures, treated the sick poor with both skill and compassion, and spoken out against the barbarities of apothecaries and barber-surgeons, published in 1628 a treatise which may well be the most important single document in the history of British medicine. William Harvey was in fact a physician rather than a witch-doctor, a comparatively rare thing in those days, and his theory of the circulation of the blood opened the way to more enlightened study of the human body and the treatment of its ailments. Interested in many questions of heredity and eugenics, he also published a lesser known but equally revealing book on embryology. He was court physician to both James I and Charles I, and would have been made president of the College of Surgeons in 1654 if he had not by then been in his late seventies and painfully ill.

A younger pioneer of clinical medicine, Thomas Sydenham,

(1)

(1) Robert Boyle, who conceived the principle of chemical elements and whose statement of 'Boyle's Law' on the properties of air was a major step forward in chemistry.

(2) The Octagon room, Flamsteed House, the old Royal Observatory. John Flamsteed was England's first Astronomer-Royal and father of modern practical astronomy.

(2)

(1) Sir Isaac Newton, the greatest scientist of the age.

(2) Sir Christopher Wren, a noted mathematician and astronomer, who earned lasting fame for his rebuilding of London after the Great Fire.

was among those who learned from the experience of that terrible year of the Plague, 1665. He prepared a treatise on fever and was the first to recognise and name scarlet fever, and recognised what now seems so obvious to us—the relationship between diet and health.

The influence of such men was incalculably great, but not immediate. The Plague died at last of cold, not from men's efforts.

The Royal Society

Other scientific activities were flourishing. Since 1645 a group of mathematicians, scientists and scholars had been meeting to discuss new philosophical concepts, and in 1662 Charles granted a charter for the establishment of the Royal Society of London for Promoting Natural Knowledge. Its members were enjoined to prosecute 'the Advancement of Natural Experimental Philosophy especially those parts of it which concern the Encrease of Commerce by the Addition of useful inventions tending to the Ease, Profit or Health of our Subjects . . . to confer about the hidden Causes of Things . . . and to prove themselves real benefactors to Mankind'.

One of the most eminent of these members was Robert Boyle, whose experiments with the compressibility of air and gases led to the formulation of Boyle's Law. He also exposed the absurdity of the long-held Aristotelian belief in four elements composing all matter, denounced the blind alleys of alchemy, and opened the way to the more rational study of chemistry. John Aubrey, the diarist and discoverer of the Aubrey Holes around Stonehenge, was another member. Isaac Newton, who had formulated the differential calculus and the law of gravity while on vacation from Trinity College, Cambridge, during a plague outbreak, was elected a fellow in 1672 and eventually became its president, from 1703 until his death in 1727. Working on the measurement of planetary orbits, he came into regular contact with the Reverend John Flamsteed, the first Astronomer Royal. Alchemy was giving way to chemistry; astrology to astronomy.

In 1675 Charles issued a royal warrant pronouncing that 'in order to the finding out of the longitude of places and for perfecting navigation and astronomy, we have resolved to build a small observatory within our park at Greenwich, upon the highest ground, at or near the place where the castle stood, with lodging rooms for our astronomical observator and assistant'. The design was executed by another member of the Royal Society, Sir Christopher Wren, and later named after Flamsteed, the first incumbent.

It was appropriate than Wren should have been chosen, since he had been professor of astronomy at Gresham College in London before turning his talents towards architecture. In that same year in which Greenwich Observatory was born, the first stone was laid for another of his creations—the one by which he will probably be longest remembered.

The Great Fire

Samuel Pepys records that he and his wife were aroused at three in the morning on a September Sunday in 1666 by a maid who told of a great blaze in the city. Pepys went to the window, but thought

(1)

(2)

(1)

the fire was far away and of no great personal consequence, so went back to bed. By dawn it was clear that this was no small localised outbreak. Starting in a Pudding Lane bakery, it spread so fast that people threw their belongings into the river and jumped in after them, or stayed stupefied on their own doorsteps until it was too late—'so that there was nothing heard, or seen,' according to that other indefatigable diarist, John Evelyn, 'but crying out and lamentation, running about like distracted creatures . . .'.

Pepys himself was asked by the king for an eyewitness account, after which Charles and his brother James, duke of York, went to supervise the destruction of houses in the path of the blaze in order to make firebreaks. But the fire was faster than the defenders. Houses were packed too closely together, there was too much wood in their construction, and the streets and lanes were too narrow and twisting for any fire appliance to be used effectively.

When the fire died, largely because there was little left to burn, it was resolved that the insanitary and all too combustible hovels in their cramped lanes should be replaced by wider thoroughfares with brick buildings and at least a rudimentary drainage system. Sir Christopher Wren submitted a comprehensive scheme for the whole city but, as was to be the case some three centuries later after the Second World War, noble ideals were overridden by other, largely commercial considerations. Nevertheless Wren put his distinctive stamp on over fifty churches, and produced his masterpiece in the

(2)

(3)

new St Paul's Cathedral. His epitaph there, written by his son, is the worthiest any man could desire: *Si monumentum requiris, circumspice*—If you seek his monument, look around.

The Dutch wars

While recording the tribulations of plague and fire, Pepys had other problems on his mind. England had taken up war with the Dutch where Cromwell had left off in 1654: unfettered expansion of trade was impossible until the Dutch near-monopoly in the East Indies had been broken, and their commercial domination of the seas about Britain eased. The North American colonies were irritatingly divided by the powerful Dutch territory of New Amsterdam, until an armed expedition seized it in 1664 and renamed it New York.

In 1665, soon after the recommencement of hostilities, an English fleet under its lord high admiral, James, duke of York, defeated the enemy off Lowestoft; but a fleet under Monck, who had been created first duke of Albemarle by Charles, was nearly annihilated the following year. Pepys at the Admiralty pushed supplies through and urged drastic reforms in the whole structure; put forward plans for the reorganisation of the dockyards; and, when promoted secretary to the Admiralty, set about abuses in the system and re-commended the promotion of long-serving officers rather than the cynical selling of places.

Dismally he noted in his diary during June 1667 that the daring

(1)

Admiral de Ruyter had sailed up the Medway into Chatham, set fire to a large part of the English fleet there, and impudently towed away the flagship, the *Royal Charles*. The following month a peace treaty was signed at Breda, and the Commons appointed a committee to see how money raised for the war had been spent by the king's ministers and commanders. Its exposure of various scandals brought down a number of Royalists—which embittered Charles against Parliament and led him to intrigue with anyone he thought might further his own interests.

He especially admired Louis XIV of France, and must wistfully have longed to be able to adopt that king's arrogant motto, '*L'Etat c'est moi*.' In 1670 he opened wary negotiations with Louis and signed a secret treaty at Dover, promising to declare himself for Roman Catholicism as soon as practicable, in return for which Louis would subsidise him and provide troops to reimpose the old faith upon England. Charles also agreed to support a French attack on Holland, where Louis was laying claim to part of the Spanish Netherlands; and when this was satisfactorily concluded, England would be given Walcheren.

In his discussions with all save a few of his ministers, Charles omitted all reference to 'Catholicity', but rumours began to circulate

(2)

and it soon became clear to the king that re-conversion of the country by armed force was out of the question. With this part of the bargain unfulfilled, he was nevertheless urged by a group of his councillors to go ahead with war against the Dutch. These men, predominantly Catholic in inclination, were Clifford, Ashley, Buckingham, Arlington and Lauderdale, their initials adding up all too appropriately to 'Cabal'—a clique of intriguers.

Charles made a token gesture towards implementation of his commitments by issuing a Declaration of Indulgence in 1672 to remove penalties against Roman Catholics—and, blurring the real issue, against Nonconformists. Two days after its issue, before any fuss could rise—the fuss came later, when Parliament forced Charles to withdraw the Declaration in 1673—war with the Dutch had been resumed.

A French army of 120,000 swept across the Netherlands, confident of success against the mere 25,000 ill-prepared men under the command of the young William of Orange. The Dutch fleet, on the other hand, was in excellent shape, and to block any English diversionary move it sallied out to attack the English and French fleets in Sole Bay, on the Suffolk coast.

Anticipating an assault in this region, the duke of York had set up his headquarters at Southwold together with his cousin, Prince Rupert, and Pepys's patron, the earl of Sandwich. When the enemy hove in sight, the French headed south, having apparently been ordered by the evasive Louis to leave their allies to it.

The slaughter on both sides was appalling. Hundreds of bodies brought ashore or washed ashore were buried in churchyards between Southwold and Ipswich. The earl of Sandwich went down with his ship, and when his corpse came in on the tide some days later it could be identified only by the star he wore on his charred uniform and by three rings in his pocket. The duke of York had to abandon first one flagship and then another.

At last the wounded de Ruyter withdrew, and England claimed a victory. John Evelyn lamented the loss of so many good men 'for no provocation but that the Hollanders exceeded us in industrie, and in all things but envy'. In effect there was stalemate. The Dutch had been unable to inflict the crushing defeat they had planned; but they were still masters of the seas, and when the French and English combined again for an attempted invasion at Scheveningen, de Ruyter's smaller fleet drove them off.

On land, the Dutch had been driven back behind the 'Water Line' of their complex of dykes and sluices. They opened the gates and flooded the countryside to slow down the enemy. Unfortunately for the defenders, this isolated them, too; and both sides settled down into damp discomfort, with inevitable outbreaks of disease. By skilful diplomacy William of Orange arranged treaties with Spain and the Holy Roman Emperor, and soon afterwards the invaded provinces were evacuated by Louis's armies.

In 1673 a peace was patched up, with many elements in England openly favouring an alliance with the Protestant Dutch rather than the unreliable Louis. Pepys and his colleague Sir Anthony Deane carried on their dogged work of reform within the navy until

(1) George Monck, duke of Albemarle, who paved the way to the Restoration.

(2) The *Royal Charles* captured by Dutch naval forces at Chatham is brought into the Texel. It was this ship which brought Charles back to England after his long exile.

Titus Oates in the pillory outside Westminster Hall after being convicted of perjury.

ignominiously dismissed, in one of the most grotesque fantasies of the time, along with many who had worked patriotically and unselfishly with the duke of York.

The Popish Plot

In return for a grant of money to keep the Dutch wars going, Charles had been forced by Parliament to cancel out his Declaration of Indulgence by a Test Act compelling all holders of office under the Crown to take the oath of supremacy and adhere to Church of England forms of worship. His own brother James, duke of York, made no secret of being a Catholic and therefore had to resign his appointment as lord high admiral. There was much bitterness about this return to religious discrimination; many rumours that the king of France was provoking Catholics to work against the nation's Protestant ascendancy; and, in 1678, the accusation that James was party to a plot to assassinate Charles and make himself king, with a team of Jesuit advisers.

The men who laid this charge were Dr Israel Tonge and Titus Oates, an Anglican chaplain who had been dismissed from various posts on grounds of vicious conduct. They swore an affidavit before

Sir Edmund Berry Godfrey, a London magistrate, that they knew
of a plot to murder the king and massacre thousands of Protestants
preparatory to James taking over. There were so many inconsis-
tencies in the story that only the confusion of the times could have led
to its being taken seriously for even five minutes. But when Sir
Edmund was found dead transfixed with his own sword, panic broke
out. On the extracted confession of a Roman Catholic silversmith,
three innocent men were charged with having murdered him and
were executed. Eminent Catholics were hounded out of office and
home; some to the Tower. The duke of York fled the country.
Titus Oates accused the queen, the Portuguese Catherine of Braganza, of treason, and Charles saved her only by dissolving Parliament before it could start proceedings. Pepys, accused of being an
accomplice in this plot, was sent to the Tower, but soon released.

It was not until 1685 that the tables were turned. Oates, who had
been granted a pension and was by now living richly in Whitehall,
was convicted of perjury, whipped through the streets behind a cart,
and sentenced to life imprisonment. In the time of William and
Mary he was quietly released and had his pension restored.

(1)

Whigs and Tories

The alarm caused by the supposed Popish Plot facilitated the rise to power of the first earl of Shaftesbury, and strengthened the distinction between the two parties already existing in Parliament. One of these, led by Lord Danby, had been consistently favourable to Charles and was known as the Court party—or, by its opponents, as Tories, a name derived from Irish robbers who preyed on friend and foe alike, and bestowed on this faction because it was thought to be implicated with the Irish and other Papists wanting James of York on the throne. The opposition emphasised its allegiance to ordinary people of the land as the Country party, and was said to favour the Covenanters: which earned it the epithet of Whig, from the Scottish 'whiggamore', a horse-drover.

Danby fell in the uproar after Oates's accusations, and Shaftesbury played on the nation-wide fear of Catholic plotters to have himself and fellow Whigs appointed to the Privy Council. He tried to force a Bill through Parliament to ban the duke of York from the throne and nominate in his place the duke of Monmouth, Charles's illegitimate son. Dryden's satirical poem *Absalom and Achitophel* mocked both Shaftesbury and Monmouth, and aimed to turn public opinion against them. In fact, despite noisy support from the London populace—or perhaps because of this very unruliness—Shaftesbury was already losing ground. He had shown himself too ruthless in hounding Catholics out of high office, some to their death, and now an attempt was made by his rivals to convict him of treason. The duke of York returned from the Continent and became high commis-

(2)

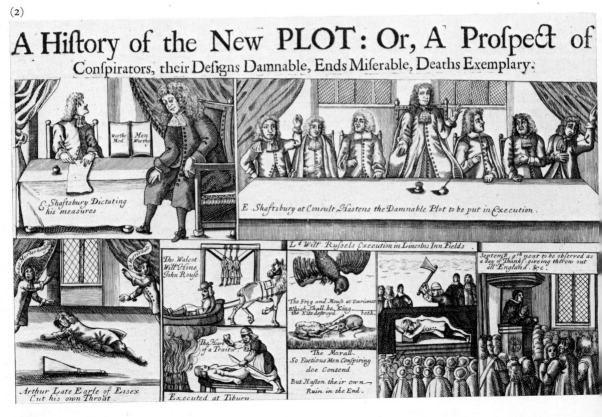

(1) Anthony Ashley, the first earl of Shaftesbury, unscrupulous, ambitious and strongly anti-Catholic.

(2) Contemporary print celebrating the demise of the Rye House plotters, 1683.

sioner for Scotland. Shaftesbury, after a spell in the Tower, saw which way the Tory wind was blowing and fled to Holland, where he died early in 1683.

In June of that year the Tories were given an opportunity to play the same game as the Whigs had played with Titus Oates. They revealed a conspiracy by a number of eminent Whigs, including Lord Russell and the earl of Essex, to assassinate the king and the duke of York as they returned one day from Newmarket. There had undoubtedly been a conference of disaffected elements still wishing to exclude James and crown the duke of Monmouth in due course, but it is highly improbable that those arrested ever had any murderous design. Nevertheless the Tories used the so-called Rye House Plot to bring down the Whigs, executing two of their leaders and several sympathisers. The earl of Essex committed suicide in the Tower. Monmouth fled abroad. The plot, said William of Orange sceptically, was 'no more than a thing contrived to destroy the most honest people in England'.

Shaftesbury had left behind him one worthy legacy: the Habeas Corpus Act of 1679. Until that time it had been difficult for an arrested man to exercise his legal rights if the king or some cunning official chose to ignore them. From now on it was established that a prisoner should be brought before the courts with a minimum of delay, and heavy penalties could be imposed for any attempt to shift such a prisoner from one place to another to avoid having to produce him.

But if Shaftesbury had succeeded in getting this safeguard against royal whims through Parliament, he succeeded in little else. Dying in 1685, Charles avowed himself a Catholic; and a loyalist Court party welcomed the duke of York as King James II of England.

James and Monmouth

James began his reign amiably enough. He announced that he would recognise the Church of England as the country's established church, and seemed so reasonable that when a motion was put forward to enforce laws against Roman Catholics more rigorously, it was felt to be an insult to the king himself and rejected.

The Whigs still did not fancy the idea of such a ruler. They urged the duke of Monmouth to come and save them, and in Holland he and an exiled Covenanter, the duke of Argyll, planned an invasion. Argyll set out first, heading for Scotland. He found that ancient Highland and Lowland jealousies made a united Scottish force impossible, and was soon captured and executed. Monmouth landed at Lyme Regis early in June 1685 and was proclaimed king, but on 5th July his makeshift forces were pitilessly slaughtered at Sedgemoor by a small but efficient army whose second in command was John Churchill, later to become duke of Marlborough.

Monmouth was clumsily executed by Jack Ketch, who had to make seven blows with his axe before the deed was done. The sadistic lord chief justice, George Jeffreys, handed out over three hundred death sentences at what were known as the Bloody Assizes and sentenced innumerable other unfortunates to transportation and slavery.

George Jeffries, King James's notorious lord chief justice.

(2)

The pitifully inadequate rebellion was used by James as an excuse for the persecution of dissidents and the advancement of fellow Catholics to high positions. Over the next year or two the Whigs' worst fears were realised. In 1687 the king put forward a Catholic nominee for the presidency of Magdalen College, Oxford, which was against their statutes, and when the Fellows persisted in electing their own nominee James bullied them into submission. Twenty-five of the Fellows were expelled from the college, whereupon the subservient bishop of Oxford was elected president, followed on his death by one of the papal vicars apostolic.

Then he boldly issued a Declaration of Indulgence to abolish laws against those who did not belong to the Church of England, and ordered that it should be read out in every church of the land. Most of the clergy refused to obey. Old Archbishop Sancroft of Canterbury, who had crowned James, said that the Declaration defied the law, whereupon he and six bishops were charged with seditious libel and sent to the Tower. Brought to trial, they were acquitted, amid great popular enthusiasm. James, disturbed by rumours that his disenchanted people were beginning to look for help from Protestant Europe, made a few concessions, including the restoration of the Fellows of Magdalen; but it was not hard to predict that the moment he felt powerful enough he would once more thrust his religious views upon the country.

The Glorious Revolution

James II had had two daughters by his first wife. The older, Mary, had married the Protestant hero of Europe, William of Orange—himself a grandson of Charles I through Charles's daughter Mary. The younger, Anne, was married to Prince George of Denmark. Both young women were Protestant and both disapproved of their father's conduct, especially when they heard reports that he was trying to find a way to exclude all Protestant heirs from his throne.

There seemed little real doubt that Mary would eventually succeed, so there was no sense of urgency. Then, to the consternation of his critics, James's second wife, the Catholic Mary of Modena, gave birth to a baby son. Attempts were made to discredit this late arrival by spreading the slander that the baby was not James's at all but had been smuggled into the queen's bed in a warming-pan. Such gossip was not enough to bar the child, Prince James Edward, from the succession. Something more drastic was needed.

Many Tories were unhappy at the prospect of a Roman Catholic dynasty and, sinking their differences, joined the Whigs in sending a formal invitation to William of Orange to come to England's aid before it was too late.

William landed at Torbay in November 1688 with an army of some fifteen thousand men, avowing that he had come only to safeguard the Reformed religion and meant no ill to his father-in-law. West-country magnates flocked to join him, after an initial hesitation largely due to memories of the fate of those who had supported the earlier rebellion in these parts. James's most distinguished commander, John Churchill, defected to the invader, and his daughter Anne slipped away to the protection of other rebels at Nottingham.

(1) James II, the last Stuart monarch.

(2) William of Orange who, with James's daughter Mary, took the throne in the 'Glorious Revolution'.

Angelanget in Engelandi, Año. 16...

William of Orange landing at Torbay 5th November 1688.

The king hurriedly sent his wife and infant son off to France. In the small hours of the morning of 11th December he himself slipped out of London, tossing his great seal into the river so that in his absence no Parliament should be summoned in his name. Captured, he was returned to London and then sent to Rochester, from where William allowed him to escape, his flight being declared the equivalent of abdication.

Both Whigs and Tories invited William to call a Convention Parliament. A chauvinistic attempt was made to appoint Mary as queen in her own right. She indignantly rejected this, and William, also refusing the idea of serving as a mere consort, made it clear that if this was the best those he had liberated could do, he would go home 'and meddle no more in their affairs'. Parliament therefore agreed to recognise them as joint sovereigns.

In return, William and Mary had to accept a Bill of Rights which clearly established the supremacy of Parliament and denied any ruler the right to suspend the laws of the land whenever it suited him. 'Divine right' was dead.

There was also a Toleration Act granting freedom of worship to Dissenters, save Unitarians and Catholics; but all holders of office were still obliged to take the sacrament according to the usage of the Church of England.

The Boyne and Glencoe

One of William's main aims in accepting his role in the 'Glorious Revolution' was to strengthen the forces aligned against France, forever threatening the Netherlands. The French did nothing to cool his antagonism by helping the exiled James II to reach Ireland and raise Catholic forces against the new king. William took charge and on 1st July 1690 crossed the river Boyne and routed the rebels. He and the Dutchmen among his forces were horrified by the savagery of the English, who massacred their Irish prisoners and drove carriages over the bodies of the wounded. The day of the battle of the Boyne has been contentiously remembered ever since, especially in Northern Ireland, as Orangeman's Day.

Many Scots also espoused the Jacobite cause, and won a victory at Killiecrankie, but wasted so much time afterwards in plundering and squabbling between the clans that they did not follow it up, and eventually dispersed. William agreed to pardon the chieftains if they would take an oath of allegiance to him before New Year's Day, 1692. Some of his advisers hoped for a refusal so that they could put the entire country to the sword and settle Scottish intransigence once and for all; but in fact all save one complied by the appointed date. Macdonald of Glencoe was six days late in taking the oath, by which time Sir John Dalrymple, Master of Stair, who hated the Macdonalds, had tricked the king into allowing him to send a force of Campbells to punish the chief. Although the Campbells too were old enemies of the Macdonalds, they arrived in the guise of visiting friends and were entertained with traditional hospitality for several days, until one morning they silently arose and massacred their hosts.

With Scots and Irish more or less under control, William turned his attention to his main concern. The imminent death of the king of Spain was likely to lead to the accession of Louis XIV's grandson, thus bringing under French influence not just Spain herself but all her prosperous colonial empire. John Churchill, now earl of Marlborough, was appointed commander-in-chief and empowered to negotiate a Grand Alliance against the French, who continued to exacerbate the situation by sheltering the defeated James II and, on his death in 1701, recognising his son as rightful pretender to the throne of England.

Thrown from his horse while riding at Hampton Court early in 1702, William did not live to see Marlborough launch the all-out anti-French campaign which had been his most burning ambition.

The need for this coming war had led to the introduction of some novel financial contrivances. There was a very unpopular window tax, some relics of which may still be seen in the bricked-up windows of old houses, and a lottery loan. In 1694 a Scottish financier, William Paterson, advised on the foundation of a Bank of England which, in return for an undertaking to raise over a million pounds from the public and lend it to the government at an interest rate of eight per cent, was allowed to issue banknotes and discount bills. The capital sum need never be repaid provided the interest was regularly paid over. Thus was established the National Debt. In 1698 a new East India Company was constituted after agreeing to lend the government money at the same rate as the Bank of England.

John Churchill, first duke of Marlborough.

The duke of Marlborough with
his staff at the battle of Blenheim.

Queen Anne

William's childless wife having predeceased him, the Crown passed
to James II's younger daughter, Anne. There was no question of
her husband being declared co-sovereign as William had been.
Prince George of Denmark was slow, insignificant, and utterly un-
interested in politics. A much more powerful influence on Anne
had always been that of Sarah, the earl of Marlborough's wife, and
now that Anne was queen the fortunes of the Marlboroughs rose to
new heights.

Marlborough was anxious to meet the French and their allies
head-on without delay. He encountered many frustrations from the

Dutch, whose field deputies had powers of veto over battles on Dutch soil and at the same time were reluctant to let the armies range too far afield, leaving Holland unprotected. Marlborough flouted all these restrictions and took fifty thousand men on a six-hundred mile march to the Danube, where French and Bavarian forces awaited them in a strong position near the village of Blenheim. By tactical brilliance and by the personal inspiration he gave his troops, Marlborough achieved a resounding victory on 13th August 1704.

When he returned to England at the end of the year he was created a duke and granted the royal manor of Woodstock with the promise that a sumptuous palace should be paid for by a grateful country and his name kept evergreen.

The architect of Blenheim Palace was John Vanbrugh, already celebrated as a dramatist, combining wit and bawdiness in such plays as *The Relapse* and *The Provok'd Wife*. Without any architectural training, he worked with Sir Christopher Wren's one-time clerk, Nicholas Hawksmoor, on Castle Howard and Blenheim, and contributed much to Greenwich Hospital. He was knighted in 1714, when Blenheim was only half finished. Although Marlborough had gone on to further victories at Ramillies, Oudenarde and Malplaquet, he offended Queen Anne by demanding to be made captain-general for life—antagonistic pamphlets accused him of aspiring to be 'King John II'—while his wife had grown so arrogant that her royal mistress finally threw her over in favour of the Tory-minded Abigail Masham, who worked hard to undermine Marlborough's status. When the commander returned at the conclusion of the war he was dismissed from all his official positions, and the Treasury showed marked reluctance to make the payments which his Sarah demanded for the lavish furnishing of Blenheim.

By the treaty of Utrecht in 1713, Britain retained Gibraltar, seized by Admiral Rooke during the fighting, and was granted full control of Hudson Bay, Newfoundland, Nova Scotia, some West Indian islands, and a part of Canada. It was also conceded that the South American slave-trade should become a British monopoly. Neither France nor Spain could now check Britain's colonial expansion.

This trading strength was an asset to Parliament in forcing through a marriage with those neighbours who had for so long balked at the idea of becoming full members of the family. Although the two countries had been under the same monarch since James VI of Scotland became also James I of England, the Scots had retained their own Church and Parliament, and carried on their own trading ventures. In 1695 William Paterson, who had provided the blueprint for the Bank of England, put up a scheme for establishing a Scottish trading centre on the Darien isthmus between Colombia and Panama, handling goods from both east and west. It was a tragic failure. When Queen Anne's ministers opened discussions for a union of England and Scotland, and the Scots refused to pass an Act invalidating Jacobite claims to the throne or to declare that henceforth both countries should automatically accept the same monarch, England framed an Aliens Act designed to place an embargo on all trade between Scotland and England. Taken in conjunction with the 1660

(1)

(2)

Navigation Act, this would have crippled Scottish commerce. Resistance crumbled, concessions were made, and in 1707 the Act of Union created the United Kingdom of Great Britain, in which the Scots kept their own Church and law courts but would share England's Parliament and trading system.

Queen Anne died in 1714. She had produced sixteen children, but none survived childhood. Towards the end of her reign she was willing to listen to suggestions that her half-brother should succeed to the throne. Parliament, however, was determined that the Stuarts should not return; so a legitimate Protestant successor had to be found.

Pens and papers

The first newspaper in the true sense of the word, the *Daily Courant*, had appeared in the opening weeks of Queen Anne's reign and was soon followed by others in London and the provinces. Previously the dissemination of news and opinion had been in the form of newsletters and pamphlets with a limited circulation, often passed slyly from hand to hand if the contents were too controversial.

In Elizabeth's day such publications had been regarded as dangerous, and all printing-presses had to be registered. None were authorised outside London apart from the Oxford and Cambridge university presses, but secret printers did risk publishing criticisms of those in authority. James I decreed that no pamphlet concerning state or religious matters could appear without licence from an archbishop, the bishop of London, or a university vice-chancellor.

Early in the Civil War John Milton addressed his impassioned *Areopagitica* to 'the Lords and Commons of England' in defence of 'the liberty to know, to utter and to argue freely, according to conscience, above all liberties'; but the Commonwealth in which he dutifully served as Latin secretary to the Council of State continued to censor printed matter, and the Licensing Act of Charles II's time stiffened controls and penalties. For years the only licensed periodical was the *Oxford Gazette*, later the *London Gazette*, which offered its subscribers nothing which the government did not wish them to read. The coming of William III resulted in a relaxation, and once

(1) Blenheim Palace (1745) built at public expense for the duke of Marlborough.

(2) Head of Queen Anne on a contemporary silver coin.

a whiff of freedom had enlivened the Press it was difficult ever again to reimpose manageable restrictions.

In 1702 Daniel Defoe published *The Shortest Way with the Dissenters*, a pamphlet in which he tried to show up the absurdities of persecution by ironically demanding intensive persecution on every possible excuse. The irony misfired: his plea was taken seriously, and he was fined, imprisoned and put in the pillory. On his release he decided to start a newspaper in which he could say what he pleased about the political, moral and commercial state of the nation, and in 1704 founded *The Review*, which he wrote almost single-handed, three issues a week for nearly ten years.

In 1709 Richard Steele founded *The Tatler* to report on 'Gallantry, Pleasure and Entertainment' from the leading coffee-houses, which were fast becoming the intellectual debating and social centres of the capital. Later he joined Joseph Addison in producing *The Spectator*, supposedly under the auspices of a club whose most distinguished member was Sir Roger de Coverley, gently satirised by his creators as the typical country gentleman of the day.

Writers were very politically and socially conscious, most of them fired by the principles of the Glorious Revolution. When the war-weary country sought a scapegoat and the Tories tried to bring down both the once-adored Marlborough and the Whig ministry, pamphleteers such as Steele, Addison and Defoe rallied to the Whigs. A Mrs Manley wrote a vindictive book attacking them with, as Steele put it in *The Tatler*, 'artificial poisons conveyed by smells', much in the manner of a modern 'scandal' magazine. Marlborough, a seasoned fighter in the open, found these verbal battles between the partisans quite a different thing, and his wife scorned the epigrammatic Matthew Prior and 'The Rev. Mr. Swift' for offering themselves so readily 'for Sale . . . both men of wit and parts ready to prostitute all they had in the service of well rewarded scandal'.

Scene at a London coffee-house.

The TATLER.

By *Isaac Bickerstaff Esq;*

From *Thursday* March 2. to *Saturday* March 4. 1709.

Sheer-Law, March 2.

[column of small print facsimile text]

(1)

Jonathan Swift, most savage and brilliant of them all, had been born in Ireland of English parents. He came to England as secretary to Sir William Temple, who had been instrumental in arranging the marriage of Mary to William of Orange. Easily inflamed by slights real or fancied, Swift returned to Ireland when he felt the influential Temple had not worked hard enough to obtain him some preferment. He was ordained there, but was soon back in Temple's employ at Moor Park, where he wrote *A Tale of a Tub* in 1704, a dour satire on religious and philosophical corruption. He was a member of the Scriblerus Club along with Pope, Gay, and his schoolfellow Congreve. When he found there was little chance of his obtaining any worthwhile appointment from the Whigs, he attacked them in derisive pamphlets and for a while edited and contributed to the Tory weekly, *The Examiner*, in which he refuted the arguments of his old friends Steele and Addison. In 1713 he returned to Dublin as dean of St Patrick's Cathedral, where, regarding life in Ireland as little better than banishment, he grew steadily more misanthropic until he sank into the darkness of insanity which he had always dreaded.

In the year of Anne's death, the collected works of John Locke were published. His defence of religious liberty, his *Treatises of Government* in 1689, laying down the responsibilities of Parliament and of a constitutional monarch, and his *Essay concerning Human Understanding* in 1690 influenced all his thinking contemporaries, and laid the foundations of a new empirical philosophy.

The ideas and attitudes of such creative and critical writers carried over into Hanoverian times. Freedom often became recklessness. Parliament worried about its debates being freely reported and freely commented on. All four Georges were to be subjected to scurrilous attacks, especially at the hands of the most brilliant cartoonists. But it was too late to check the increasing circulation of newspapers and magazines of all kinds. As the pseudonymous 'Junius' was to affirm later in the century, 'The liberty of the press is the Palladium of all the civil, political, and religious rights of an Englishman.'

(2)

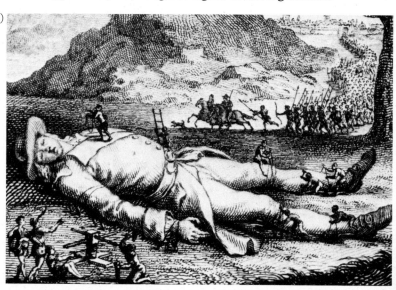

(1) A page from *The Tatler*, 1709.

(2) Gulliver in Lilliput; illustration from a French edition of Swift's *Gulliver's Travels*, 1797.

OPPOSITE William Pitt the Younger in the House of Commons, 1793. Pitt was the son of another great prime minister, William Pitt, earl of Chatham, and was trained from his childhood to succeed his father.

170

The Georgian Era

The Georgian Era

However firmly a progressive society and its writers might set themselves against a Jacobite revival, with the inevitable suppression of free religious and philosophical debate which would follow, they were none too enthusiastic about the alternative. The Crown had been offered to the elector of Hanover, descended from James I through his daughter, the Winter Queen of Bohemia. But although George accepted the English succession as his due, he spoke no English and naturally enough cared more for Hanover than for England; it was a couple of months before he had arranged for the government of Hanover in his absence, and made his way to London, arriving in thick fog. He soon became the butt of the wits, and conniving members of Lords and Commons hoped they might play on his ignorance of the language and customs of the country to run it much as they pleased. Heavy-going as he might be, George I was not that stupid: he brought with him two shrewd Hanoverian advisers, though this did little to endear him to his English ministers or his new people.

The Jacobites soon decided the time was ripe for removal of this ponderous German, who had divorced and imprisoned his wife, was on the worst of terms with his son and heir, and showed few signs of winning the hearts of the populace.

The Old Pretender, James Edward Stuart, had tried an abortive invasion of Scotland shortly after the Act of Union, so absurdly bungled that it caused Queen Anne scarely a tremor. Now, in 1715, another rebellion was stirred up by the earl of Mar and a number of Highland chiefs. Mar raised James's standard and marched south towards the Border. An attempt was made to seize Edinburgh Castle, the Government's main arsenal in Scotland, but went awry because the conspirators spent too long drinking to their own brilliance in a local tavern. News arrived of the death of the king of France, on whose support the rebels had been relying. The Old Pretender himself did not appear until the end of December, by which time Mar had fought an inconclusive battle at Sheriffmuir, and Jacobite forces pressing on into England had been defeated at Preston. Accompanied by Mar, James Edward returned dismally to France.

Prime minister and Cabinet

It would have been hard to find a more fittingly 'Country party' member of the House of Commons than Sir Robert Walpole. A Norfolk squire who believed the nation's well-being depended on sound investment and the flow of trade rather than on war, he was incongruously made secretary for War in 1708, but after a brief lull when the Tories were in power devoted himself to steering the country on a course of peace and prosperity. As chancellor of the

Robert Walpole, first earl of Orford, by Van Loo, c. 1740. He was the pre-eminent politician of his day and has been called Britain's first 'prime minister'.

Exchequer he devised a Sinking Fund to back up the National Debt and give the public the confidence to invest. When taxes deflected into the fund proved higher than had been estimated, Walpole as a landowner himself was glad to relieve his fellows of the burden of increased land taxes by raiding the fund for governmental expenditure.

There were few restrictions on a minister juggling public funds for his own gain or accepting bribes for the distribution of public contracts. Walpole did handsomely out of such practices; but the country itself benefited. In the interests of the industrial and merchant classes he represented, it made sense to simplify customs dues and remove many duties from exports and imported raw materials.

A dispute arose within the Whig ranks. Walpole felt sure that the aggressive policies of Stanhope and Sutherland, effective leaders of

The BUBBLERS MIRROUR; or ENGLANDS FOLLY.

A satirical print of 1720 showing a ruined investor in South Sea stock.

the party, would lead to war and bankruptcy. Dismissed from office, he attacked also their attempts to limit the royal prerogative in the creation of peers. He had to be reinstated, and so was in power at the moment when he was most needed—when a bubble burst.

In 1710 the South Sea Company had been granted a trade monopoly in the Pacific and along the eastern coast of South America, largely concerned with the slave traffic. It prospered so well that in 1720 it offered to pay off the entire National Debt and buy up the irredeemable annuities, provided it had exclusive handling of the consolidated fund. The king's German mistresses and a number of leading politicians received shares in the company to persuade them to back this scheme.

Once the Government had announced its approval, the public rushed to buy shares. Rival companies were set up on the flimsiest pretexts. There were a few get-rich-quick months, then a catastrophic drop. A few speculators who sold out in time made a fortune. Most were ruined.

Stanhope and Sutherland left Walpole to sort out the mess. He evolved a scheme of assigning some South Sea stock to the Bank of England, some to the East India Company, and repaid the bonus which had earlier been paid over to the Government. This way, creditors got about a third of their money back. Many politicians and courtiers involved in the disaster thought it wise to retire, Sutherland among them; and Stanhope died of apoplexy. Having saved the day, Walpole was now the most powerful of the Whigs, utterly at home as first lord of the Treasury and chancellor of the Exchequer.

George I's reluctance to learn English made it impossible for him to preside effectively over meetings of his ministers. In his absence it was inevitable that one man should set the pace and tone of such meetings and eventually assume precedence. Soon it was said that here was not just one minister among equals, but one aspiring to be 'prime minister'. The description was not yet officially applied, but from now on there would invariably be such a first minister, surrounding himself with an administrative entourage which was to develop into the present Cabinet.

Walpole ensured the solidarity of his team by straightforward bribery. This was not regarded as being especially heinous at the time. There was no nonsense about the Simon Pure integrity of the people's delegates. Only a limited number of people had the vote, and this vote was usually for sale. Elections were expensive, but with a large enough outlay the results were seldom in doubt. In areas where supposed freemen were in fact under the eye of a squire or noble landowner who could throw them out when he chose, they tended to vote as they were told. Once in Parliament, the member would find that loyalty to Walpole and his policies was a way to advancement. Defection meant immediate loss of all perks.

The newspapers did not fail to draw attention to this army of placemen or to the remarkable number of Walpole's relatives in lucrative offices. His ministry was dubbed 'the Robinocracy'. When George II came to the throne in 1727 there were hopes in certain quarters that Walpole might be brought down; but although the

A medal depicting George I, by John Croker.

(1) 'Bonnie Prince Charlie', Charles Edward Stuart, was grandson of the last Stuart king, James II.

(2) George II at the battle of Dettingen, 16th June 1743.

new George disliked his first minister, Queen Caroline thought him the soundest man for the job and persuaded her husband to retain him.

The war of Jenkins' ear
Always parsimonious with military expenditure, Walpole was not ready for war when it came.

Spain, angry over the expansion of British trade and particularly its operations in America, had been protesting repeatedly about the semi-piratical exploits of some adventurers. In 1731 a Captain Jenkins carrying on illegal trade in the Spanish colonies was intercepted by the Spaniards and, he claimed, had his ear torn off. This ear he produced in the House of Commons in 1738; by 1739 Britain was at war with Spain, and soon the conflict spread until Britain, Hanover and Austria were lined up against Spain and France. In 1742 Walpole, incapable of coping with a conflict of this scale, resigned. Created earl of Orford, he died within three years, blamed by many for the country's unpreparedness.

In 1743 George II himself commanded the army protecting Hanover. The battle of Dettingen was the last in which a British monarch took any part in the fighting.

The Young Pretender
Disaffected elements in Scotland, incensed by the conviction that London and its Germanic court cared little for what went on north of the Border, saw a chance of using the war for the restoration of their 'king across the water'.

James Francis Edward, still King James III in some minds, was fifty-six in 1744, living in Rome on such pittances as reached him from devout loyalists. His son, Charles Edward, was in his early

(2)

(1)

twenties—courageous and impetuous, very much the 'Bonnie Prince Charlie' of legend. Born and brought up in Rome, he distinguished himself at the siege of Gaeta and—probably with much personal satisfaction—during the battle against George II at Dettingen. He was delighted by the prospect of invading England with French help: from the French point of view, the diversion would help their operations in Europe, and from Charles Edward's point of view the claims of his father to the Crown could be reasserted. In March 1744 he hurried from Rome to Paris and on to Gravelines, near Dunkirk, boasting that friends in England were 'certain of my meeting with no resistance'.

A gale then blew up which made the crossing impossible. The Young Pretender settled down in Paris to await more favourable conditions. As time went on it dawned on him that French enthusiasm for the project was waning. In mid-1745 he impatiently pawned some of his valuables, raised enough money to buy muskets, swords, ammunition and twenty small guns, and hired two ships to take him, his followers and his supplies to Scotland. The ship carrying the arms and ammunition was intercepted by a British man-o'-war and driven back to France. The prince continued and landed on the isle of Eriskay in the Outer Hebrides with only seven men—two Scots, four Irishmen, and an Englishman.

Even those supporters who had longed most ardently for Prince Charles Edward's arrival were dismayed by the loss of supplies and the lack of French assistance. But the Young Pretender rallied the clans round him and marched them to Edinburgh to proclaim his father king. After a victory at Prestonpans he penetrated England as far south as Derby.

There was alarm in London. Actors at Drury Lane Theatre spontaneously added a song called 'God save the king' to their

(1)

(1) An anti-Jacobite print issued after the battle of Preston showing rebel prisoners being herded to London.

(2) The execution of Jacobite rebels on Tower Hill.

(2)

The battle of Culloden, 16th April 1746; the duke of Cumberland directs the battle as the English redcoats repel the highlanders' charge.

programme, in a setting by Thomas Arne, leader of the orchestra. It was taken up in other theatres, and eventually established as the National Anthem.

Bonnie Prince Charlie found no sign of the general uprising he had anticipated. His advisers began to urge retreat. Armies of over nine thousand were threatening to close in on their mere five thousand. The prince, accusing his officers of betraying him, nevertheless bowed to their wishes. The Jacobites turned back.

Troops had been recalled from the Continent, including large Dutch and German detachments, and under the duke of Cumberland drove the rebels northwards until they had to stand and give battle at Culloden, near Inverness. By this time Charles was surly and dis-

illusioned, and his men, according to one of their officers, 'seemed to think of nothing but sleep . . . prodigiously tired with hunger and fatigue'. Many drifted away to eat and drink in Inverness, and others spent the night with friends in the neighbourhood.

Cumberland's trained army made short work of its opponents. The killing did not stop with the defeat of the Jacobites: the Hanoverians in particular went about the field slaughtering the wounded, 'dabbling their feet in the blood and splashing it about one another . . . like so many butchers', and hunting down anyone hiding in houses or crofts in the region. Cumberland's callous encouragement of these excesses earned him the title of 'Butcher' Cumberland.

Bonnie Prince Charlie himself dodged from one hiding-place to another for several months, with a price of £30,000 on his head. On one occasion a supporter, Flora MacDonald, had to disguise him as her maid to get him safely from one of the Western Isles to another. At last he escaped to France, but was expelled and forced to trail from one country to another, lapsing into drunkenness. He married in 1772 but produced no heir. There would be no more Stuarts to perturb the rulers of Britain.

Eastern colonies

After Walpole's downfall and the collapse of 'the 45', George II had to accept a forceful man of very different character to run his government: a difficult man, nearly impossible to work with but impossible to do without.

William Pitt was the grandson of a bluff, reputedly unscrupulous merchant who had made a fortune in India. They both believed that their country's future depended on establishing a firm hold on world trade. Walpole had felt the same, but tried to achieve expansion by negotiation and financial juggling. Pitt was sure it depended on force. A trade rival was as much an enemy as a military opponent.

(1) Flora Macdonald, who disguised Prince Charles as her maid and led him to safety on the Isle of Skye.

(2) Clive of India, whose victory at Plassey proved the foundation of British power in India.

(3) A sale at the East India Company portrayed by Rowlandson.

1) British prisoners in the 'Black Hole of Calcutta' struggle to reach the windows. They had been captured by Siraj-ud-Daulah (2) an Indian prince who favoured the French.

1)

(2)

Any method which added to Britain's income and territories was justified. Incorruptible himself, Pitt persuaded not by bribery but by rhetoric: a superb orator carried occasionally by fervour or apocalyptic gloom to the brink of madness, he inspired in even his most sceptical contemporaries a sense of Britain's almost holy responsibility to impose her traditions and her merchants on the undeveloped countries of the known world.

One thing Pitt never doubted. The main competitor was not Spain, whose grip on the riches of South America and the Caribbean had been progressively weakened, but France. A peace treaty patched up at Aix-la-Chapelle meant nothing. There would be some kind of European war again before very long; and overseas there had never really ceased to be one.

The East India Company had grown in stature since James I's grant of a permanent charter. Although a purely trading venture, it had found it necessary to build forts and maintain its own troops, never knowing which way the quarrels of local potentates might go or what pressure other nations might exert. When Britain and France were at war between 1744 and 1748 the governor of French possessions in India, Joseph Dupleix, thought this a good time to enlist the aid of some powerful princes in an attempt to drive the British out altogether. Within a few years he seemed in sight of success, with almost the whole of the Carnatic and the Deccan under French control.

A diversion was staged by a young officer, Robert Clive. Clive had joined the East India Company as a clerk, but transferred to the military wing and was swiftly promoted to captain. He volunteered to attack French-held Arcot with some five hundred men, over half of them Indian sepoys, and succeeded in taking the town. The much greater French army was unable to dislodge him, and Dupleix, losing the support of the local princes, was duly recalled to France in disgrace in 1754. Clive, in contrast, returned home in 1753 as a hero. His dealings with local princes had made him a fortune, but he soon squandered it, and in 1756 returned to India.

Siraj-ud-Daulah, a young prince who still had leanings towards the French, seized the British trading post at Calcutta and crammed 146 prisoners into a guardroom—'the Black Hole of Calcutta'. By morning there were only 23 survivors. Ordered to recapture the post, Clive did not just leave it at that but went on to defeat Siraj-ud-Daulah utterly at the battle of Plassey in 1757. He became governor of Bengal, and amassed another fortune. Later he loftily repudiated criticism of his methods of acquiring such wealth by declaring at a parliamentary inquiry, 'I stand amazed at my own moderation.'

In 1770 a terrible famine which killed a third of the population of Bengal showed up the glaring gulf between these 'Nabobs' and the peasantry. Parliament decided that, while the East India Company should be allowed to continue its trading operations as before, administration must be transferred to the Crown. In 1772 Warren Hastings, who had worked his way up through the Company's service, was appointed governor of Bengal, and a year later designated governor-general with the task of bringing order out of anarchy, checking abuses, and disentangling the strands of Clive's system.

(1)

(1) The Englishmen in India travelled in style. Those who returned home with huge fortunes were disparagingly nicknamed 'nabobs' by their envious countrymen.

(2) A detail from *The Election* by William Hogarth, showing a parliamentary candidate and supporters impeded by a busker.

Not all the councillors sent out to support him agreed with his methods. One of them, Sir Philip Francis, he wounded in a duel.

Hastings was a fervent patriot, dedicated to the expansion of British rather than personal interests; but his autocracy and the expense of his far-ranging administration brought the mounting disapproval of powerful opponents. In 1788 he was impeached for corruption and cruelty. The trial lasted for seven years, ending in his acquittal. Hastings spent every penny he had in his own defence— and, unlike his predecessors, he had built up no great illicit fortune. The East India Company came to his rescue with the grant of a large pension.

(1)

The Seven Years' War

In 1756 hostilities had broken out in a European war which was to make Frederick the Great's Prussia as important as Austria, and provide the cornerstone of a new Germany. Alarmed by threats from Russia and France, Frederick entered into mutual guarantees with Britain, which prompted France to conclude a deal with Austria and, overseas, to make threatening moves towards British colonies.

Pitt, briefly out of favour because of his fulminations against military expenditure favouring Hanover rather than England, had now to be given his head. His own boast was accepted: 'I know I can save the country and that I alone can.' Only confidence of this order would carry him through.

In 1756 Admiral Byng was despatched from Gibraltar to relieve a garrison on the island of Minorca, under attack from the French. He returned after a half-hearted naval skirmish, leaving them to surrender; and was rushed home, court-martialed and executed. In Voltaire's words, 'it is thought well to kill an admiral from time to time to encourage the others'. Until Clive's triumphs at Calcutta and Plassey, India was in grave danger. In North America, attempts of Virginian settlers to establish a fort at the confluence of the Allegheny and Monongahale rivers had been thwarted by the French, who established their Fort Duquesne and held it against a British assault.

Fighting a war on three widely separated fronts, Pitt was especially aware that the balance of power in the American colonies had reached a crucial pitch. The French and their allies among the Indian tribes made British expansion westwards impossible. They would soon dominate the eastern regions as well, and so control all commerce in and out of the New World.

In 1758 the tide began to turn. The capture of Fort Frontenac brought control of the Lake Ontario region. An attack on Ticonderoga failed, but the port of Louisburg, once before captured from the French and then returned under the treaty of Aix-la-Chapelle, was now retaken by young General Wolfe. Unorthodox and none too deferential towards his seniors, Wolfe aroused some antagonism, and it was hinted that he was mad. In which case, observed George II, 'I hope he'll bite some other of my generals.'

Another attack on Fort Duquesne, forcing the garrison to blow it

(1) The invasion of Cape Breton island by English forces, 1745, leading to the capture of the French fort of Louisberg.

(2) William Pitt, earl of Chatham, believed in using force to extend Britain's trading interests overseas.

up, was a success. It was renamed Fort Pitt after the prime minister, and later Pittsburgh.

In Europe, English and Hanoverian troops inflicted a heavy defeat on the French at the battle of Minden. Pitt poured money into the building up of the navy, which imposed a tight blockade on the coasts of France and her Spanish ally, and checked the flow of reinforcements to America. In August 1759 a squadron from Toulon tried to link up with forces at Brest, but was pursued and destroyed by Admiral Boscawen in Lagos Bay. In November the Brest fleet itself came out, only to be driven into Quiberon Bay and shattered by Admiral Hawke.

From June to September a large British fleet and army had been tied down in the St Lawrence river below Quebec. This and Montreal were the two keys to French Canadian power, and must be taken. But the commander at Quebec, General Montcalm, seemed in an impregnable position. French fire-ships were unable to drive the British ships away; but British troops could not get to grips with the enemy save by attacking up precipitous cliffs, which would be suicidal.

Finally Wolfe detailed a squadron to set sail up-river as though making for Montreal. The body of the fleet remained to bombard the banks below Quebec. Then, under cover of darkness, Wolfe landed over four thousand of his men in a cove north of the city, from which they climbed in single file up the Heights of Abraham. When dawn broke, Montcalm found the British on his doorstep. In the ensuing battle both the French and British commanders were killed; but Wolfe died in the knowledge that he had been victorious.

In the following year the French governor in Canada formally surrendered when Amherst captured Montreal. In that same year, 1760, George II died.

George III at a review of troops in 1797; painted by Beechey.

Wilkes and Liberty

Frederick, Prince of Wales, had died before his father, so George's grandson became George III. An introverted, petulant young man filled with ideas of restoring as nearly an absolute monarchy as he could achieve, he was in fact at the age of twenty-two still under the spell of his mother and her friend the earl of Bute. Insisting on choosing his own ministers (after deferential consultation with Bute) he had no time for men set on driving the country to ruin—such as Pitt. Pitt's achievements and the rich conquests overseas meant little to him. The war must be ended; obligations to Prussia and Hanover rescinded.

In 1763 the treaty signed after cessation of hostilities gave back to France many possessions acquired by Britain, including the West Indian sugar islands and Dakar, key port in the West African gum and slave trade. Even off Newfoundland the French were granted renewed fishing rights. Pitt, so near to collapse at this reversal of his policies that he had to be carried into the House for debates, warned that in restoring so much to France 'we have given her the means of recovering her prodigious losses and becoming once more formidable to us at sea'.

He was not the only one to be appalled. Among the king's most

The taking of Quebec, 13th
September 1759. Boldly conceived
and executed Wolfe's victory
established English control of
Canada.

vitriolic critics was John Wilkes, a journalist and member of Parlia
ment, who founded a newspaper called the *North Briton*. In it
forty-fifth issue he attacked not just the vacillations of the Govern
ment but the character of the king himself. He was arrested and pu
in the Tower to await trial on a charge of seditious libel. In a few
days he was released, claiming privilege as an M.P. He then sued
the Government for wrongful arrest and for damage done to hi
property, declaring that the principle of the general warrant unde
which he had been arrested was illegal. He won his case and damages
'Wilkes and Liberty' became the slogan of all those dissatisfied with
venal authority and with attempts to stifle free comment.

Wilkes fought a duel with a man who claimed to have been
slandered in the *North Briton*, and while away in France recupera
ting had a warrant issued for his arrest. He was formally expelled
from the House of Commons, but after a lull came home to put him
self up for re-election. When he won with a large majority, he was
arrested on the warrant issued in his absence, and forbidden to take
his seat. Freed, he stood again; and again was the winner. Again he
was expelled; and again won the ensuing election. By now the public
loving a good fighter, was behind him. Pitt spoke on his behalf

The battle of Lexington, 19th April 1775, was in fact a small skirmish in which eight Americans died opposing a British force sent from Boston to destroy military stores. However, the bloodshed inspired the colonists to full-scale revolution.

Appointed as a city magistrate, Wilkes acquitted a printer charged with printing Parliamentary debates for the edification of the electorate. Ordered to appear before the House of Commons, he refused; and the Government, belatedly sensing the mood of the country, let the matter drop. Wilkes became lord mayor of London and at last took his seat in Parliament, where he continued to criticise the king and the party of the 'King's Friends' in fine style.

He was a libertine and a drunkard, and many of his resounding pronouncements were occasioned by little more than a zest for stirring up trouble for its own sake. But whatever his motives, he established the right of the press to report Parliamentary debates, and the right of a duly elected member to take his place in Parliament against any opposition which a ruling clique might offer.

The Wesleys and Methodism

Around the middle of the century other voices advocated other, higher truths—not in press or Parliament but in prisons and from wayside pulpits.

While still a scholarship student at Oxford, young Charles Wesley, son of a poor Lincolnshire clergyman, had formed a group

of pious friends. Soon joined by Charles's older brother John, they practised self-denying austerities so rigorously that they came to be known as 'Methodists'. There was little joy in this asceticism, however sincere, until John, coming in contact with the deeply personal religion of the Moravian sect, had a shining revelation: 'I felt that I did trust in Christ, Christ alone for salvation; and an assurance was given me that He had taken *my* sins, even *mine*, and saved me from the law of sin and death.'

It was his duty to show others the way to the light. Although neither he nor his brother wished to break away from the Church of England, they found few parsons willing to lend their pulpits for the preaching of their emotional doctrines, so they went out into the fields and highways. 'The world is my parish,' said John. In the fifty and more years of his ministry he journeyed about a quarter of a million miles, much of it on horseback, preached over forty thousand sermons—often reviled, stoned, and in danger of death—and built over three hundred and fifty Methodist chapels. Charles excelled in the composition of thousands of tunefully simple hymns.

Although the Wesleys' own politics were conservative, their teaching of the individual search for salvation appealed most to those who, mistrustful of the established Church as the province of the squirearchy, needed just such a personal challenge to strengthen their self-respect under the darkness of indifference and exploitation.

(I)

The Gordon riots

Religious bigotry was still, as the Wesleys had discovered, a force to be reckoned with. After a mild measure in Parliament to ease restrictions on Catholics, the half-mad Lord George Gordon assembled a mob about him in June 1780 and, with the old cry of 'No Popery', marched them towards the House to demand repeal. The rabble got out of hand, pillaged Catholic chapels, broke open prisons, and set fire to a distillery, proceeding to get drunk and in a

(2)

(3)

(1) An etching by Hogarth of John Wilkes, whose racy wit and outspoken radicalism brought him into repeated battles with the government.

(2) The founder of Methodism, John Wesley, painted in 1766.

(3) A detail from 'A Midsummer Afternoon with a Methodist Preacher' by de Loutherbourg.

(4) The burning of Newgate during the Gordon riots, 1780.

(5) The failure of the Stamp Act (1766) lampooned in a contemporary cartoon. The Act is carried in a coffin by a member of the funeral procession. Behind are ships and warehouses full of goods for America.

(4)

few instances burning themselves to death.

The orgy of destruction lasted for a week, though full order was not restored in London for another three days, and almost five hundred people were killed or wounded. Those sworn enemies John Wilkes and George III collaborated for once, and called out enough troops to clear the streets and restore order. What was conspicuously lacking was any civil police force—a lack which was not to be adequately dealt with for another half-century.

Lord George Gordon was sent to the Tower and charged with treason, but acquitted. In 1793 he died of gaol fever in Newgate Prison, where he had spent the last five years after being convicted of a libel on the French queen, Marie Antoinette.

The War of Independence
After the conquest of Canada, and even after the ill-managed peace treaty, the colonies were in little further danger from the French. It came as a shock to them to learn that they were expected to pay heavy taxes to Britain as their share in the operations which had brought them this security, and to support a standing army which,

(5)

(1)

These two paintings reflect the
formal elegance and grace of 18th-
century portraiture.

(1) John Peyton, Baron Willoughby
de Broke, with his family, painted
by Johann Zoffany.

(2) The celebrated actress, Mrs
Siddons, painted by Thomas
Gainsborough.

though ostensibly created to repel Indian attacks, was suspected a
being there to pacify the settlers, too.

Of the original thirteen colonies, some had preserved their sel
governing status. Others were administered by governors appointe
by the Crown. By the middle of the century the actual day-to-da
work was carried on by the colonists' own assemblies, which raise
necessary revenue and had virtually taken over control of expenditur
from the figurehead governors.

Britain had made various attempts to raise money from thes
regions, but the Stamp Act of 1765, ordaining that colonists shoul
pay duty on a wide range of legal documents, was the first direct ta
imposed by Parliament on its faraway cousins. Even in Londo
there were doubts about it. 'The British Parliament has no right t
tax the Americans,' declared Baron Camden in the House of Lords
'taxation and representation are inseparably united.' It was to be
come almost a war-cry: 'No taxation without representation.' Th

(1)

(1) A cartoon on the Boston Tea Party.

(2) George Washington, the commander of the victorious American forces and the first President of the United States.

Act was repealed the following year, but Parliament rebuked the protesters by passing a Declaratory Act affirming its full jurisdictional rights over the colonies, and imposed further duties.

Customs officials found themselves often having to call in troops for their protection. Merchants in some American cities refused to import any British goods until taxes were repealed. The Virginian House of Burgesses in 1765 had pronounced that only the governor and provincial legislature were empowered to tax Virginians. When Lord North became prime minister in 1770 he withdrew all duties except that on tea, while at the same time allowing the East India Company to undersell all rival traders. Defiantly the colonists smuggled tea in from other sources.

On 16th December 1773 a number of men disguised as Mohawk Indians boarded an English ship in Boston harbour and threw its entire consignment overboard. Parliament ordained that the East India Company and the Customs authorities should be recompensed for this Boston Tea Party. Wide powers were given to officials involved in suppressing riots. The individual states, still trying to avoid an irreparable clash with Britain, joined in a Continental Congress in 1774. But by 1775 Patrick Henry, declaring himself not just a Virginian but an American, was prophesying imminent war and saying, 'Give me liberty or give me death.'

A second Congress appointed George Washington commander-in-chief of its mobilising forces. Further peace overtures were made to Britain; but after a rebuff from the king, Congress renounced allegiance to the mother country and on 4th July 1776 issued the Declaration of Independence.

King George III had grown more stubborn as the years went by. These argumentative colonists must be put in their place. His prime minister, Lord North, was an indolent and confused man ready to say yes to whatever his royal master might thunder. Recent medical research tends to absolve George from the charge of out-and-out insanity and to attribute his mental disturbances to a rare disease, porphyria; but whatever the clinical explanation, there is no doubt that when the king lost his temper and his reason he lost them with devastating effect. He was a pig-headed man rather than a tyrant—but from America the distinction was not clear to the naked eye.

John Wilkes and Charles James Fox, a witty and ardent young Whig already in the king's bad books, warned that all England's enemies would rush to the aid of the rebels. Pitt, now elevated to the peerage as first earl of Chatham, uttered dire warnings in the House of Lords. King George and Lord North floundered on, clinging desperately to each other, although at one stage North longed to resign, and George in a fit of black depression considered abdicating because everybody was letting him down.

British officers had so frequently expressed their contempt for colonial militiamen—'all so nearly on a level, and a licentiousness, under the notion of liberty, that they are impatient under all kind of superiority and authority'—that the early subjection of the rebels was taken for granted. The American forces, however, inflicted repeated defeats on those sent to quell them. American approaches to France brought offers of assistance, and Spain and the Netherlands

 (1)

(2)

(1) The raising of the siege of Gibraltar, 1780.

(2) Charles James Fox, the brilliant Whig M.P. who opposed first the elder William Pitt and then his son.

weighed in. Too late, North decided to talk peace with the revolutionaries. Seeing their independence within reach, they would not parley.

In October 1781 Lord Cornwallis was trapped in Yorktown with the last sizeable British force still in operation. Unable to break out, he was compelled to surrender. Reinforcements were on their way, but turned back when the news reached them.

Early in 1782 Admiral Rodney, who had previously defeated a Spanish fleet off Cape St Vincent and relieved pressure on Gibraltar, saved British possessions in the West Indies by a brilliant engagement with a combined Spanish and French fleet in the battle of the Saints, off Dominica. But it could now have no appreciable influence on the crumbling campaign on the mainland. Parliament demanded an end to the war; Lord North resigned; and on 3rd September 1783 treaties were signed at Versailles. France retained her West Indian possessions and in addition was given Tobago. Forts and factories in India were restored to her. Spain got Florida back after twenty years of British control (but later sold it to the United States). Britain retained Canada and the West Indian islands safeguarded by Rodney. And the thirteen rebellious states were recognised as the United States of America.

Captain James Cook, remembered not only for his discovery of Australia but for saving his seamen from scurvy by the introduction of citrus fruits into their diet.

The Spirit of the Age

As has so often happened, the wars and ferments of the mid-eighteenth century threw off many scientific and intellectual side issues. The firmer Britain's mastery of the seas, the wider her explorers and traders could range. The more contentious her political entanglements, the more vigorous the debates in the fashionable coffee-houses and the press. Kings and barons no longer disappeared for years on end, leaving their people with no news of the war until it was all over. Communications were swifter; speech was freer.

Between 1740 and 1744 George Anson, later Lord Anson, in charge of the South American squadron fighting the Spaniards, had gone right round the world, almost inadvertently. His chaplain kept and later published valuable records of the voyage.

A gifted naval surveyor, James Cook, who had done magnificent work for Wolfe at Quebec by charting the St Lawrence river from the capital to the sea, later surveyed the coast of Newfoundland and as a result was invited by the Royal Society to make observations from the South Seas on the transit of Venus. Operating from

Tahiti, he prolonged his expedition in the hope of finding the continent which it had long been believed must exist somewhere in the south. He established the location of New Zealand and landed on the coast of Australia, claiming it for Great Britain as New South Wales. On his return he reported on possibilities of colonisation. His landing-place, Botany Bay, was to become a grim penal colony for felons transported from the homeland.

Promoted to captain, Cook continued mapping and opening up little-known territories until killed in 1779 during a misunderstanding with natives in Hawaii.

Captain Cook is killed by natives in Hawaii.

Men who were part philosopher, part scientist were also exploring, in physics and chemistry. The radical Joseph Priestley made early experiments with electricity, and isolated oxygen. His work and theological speculations were regarded as so dangerous that a Birmingham mob burned his house, books and instruments. Henry Cavendish, a millionaire recluse, followed up by breaking water down into oxygen and hydrogen, which led to the use of hydrogen in early balloon tests, and studied the density of the earth. The properties of electricity and its storage and control were being examined all over the world: when George III took over Buckingham House as his London palace, he added one of Benjamin Franklin's inventions—a lightning conductor.

The writers of the time did not live in ivory towers. When Dr Samuel Johnson helped to found the Literary Club in 1764 it included not merely the poet and playwright, Oliver Goldsmith, and Johnson's disciple and biographer, Boswell, but Edmund Burke, shortly to enter Parliament and use all his oratorical skills to convey his views on free trade, Catholic emancipation, and the

(1)

(2)

freeing of Parliament from royal interference. There were also the historian, Edward Gibbon, and the portrait-painter, Joshua Reynolds. In 1768 the Royal Academy of Arts was founded, and Reynolds became its first president, receiving a knighthood in the following year.

In poetry, a new style of romantic naturalism was taking over from the stylised forms which had been practised for so long. Towards the end of the century Robert Burns spoke with his own, individual voice, while in England Samuel Coleridge and William Wordsworth combined to publish their *Lyrical Ballads* in 1798, with Wordsworth in particular striving 'to give the charm of novelty to things of every day'. Academic critics heaped scorn on these new departures; but they reflected, as all truly creative literature does, the real 'Spirit of the Age'—a title the acute critic and essayist, William Hazlitt, was to give to his volume of penetrating studies of his most significant contemporaries.

It was a restless spirit, demanding freedoms which to those in authority could look too much like anarchy. The American War of Independence had fired many a radical imagination. In 1789 came an upheaval which was to arouse even more enthusiasm, and even more fear.

1) Mutineers on H.M.S. *Bounty* turned adrift their officers in an open boat, which drifted for 41 days before reaching land. It was an accident typical of the unrest of the age.

2) William Wordsworth lived most of his life in the Lake District where the beautiful surroundings inspired much of his poetry.

3) The cartoonist Gillray depicts the scene in the House of Commons if a French invasion were to take place.

The French Revolution

'Bliss was it in that dawn to be alive,' Wordsworth was later to recollect, 'But to be young was very heaven!'

The idea of absolute monarchy which had been steadily chipped away in Britain still flourished in France. Blind to the need for reform in his almost bankrupt country, Louis XVI put off until the last minute any attempt to set his finances straight. When he finally summoned the States-General to meet at Versailles in 1789, members representing middle-class interests rather than those of the nobility and clergy formed a National Assembly and demanded Liberty, Equality and Fraternity. Workers stormed the Bastille on 14th July to seize arms stored there. Discussions on limitations of the king's authority were begun, but, as in America, the people's taste for freedom from old restrictions outran the rulers' willingness to make concessions.

Louis and his family tried to flee Paris but were brought back. A republic was declared, and in 1793 the king and Marie Antoinette,

3)

his queen, were guillotined—two among the thousands who suffere[d]
during the Terror.

Republican and egalitarian sentiments rippled out across Europ[e].
But the violence of the revolutionary leaders and the mob whic[h]
egged them on brought a wave of disenchantment. Men of goodwi[ll]
who had welcomed the ideals of the new republic were sickened b[y]
the unrelenting work of the guillotine. 'The glory of France [is]
extinguished for ever,' declared Edmund Burke in his *Reflection[s]
on the Revolution in France*, and he warned: 'Kings will be tyran[ts]
from policy, where subjects are rebels from principle.'

There were many, however, who still believed that good coul[d]
come out of this horror. Thomas Paine, an Englishman who ha[d]
emigrated to Pennsylvania in 1774, served under Washington, an[d]
returned to England after visiting France, published a plea fo[r]
universal suffrage and a democratic constitution in *The Rights of Ma[n]*,
framed as an answer to Burke's tirades. His appeal for the creation [of]
a British republic in alliance with those of America and France wo[uld]

(2)

(1)

(1) The French method of disposing of the aristocracy was to lay them beneath the guillotine.

(2) William Pitt the Younger shown dominating Parliament in 1797. He became prime minister at only 24 and, apart from a short break, remained in power until his early death at 47 from overwork and overdrinking.

popular acclaim, but fearing he was in imminent danger of arrest he went off to France and took up French citizenship. In 1794 he was imprisoned because of his outspoken disapproval of the execution of the king and queen, and in daily expectation of death wrote the second part of his book *The Age of Reason*. Released after Robespierre's downfall, he returned to America, but even the young republic found him too extreme, and he was shunned as a dangerous radical and anti-Christian.

British dissidents kept in touch with France and hoped the day was not far distant when their own rulers could be overthrown. Alarmed by intimations of working-class rebellion, the Government twice suspended the Habeas Corpus Act, arrested the leaders of various groups, and had many transported to penal servitude on grounds of sedition. The Combination Acts, which declared that working men who combined to form societies or unions to press for higher wages or better working conditions were guilty of conspiracy, were manipulated to suppress discussion of any provocative topic whatsoever.

The French announced that they would support, with military might if necessary, any movement towards freedom within other nations. Austria and Prussia were already at war with her when she annexed Belgium and part of the Rhineland. Britain, anxious to remain neutral, nevertheless insisted that France must withdraw her troops; whereupon France declared war on Britain and also upon Holland.

Britain remained divided. George III wanted swift action to crush the republicans and restore the monarchy. William Pitt the younger, son of Chatham, had become prime minister at the age of twenty-four and shared most of his king's opinions on administration, finance and sedition. He, too, was utterly opposed to the French Revolution. Yet it was Pitt who, in the cause of economy, had cut down on armaments and neglected the navy which his father had done so much to strengthen.

John Bull, the typical Englishman, scratching his head over the intricacies of income tax. Pitt, who introduced many new taxes, is portrayed as guardian angel.

The Union Jack

During the American fight for independence the Irish had raised a force of United Volunteers which, announcing its loyalty to the Crown and its readiness for any possible French invasion, used its influence to win a nominally independent Irish Parliament. Being Protestant and basically English, this was hardly representative of the large part of the country, and after some bloody clashes between Catholics and Protestants, in which the Catholics invoked the aid of the French, Pitt came to the conclusion that direct rule from London was the only solution. The Commons of Ireland were persuaded by a lavish distribution of peerages and bribes to surrender their legislative powers, while the Catholic gentry and peasantry were offered warm, if unspecific, promises of a limited measure of emancipation.

On 1st January 1801 Great Britain and Ireland were formally united, with seats for one hundred Irish members in the Commons, and twenty-eight temporal and four spiritual peers in the Lords.

One result was the completion of the national flag as we know it today. A 'Union flag' bearing the crosses of St George and St Andrew

Jack Tar, representing British sea power, knocks Napoleon off the globe.

had been in existence since the union of England and Scotland in 1707. Flown from the jackstaff of men-of-war, it became known as the Union Jack. Now, in 1801, the red saltire of St Patrick on a white ground was incorporated.

Other results were none too happy. George III refused to allow any gesture towards Catholic emancipation. Pitt, stricken by this obduracy, resigned. Irish Catholics added it to the catalogue of what they regarded as characteristic English betrayals.

Napoleon Bonaparte

Napoleon Bonaparte was a young Corsican officer who distinguished himself in December 1793 by retaking Toulon, the Mediterranean naval base, from the British, who had occupied it in August. A general by the age of twenty-six, he carried on a brilliant campaign against the Austrians in Italy and returned to Paris a national hero. Alarmed by these symptoms of what would now be called a personality cult, the Directory hurried him off with instructions to conquer Egypt, which he might well have done had not his fleet been smashed by Admiral Nelson at the battle of the Nile. Napoleon made his way home again, saw that a strong man was needed to reorganise the chaotic administration, and by a *coup d'état* in 1799 set himself at the head of the government as first consul. In 1804 he assumed the title of emperor, which lost him most of his remaining admirers in Britain and elsewhere.

A peace had been patched up between Britain and France in 1802, but war broke out again in 1803 as a result of Napoleon's intervention in Swiss and Italian affairs, and Britain's delay in relinquishing Malta according to the terms of the treaty. William Pitt had to be recalled.

His main antagonist in and out of office was Charles James Fox, close friend of the Prince of Wales and therefore mistrusted by King George, who followed the Hanoverian tradition of being forever at loggerheads with his heir. Fox in power did all he could to limit royal prerogative. Fox out of power continued to speak up for republicanism and for peaceful relations with democratic France. It was not until Napoleon was crowned that Fox sadly accepted the collapse of those ideals which all liberals had admired. Then he offered to serve with Pitt, but was excluded by the continuing animosity of the king.

Whatever Pitt's earlier reluctance to go to war, once hostilities were inevitable he adopted many of his father's tactics. The fleet roamed far and wide to protect Britain's overseas possessions, and a blockade was imposed as tightly as possible on French ports. Money and supplies were offered to hard-pressed allies on the Continent. But while the sea war went well, resistance to Napoleon on land weakened until the emperor was free to turn his attention to the problem of invading England across the Channel.

In anticipation of such an invasion, a string of small round forts known as Martello towers was set up along the southern and East Anglian coasts, and Pitt ordered the digging of a defensive ditch, the Royal Military Canal, across the vulnerable expanse of Romney Marsh. Napoleon assembled a fleet of rafts and barges, some carrying strange devices like windmills to drive them, and an army of

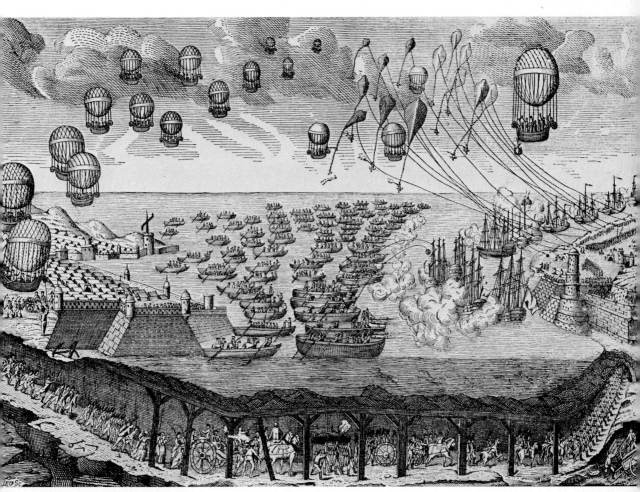

A French print of 1803 showing a plan for invasion forces to cross the Channel by boat, balloon and tunnel.

(1) The guns of H.M.S. *Victory*, Nelson's flagship at Trafalgar.

(2) Nelson lies mortally wounded on the deck of the *Victory* which is locked against the French ship *Redoutable*.

(1)

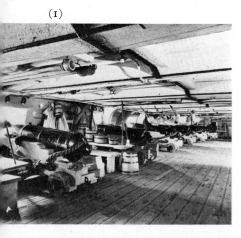

ninety thousand waited at Boulogne for embarkation orders. As with the Spanish Armada, what was needed was a fleet strong enough to cover the passage of these troops across the Channel. 'Let us be masters of the straits for six hours,' declared Napoleon, 'and we shall be masters of the world.'

His admiral, Villeneuve, was ordered to lure the British fleet out to the West Indies and then shake it off and hurry back to Boulogne. The ruse began successfully. Admiral Lord Nelson gave chase, but suspected Villeneuve's intentions. A brig sent to report to the Admiralty had a stroke of good fortune: in the vastness of the Atlantic it saw Villeneuve's ships on their way back, and reached England in time for Admiral Calder to sail out with a squadron and drive the French into the Spanish port of Ferrol.

Meanwhile Nelson was returning. Ill and due for leave, he handed over command to Admiral Collingwood and went to report to the Admiralty. While on leave he heard that Villeneuve had sailed out of one harbour only to be chased and penned in another, Cadiz, by Collingwood.

England expects . . .

With no ships arriving to cover his landing, Napoleon had to call off the invasion. In a fury at Villeneuve's failure, he ordered the admiral's dismissal. When Villeneuve received the news he decided to go out in a blaze of glory, and left harbour to meet the British at Cape Trafalgar.

Nelson, eager to come to grips with the main body of the French fleet at last, sailed in his flagship *Victory* from Portsmouth on 14th

(2)

(1)

(2)

(1) Admiral Lord Nelson, beloved by his seamen and by Emma, Lady Hamilton (2), his mistress.

September 1805. As he approached Spain he issued a Fighting Memorandum ordering that if the Franco-Spanish fleet could be drawn into battle, British ships would not attack in line ahead but would form two columns, try to break through the enemy line, and surround and destroy them in batches.

On 21st October Nelson put on his admiral's uniform and all his decorations, and hoisted the signal: 'England expects that every man will do his duty.'

The tactics were successful. With Nelson himself at the head of one column and Collingwood leading the other in the *Royal Sovereign*, the British chopped through the enemy. The fleet was smaller than Villeneuve's, but its ships were faster and the broadsides it poured from close range into the hulls and even the cabin windows of its opponents were devastating. Fewer than five hundred British seamen were killed, against some four thousand, four hundred French and Spanish. Villeneuve was forced to surrender.

In the hour of triumph England suffered a blow which, said *The Times*, 'was too great a price for the capture and destruction of twenty sail of French and Spanish men of war'. When in the heat of battle the *Victory* was locked against the French *Redoutable*, Nelson's resplendent uniform made him a perfect target for a marksman in the enemy's rigging. A bullet passed through his shoulder and chest into his spine, and he was carried down to the cockpit to die. All his preparations for the battle, including the addition of a codicil to his

(2)

(1)

(3)

(1) A handsome jug inscribed to Nelson.

(2) The funeral of Nelson at St Paul's cathedral was an occasion of great pageantry but his request that Lady Hamilton should be cared for was ignored.

(3) Rowlandson's picture of seamen off-duty in Portsmouth.

will asking his king and country to look after his mistress, Emma, Lady Hamilton, and their daughter Horatia (a request which was callously ignored), suggest that he had expected this end—almost that he had come to desire it.

His body was brought home in a brandy-filled cask, and buried in St Paul's Cathedral in a coffin made from the mast of the French flagship. Villeneuve was allowed parole to attend the funeral of his great antagonist.

England had been saved from invasion, but it could not be taken for granted that Napoleon would not try again. There would be no real safety until he was crushed. It was a daunting prospect: he had reached out all over Europe, seizing Hanover, humbling Prussia, and in December 1805 inflicted such a defeat on the Austrians and Russians at Austerlitz that Pitt said of the map of Europe he had been studying: 'Roll up that map—it will not be wanted these ten years.'

The Peninsular War

In 1808 an army was sent to help Spanish and Portuguese resistance. Napoleon had forced the abdication of the Spanish king and set his brother Joseph on the throne, and ranted, 'If Portugal does not do what I want, the House of Braganza will not be reigning in Europe in two months.'

Sir Arthur Wellesley landed in the Peninsula and achieved a telling victory at Vimiero. He was superseded in his command, however, and his successor (or successors—he was the first of three men to hold command in the space of twenty-four hours) concluded the Convention of Cintra, whereby the defeated French army was allowed to leave Portugal with all its arms and equipment. Sir John Moore, who finally took over command, carried on a courageous campaign against superior forces until killed during the evacuation of Corunna. Wellesley was hurried back, and dug his men in behind fortifications constructed at Torres Vedras.

The British victory at Vimiero in the Peninsular War.

The French were too numerous for a direct confrontation to succeed. But by tying down such large numbers in Portugal, Wellesley was sapping Napoleon's strength elsewhere. When the French, deprived of supplies and unable to live off the inhospitable land, finally began to move out he emerged to defeat them at Salamanca in 1812 and then marched on into Spain and a further victory at Vittoria the following year. The retreating enemy were pursued over the Pyrenees, and the Peninsular War flowed on into France itself.

In 1812 Napoleon decided to add Russia to the nations under his sway. He took his *Grande Armée* as far as Moscow, but the Russians burned their city, and by the time the emperor decided to retreat, winter was setting in. Only a sixth of his men survived the long return through the snows. Attacked by Russians, Prussians and Austrians at Leipzig, and deserted by the Saxons who had been beside him at the outset of the battle, he fell back across the Rhine. The allies kept up the pressure towards Paris, while British forces closed in from the south. On 11th April 1814 Napoleon abdicated and was exiled to the Mediterranean island of Elba.

(1)

(2)

(1) Field-Marshal von Blucher, the Prussian leader and (2) the duke of Wellington. Together they defeated Napoleon at Waterloo.

(1) On board the *Bellerophon* Napoleon travels to his final exile at St Helena.

(2) French cuirassiers charge a highland regiment at the battle of Waterloo.

(1)

(2)

(I)

(2)

The younger brother of the guillotined king had been living in England. He now returned to France as Louis XVIII, the titular Louis XVII, son of Louis XVI, having mysteriously died or disappeared during the early years of the republic. The British ambassador to his court was Wellesley, created earl of Wellington in 1812 and duke of Wellington in 1814. Wellington also represented Britain at the Congress of Vienna, assembled to decide territorial settlements throughout war-ravaged Europe. Among its decisions was the formation of a German Confederation of thirty-nine states in place of the many tiny principalities which had existed prior to the Napoleonic Wars.

The Hundred Days

While the Congress was sitting, Napoleon escaped from Elba, landed in France, and rallied enthusiastic followers for a march on Paris. Louis XVIII fled to Ghent and remained there during the struggles of the Hundred Days, when the disbanded armies of the allies were hastily reconstructed under Wellington's command. A Prussian force under Blücher was defeated at Ligny, but regrouped and marched to link up with Wellington near the Belgian village of Waterloo.

On 18th June 1815 Wellington, sceptical of the calibre of his troops, prepared for a defensive battle. The French attacked before Blücher arrived, and for some hours things went badly for Wellington. The Belgians collapsed under the first French assault, and only a spirited charge by a cavalry brigade made up of the Royals, the Scots Greys and the Inniskillings prevented enemy infantry from breaking through the centre. Their advantage was then wasted: pursuing the fleeing men, they got bogged down in mud and were slaughtered by the French cavalry. The British infantry, however, stood firm against the enemy cavalry, forming squares and shooting down horses and riders as they vainly tried to break the formation. By the time the Prussians arrived, even the crack Imperial Guard could not save the day. Napoleon, agonisingly afflicted with piles, was unable to concentrate, and had to watch his army scatter.

The British lost over fifteen thousand men, the Prussians about seven thousand; but more than forty thousand Frenchmen died. Again Napoleon abdicated, and this time was sent to the lonely Atlantic island of St Helena, where he died six years later.

The Regency

Wellington, the 'Iron Duke', was granted £200,000 by a grateful country, bought himself a mansion and estate in Hampshire, and in 1819 became a member of Lord Liverpool's Cabinet. A staunch Tory, he viewed George III's sons as 'the damndest millstones about the neck of any Government that can be imagined', and was especially incensed by the Whig leanings of the Prince of Wales, appointed Prince Regent in 1811 because of his father's insanity.

The Hanoverian monarchs had all so far had antagonistic sons who set up 'shadow courts' while waiting their time to inherit— and then, having inherited, viewed their own offspring with similar mistrust. George III's heir was an unashamed pleasure-seeker and

(1) 'A Wellington Boot'—a cartoon of the duke as head of the army.

(2) The Prince Regent, later George IV, was notorious for his excesses with food, wine and women. This cartoon shows his distended stomach after a huge meal.

a boon companion of Fox, who championed not only freedom of the press and people but also freedom of conduct which scandalised many of his contemporaries. He was a compulsive gambler; and, emulating his idol in everything, the Prince of Wales proved just as spendthrift. Time and again Parliament was asked for large grants of money to cover his expenditure. By the beginning of his Regency he had piled up half a million pounds' worth of debts.

Not all this money was squandered on unworthy dissipations. The years of the Regency and later of his monarchy were years of adventure and achievement in all the arts. Sir Walter Scott was the best-selling novelist of the day, while Jane Austen concentrated on the 'little bit of ivory on which I work with so fine a brush'. In poetry Byron and Shelley were speaking out for what they considered freedom and their detractors called licence. Lawrence and Turner were at the height of their powers as painters, and after early frustrations the genius of John Constable was at last being recognised. But George's own passion was for architecture, and the money he lavished on the schemes of his personal architect, John Nash, was certainly not wasted.

Two Scottish brothers, Robert and James Adam, had already set new standards of building in London, including the Adelphi, Portland Place and Portman Square, and outside London enriched Kenwood, Osterley, and Syon House. Robert Adam rebuilt Drury Lane for the actor, David Garrick; and then Henry Holland altered it for Sheridan. But these were scattered individual efforts. John Nash, who had started his career as a builder and then set up as an architect in Wales, later collaborating in and around London with the landscape-gardener, Humphrey Repton, was given the opportunity of re-creating whole segments of the capital.

His work on Buckingham Palace was not a success, and parts had to be pulled down and reconstructed: after the death of his

Two of the great romantic poets of the early 19th century: (1) John Keats and (2) Lord Byron.

(3) The tapestry room at Osterley Park.

patron in 1830, another architect was put in charge. (The façade with which we are familiar today dates only from 1913.) But elsewhere Nash achieved wonders. He planned to sweep away the tangle between Carlton House, remodelled by Henry Holland as the prince's home, and Marylebone Park. A sumptuous 'royal mile' was conceived between the northern park, now renamed Regent's Park, and St James's Park in the south. The Regent's Canal was cut, and St James's re-landscaped. The main thoroughfare became, predictably, Regent Street. The whole would give, according to a contemporary diarist, 'a sort of glory to the Regent's government which will be more felt by remote posterity than the victories of Trafalgar and Waterloo'. Trafalgar was nevertheless not forgotten, for part of Nash's scheme involved opening out the west end of the Strand and providing a square which in 1829 became Trafalgar Square, though its victor's column was not erected until 1849.

Rumour had it that Nash's wife was one of the prince's mistresses and that George was the father of some of her large brood of children. Whether this was true or not, Nash assuredly had favours showered on him and became a man of some wealth in a very short space of time.

He was also let loose on Brighton, with which George had fallen in love on his first visit and where he ordained the building of a Royal Pavilion in which he could spend several months of the year. Henry Holland laid down the original classical form, but it was Nash who garnished it with pinnacles and minarets, following the current fad for Eastern décor. Such flamboyance, and the lavishness of the dinners served to guests in the pavilion, caused mounting resentment in a country suffering from poverty and unemployment. In 1817 there was an attempt to assassinate the prince. Once more there were rumblings of radicalism and republicanism.

In 1820 the deranged George III died. The Prince Regent became King George IV, and did not improve his already tarnished image in the eyes of his subjects by trying to divorce his hated wife. They had lived apart for years: he found her smelly, immoral and foul-mouthed, and had married her only to provide an heir to the throne and have some of his debts paid off by the parliamentary grant

(1)

(1) In 1814 the Prince Regent commissioned John Nash to reconstruct the Brighton Pavilion. Nash turned it into an oriental palace topped with onion-shaped domes.

(2) 'Flatford Mill' by John Constable. His pictures caused a sensation when first shown because their restraint and simplicity was in great contrast to the posed and idealised styles which preceded them.

invariably made upon such a marriage. In 1805 there had been un-savoury rumours of her adulteries and even of the existence of a son by another man, leading to a 'Delicate Investigation' by the Privy Council. Although Caroline was cleared of accusations and had many supporters among the Whigs and the public, she found life in England more and more distasteful, and eventually went abroad, leaving George to his sweeter-smelling, more amenable mistresses. But now that her husband was to be king, she announced that she would return and claim the privileges due to her as queen.

She was offered an allowance to stay away, but spurned it, and returned to London amid cheering crowds. Lord Liverpool's government hastily brought in a Bill to deprive her of all regal privileges on the grounds of adultery and scandalous behaviour with her Italian major-domo.

For two months the House of Lords met to hear evidence, and for two months there was an industrious outpouring of scurrilous newspaper articles, cartoons and pamphlets. Revulsion grew within the Cabinet, and before a verdict was reached the Bill of Pains and Penalties was withdrawn. Queen Caroline agreed now to accept a generous allowance. George was furious. At his coronation she tried to force her way into Westminster Abbey, but was repulsed; and to the relief of all concerned died the following year.

The only child of the marriage had been Princess Charlotte, who died in producing a still-born son. The successor to the throne was George IV's younger brother William Henry, who became King William IV upon George's death on 26th June 1830.

(1)

(1) 'Approach to Christmas' painted by James Pollard.

(2) 'The Blacksmith Forge' by Joseph Wright.

The Industrial Revolution

The Industrial Revolution

The years between 1750 and 1830 are generally spoken of as the crucial years of the Industrial Revolution. The phrase is misleading. Industrial revolution has been a continuing process throughout history—one might almost say, risking the unavoidable pun, since the invention of the wheel.

Stone gave way to bronze, and bronze to iron. The charcoal-fed ironworks of the Weald of Kent, Sussex and Surrey worked spasmodically in Roman times, vigorously through the Middle Ages, and on into the eighteenth century, to be superseded by new foundries closer to the developing coalfields. East Anglian weavers prospered until the introduction of fulling machines worked by water instead of by foot caused a trade drift towards the livelier water-

Robert Bakewell on horseback by J. Boultbee. Bakewell is renowned for his improvement to stock by new breeding methods and for use of irrigation.

courses of the west. The fashion for silk threatened the entire wool industry so direly that Queen Elizabeth decreed her subjects should all, at burial, be wrapped in woollen shrouds. Later there was to come an influx of cotton from the United States of America. New processes, new problems.

Nevertheless it is true that from the middle of the eighteenth century onwards there was a striking increase in the speed of technical development, offering the country opportunities—and miseries—such as it had not known before. During the Napoleonic Wars Britain set up the machinery of 'the workshop of the world', and at the same time was applying sweeping changes to her farming methods.

(1) A stage wagon in 1820 by
J. L. Agasse.

(2) The May sheep fair in Boston,
Lincolnshire, by George Northouse.

(1)

(2)

The Land

The open-field farming of the Middle Ages had been under attack for some time, but the pace of land enclosure quickened in the middle of the eighteenth century. Early enclosures had been made for the benefit of sheep-farmers and the export trade in wool. With a rising population there was a demand for more home-grown food, intensified when the country was at war and especially when Napoleon set about cutting Britain's links with the Continent. Between the beginning of the eighteenth century and the middle of the nineteenth some seven million acres were enclosed, and the landscape took on the pattern we associate with our rural England—squarish fields marked out by hawthorn hedges and clumps of trees, for mixed sheep and cattle grazing and the planned rotation of crops. Arable farming spread out across what had been heathland. Stricter control of animal movement cut down transmission of infection.

The second Lord Townshend became known as 'Turnip Townshend' because of his encouragement of turnip-growing and the use of root crops to cleanse the soil in a new four-stage rotation of crops. There were no fallow periods in this sequence: a field would bear wheat one year, roots such as mangolds or turnips the next, a spring-sown cereal such as barley or oats in the third, and in the fourth stage peas, beans or clover.

Thomas Coke—'Coke of Norfolk', later earl of Leicester—turned the barren, sandy heathland of his Holkham estate into fertile cornfields by spreading marl over the arid topsoil. Within fifteen years his tenants were quite happy to pay quadrupled rents, for he offered long leases to those who would work the land according to his principles, and they found that they all prospered.

However beneficial these measures might be in the long run to the community at large, they often meant tragedy for small farmers and labourers. The cottager who had relied on common grazing rights and cultivation of a small strip of land now had to hire him-

New methods of farming brought great prosperity to Thomas Coke in Norfolk.

self out as a labourer in a market where the cost of living rose while wages were falling.

In 1795 a bad harvest pushed up the price of bread. Many local authorities began to adopt a scheme evolved by Berkshire justices of the peace meeting at Speenhamland, near Newbury. This was a well-meaning but misguided attempt to provide poor families with a scale of relief related to the price of bread and the size of the family itself. What it really provided was an incentive to farmers to drop wages even further and leave the ratepayers to make up the difference. The conscientious labourer willing to work hard for a fair wage found himself at a disadvantage: the farmers preferred cheap labour subsidised from the rates. Even those benefiting from payments related to bread prices could still find themselves close to starvation, since other prices rose just as steeply without any allowance being made.

It was not until 1834 that a Royal Commission on the Poor Law proposed that the onus for paying relief should be transferred from individual parishes to a 'Union' of parishes who would set up a board of guardians for the area. Assistance was granted to able-bodied men only if they entered a workhouse, such establishments being deliberately administered as 'uninviting places of wholesome restraint', in the words of the social reformer Edwin Chadwick. The abuses to which such a system was open remained basically unchanged until 1929, when a Local Government Act introduced public assistance committees to supervise relief, themselves under the aegis of county or borough councils.

The Corn Laws worsened the plight of the lower-paid. Parliament was still largely the province of substantial landowners, who profited during wartime from the high price they could get for their grain and did not care to watch this price slump when imports from the Continent were once more possible. In 1815, despite opposition from merchants and town and city elements in Parliament, a law was passed permitting foreign corn to be imported free of duty only when home wheat prices had reached eighty shillings a quarter. This artificial maintenance of high prices kept farmers solvent, but bore hard on many of their own workers.

In his poem, *The Deserted Village*, Goldsmith observed:

> . . . a bold peasantry, their country's pride,
> When once destroyed, can never be supplied.

To avoid their own destruction, many of the peasantry chose to move into the rapidly expanding towns.

The Factories

By 1811 Manchester was second only to London in size and population. Over thirty years later Benjamin Disraeli was to say in his novel *Coningsby*: 'Rightly understood, Manchester is as great a human achievement as Athens.' Liverpool, too, had grown and prospered on its two-way traffic—slaves to the American cotton plantations, and raw cotton back from the plantations to the English cotton-mills, concentrated in the humid Lancashire atmosphere so essential for spinning and weaving.

(1)

(1) New machinery is demonstrated at a meeting of the Royal Agricultural Society at Bristol in 1842.

The harnessing of steam power made possible new and faster means of travel. (2) A steam carriage, 1827. (3) Steamboats designed and constructed by B. R. Dodd, 1817.

In 1721 the wool manufacturers had tried to block the competition of imported cotton cloth. Parliament passed an Act to keep finished material out, but raw cotton was imported in increasing quantities. There was a desperate demand for labour; or for faster processing techniques.

In 1733 John Kay, born in Bury, Lancashire, was supervising weavers in Colchester, and working out ideas for speeding up the hand-threading of the shuttle which carried the wool in and out of the threads of warp on the loom. He came up with the 'flying shuttle', doing the same job as the tug of a string. The men refused to use it, fearful of doing themselves out of work. Kay found more co-operative workers in Leeds, but was unable to get any payment for his invention. He retired, disillusioned, to his birthplace, but when he learned that his shuttle was using thread faster than the spinners could provide it, he set to work to devise a faster spinning-wheel also. The mere rumour of this brought a mob into his house to smash his equipment. This time Kay had had enough. He left England for good, and died a pauper in France.

It was left to James Hargreaves of Blackburn to come up with the necessary machine. Knowing of Kay's fate he tried to work in

(1) The first processes of the woollen industry: sheep shearing, washing, beating and combing.

Two of the early spinning machines by Hargreaves (2) and by Arkwright (3).

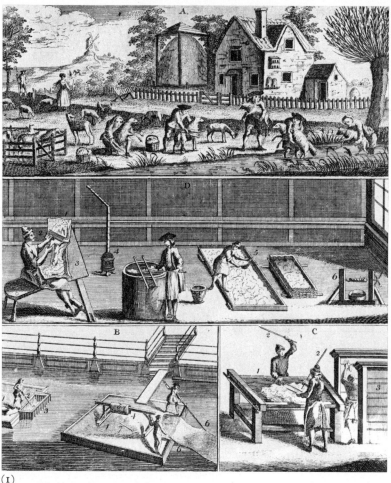

(1)

(2)

(3)

secret, but word got round and his invention also was destroyed. In 1768 he moved to Nottingham, took out a patent on what he called a 'spinning jenny', after his wife Jenny, and set up his own mill there.

A more ambitious machine to do the same work was being developed at the same time by Richard Arkwright, a Preston man whose devices suffered not at the hands of apprehensive neighbours but those of his wife. Scared that his neglect of his barber's business would reduce them to penury, she broke up some of his models, which led to their separation. Moving to Nottingham, Arkwright succeeded in creating a spinning-frame which would produce stronger thread than any of its predecessors. One feature was of great significance for the future of the industry: too heavy to be worked by hand, it relied at first on horsepower and then on a waterwheel, which meant that it was of no use to cottagers but had to be installed in a factory close to running water.

Arkwright was shrewd enough to profit from his own invention by running his own mills, and although his patents were infringed by others he amassed a reasonable fortune and in 1786 received a knighthood.

Less fortunate was Samuel Crompton of Bolton, whose 'mule'

spun a finer yet equally strong thread, a great advance on the water-frame. He was cheated out of all the profits of his invention, and when at last Parliament voted him £5000 he invested it unwisely and lost it all.

For a while there was still a need for the domestic weaver, picking and spinning at home; but weaving was increasingly concentrated in factories, at first small and local but then larger and more highly mechanised. There was a demand for increased output, which meant increased power. It was a demand shared by other industries.

In the early 1700s Thomas Newcomen had invented a primitive steam-engine, invaluable for pumping out mines, but wasteful in operation since it used most of its steam for heating the cylinder and only a fraction for filling it. This drawback was not overcome until in 1764 a model of the engine was sent for repair to James Watt, an instrument-maker at Glasgow University. He introduced a separate condenser and, going into partnership in 1774 with Matthew Boulton, owner of an engineering works in Birmingham, applied himself to the construction of steam machinery for every possible use. His 'stupendous steam-engine' was installed at Whitbread's Brewery in London in 1775 to grind malt and raise the liquor, taking the place of a huge wheel which had needed six horses at a time to turn it. 'We put aside', the company recorded, 'full 24 horses, which to keep up and feed did not cost less per annum than £40 a head. The expense of erection was about £1000. It consumes only a bushel of coals an hour.' The fame of this machine prompted a visit by King George III and Queen Charlotte.

In 1798 Fry's, the chocolate firm, invested in a Boulton and Watt engine to grind their cocoa beans. And of course the insatiable cotton-mills were eager to increase output still further. As a result of visiting Arkwright's mills, the Reverend Edmund Cartwright

(1)

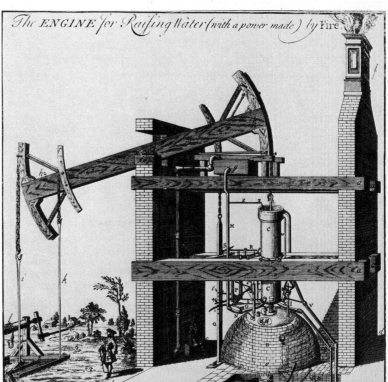

The ENGINE for Raising Water (with a power made) by Fire

(2)

(1)

(3)

(1)

(2)

had turned his mind to the invention of a power-loom, and by the beginning of the nineteenth century Boulton and Watt were at work all over the North and Midlands.

Each new advance met with a wave of protest, as men feared their own displacement by machines. There were particularly destructive riots in 1811 among hosiers in the Midlands, soon spreading north. Stocking-frames and power-looms were wrecked, and the rioters appealed to Parliament to legislate on fair wages and hours of work instead of allowing employers a free hand to impose their own oppressive regulations. These protesters called themselves 'Luddites' and signed many of their proclamations 'King Lud' or 'Ned Lud', supposedly after a Leicestershire simpleton who smashed some machinery in a rage after quarrelling with someone who had provoked him.

More machinery meant a demand for more iron. Foremost among the pioneers of smelting iron by the use of coke from coal, in place of charcoal from wood, was the Quaker family of the Darbys. In their blast-furnaces of Coalbrookdale, Shropshire, they overcame the problem of impurities in coal which had hitherto contaminated the iron, and developed more powerful blasting methods. In 1777 the third Abraham Darby erected the world's first cast-iron bridge across the Severn near his factory, giving the place its present name of Ironbridge.

The iron industry flourished where coal and iron could be found together. A 'Black Country' grew in the Midlands and there were dark concentrations in Yorkshire, Lancashire and South Wales. Another coincidence of local raw material and fuel led to the establishment of Josiah Wedgwood's 'Etruria' factory at Burslem, Staffordshire. Small potteries had existed there since the seventeenth century, but it was not until Wedgwood's combination of high quality and mass production forced his rivals to copy his methods that the characteristic bottle ovens multiplied into a forest. The complex known as 'the Potteries' took in the 'Five Towns' of Burslem, Hanley, Longton, Fenton and Tunstall—vividly re-created in Arnold Bennett's novels—now incorporated into Stoke-on-Trent.

Communications

To speed his goods on their way, Wedgwood financed the cutting of canals. They were safer and cheaper than the roads, and a lot smoother when it came to moving pottery and porcelain. Even heavier goods fared better on water: the roads then in existence were quite inadequate to bear the weight and bulk of iron and coal shipments.

The great pioneer of canal-building in England was the third duke of Bridgewater. With his engineers, John Gilbert and James Brindley, he devised a waterway from his coalfields at Worsley to Manchester, with his eye also on a route to Liverpool. To keep it level it had to be taken through tunnels, along newly raised embankments, and along aqueducts such as the two hundred-yard stretch of Barton Bridge above the river Irwell. Even before this was finished, work began on a Grand Trunk Canal, with the overworked James Brindley as its engineer. Taking some eleven years to complete, it

1)

(2)

1) The Duke of Bridgewater points to the Barton Aqueduct which carried his canal across the river Irwell.

2) A boat sails over the aqueduct.

needed five tunnels through the hills between the Trent and the Mersey, the most remarkable being the 2880-yard Harecastle Tunnel, more than two hundred feet below the surface.

There came a time when no town of any size in England was more than fifteen miles from a canal. At the junction of the Staffordshire

In a procedure of coaches the
Wootton Bassett electors escort
their member of Parliament back
home after the election.

and Worcestershire Canal with the river Severn, wharves and warehouses provided the foundation of a completely new township, Stourport.

Other eminent engineers included two Scots, John Rennie and Thomas Telford. Rennie worked with Boulton and Watt on the machinery of the Albion flour-mills, Blackfriars, then turned his attention to canals; he was also responsible for the Waterloo Bridge replaced in 1944, and the London Bridge which is now a tourist attraction in America. Telford was responsible for the Ellesmere and Caledonian canals, the magnificent Pontcysyllte Aqueduct over the river Dee, and a new tunnel parallel to Brindley's old Harecastle Tunnel.

Telford also worked on road improvement, and was responsible for more than a thousand miles in Scotland alone. His Menai suspension bridge transformed the London–Holyhead road.

From the time of the Romans it had been taken for granted that a highway carrying regular heavy traffic must have deep, solid foundations. John MacAdam introduced a surfacing of hard stone chippings which, weather-resistant, bore its load better than the less resilient solid construction, and was strengthened rather than weakened by the constant pressure of wheels and horses' hoofs.

Fast coaches were designed for these improved turnpikes, paying

A Rowlandson print of the turnpike gate just north of St James's chapel in what is now Hampstead Road.

a fee at toll-houses along the route to maintain the highway and provide profit for the magnate or local authority across whose land it went. Turnpike trusts were organised to collect dues and supervise maintenance, and also to set up milestones for the benefit of travellers and to mark the parish boundaries.

The most adventurous development in transport, however, was that of the iron road.

Railway mania

In his later years James Watt considered the feasibility of using steam as a method of propulsion as well as for powering static engines, but did not follow it up. It was a Cornishman, Robert Trevithick, who first constructed a steam locomotive and displayed it running round a circular track at Euston in 1809. In 1813 William Hedley introduced his colliery tramway locomotive, *Puffing Billy*, at Wylam in Northumberland. This ran past the cottage in which had been born, in 1781, George Stephenson, who himself began to build locomotives including *Locomotion* for the Stockton–Darlington Railway, opened in 1825. In 1829 George and his son Robert won a competition sponsored by the Liverpool and Manchester Railway with their *Rocket*, capable of travelling at almost thirty miles an hour.

Cheap Irish labour had facilitated the cutting of the canals. Now it swelled the work force on railway cuttings, embankments, tunnels and viaducts. These 'inland navigators' or 'navvies' were often drunken and uncontrollable, and districts through which they drove their iron highway feared them as an invading army. Thomas Carlyle, however, commented: 'The postman tells me that several of the poor Irish do regularly apply to him for money drafts, and send their earnings home. The English, who eat twice as much beef, consume the residue in whisky, and do not trouble the postman.'

In the year before the *Rocket* a young civil engineer, Isambard Kingdom Brunel, had been sent to Clifton to convalesce after being injured during an inundation of the new Thames Tunnel. Even during this enforced rest his mind could not remain inactive. He worked on designs for a suspension bridge across the Avon Gorge, one of which was eventually accepted. (Owing to lack of funds the bridge was not built until, after his death in 1859, old friends and colleagues of the Institution of Civil Engineers formed a company

225

(1)

to carry the project through as a fitting tribute to his memory.)

Recuperating from his injuries, Brunel became at the age of twenty-seven chief engineer to the Great Western Railway. H committed the company to a broad gauge of 7ft 0¼in on the ground that this made for faster and smoother running. But other regional companies favoured Stephenson's choice of 4ft 8½in between th rails. 'The battle of the gauges' went on for years, with some system overlapping on double-gauge track. As the railway network grew and there was more need for interchange of passengers and rollin stock between one system and another, it became obvious that th width would have to be standardised. Brunel and the Great Western lost: in 1846 Parliament made it illegal to build any more broad-gaug track, though it was not until the end of the century that the Grea Western itself completed the changeover to narrow gauge.

In 1837 young Princess Victoria saw her first steam train and marvelled at its 'surprising quickness . . . enveloped in clouds o smoke & making a loud noise'. Within a few months she becam queen, and some five years later made her own first rail journey, whe she and her husband returned from Windsor by way of Sloug Station—with Brunel on the footplate of the engine. The journe to Paddington took twenty-five minutes, 'and on Her Majest alighting she was received with the most deafening demonstration of loyalty and affection'.

Speculators possessed by 'railway mania' subscribed to innumer able companies, some so improbable that *Punch* could justifiabl dream up 'John o' Groats and Land's End Junction, with branche to Ben Lomond and Battersea'. But the growth in railway mileag did simplify the efficient and economic expansion of industry. Ther were about two thousand miles of track in 1843; within thirty year there were fourteen thousand miles, and in that same period pas senger traffic had increased fourteenfold.

In addition to all his work on land, the indefatigable Brune designed three famous ships, each the largest in the world at th time of its launching. The *Great Western*, named after the railwa company for which he worked, and conceived as an extension t carry the route on from Bristol to New York, was a wooden paddle

(2)

(1) Stephenson's Patent Locomotive Engine.

(2) A steam locomotive emerges from the engine house at Camden Town, 1839.

steamer. His second giant, the *Great Britain*, was an iron, screw-driven steamship, the world's first. The third, the *Great Eastern*, used both paddles and screws. It had a run of mishaps and lost so much money that it was taken out of passenger service and chartered to a company laying the first transatlantic cable. After completing this, it went on to lay thousands more miles of cable under the seas of the world.

Reformers

Improvement of roads made travel easier and cheaper. The railways, too, soon found there were profits to be made from cheap excursions and bulk transport of human beings in Third Class accommodation. Those with a reasonable income could travel to the nearest town to do their shopping, or even to London. Those with little money could at least scrape together enough to pay the fare to a town or city where they might find employment.

Belated attempts were made to halt the drift from the land into industrial areas. Parliament passed a series of Acts to replace the allotments and smallholdings of which the agricultural worker had been deprived by the various forms of enclosure. But families continued to leave the villages; and few came back. Exploited as they might be, and squalid as living conditions might be, they were still better off than in their country hovels. Also there was the temptation of self-advancement: a farm labourer stood little chance of becoming lord of the manor, but in the brash new towns there were many stories of self-made men climbing to the top.

A lot of this climbing was done over the bodies of women and children. In cotton-mills they supplied the cheapest labour, working in the stifling atmosphere for twelve or more hours a day. In coal-mines women were chained to trucks and hauled them like beasts of burden. Children aged five and upwards dragged similar trucks through spaces too small for a man to squeeze through. Thousands of boys slaved in the Potteries, dragging moulds to the furnaces, up to fifteen hours a day.

In 1815 Peel tried to carry a Bill limiting children's working days to ten hours. It failed. Employers claimed that children were better

(1)

(1) From left to right, John Scott Russell, Henry Wakefield, Isambard Brunel, and Lord Derby awaiting an attempt to launch the *Great Eastern* (2).

(2)

occupied doing useful work all day than running about getting into mischief. Parish authorities thought it quite reasonable to contract workhouse boys of eight and upwards to work in the mines for periods of up to twelve hours.

Not all employers or administrators were so callous. The wider the spread of greedy exploitation, the more vigorous the growth of a social conscience.

The Welshman Robert Owen, partner in the New Lanark Mills, refused to employ young children and instead set up an infant school for them. He provided further education for the older ones, and showed how an enterprise such as his cotton-mills could improve working conditions, wages, and the over-all welfare of the community, and still make a profit. He introduced a co-partnership system and a co-operative store, in contrast to those employers who forced workers to take part of their wages in the form of overpriced goods from a 'tommy shop' on the premises.

Owen urged the Government to apply his principles throughout the country. He lent his weight to the Factory Act of 1819, forbidding the employment of children under nine in cotton-mills; but this and other legislation allowed too many loopholes for employers skilled in the evasion of regulations.

It was not until 1833 that the philanthropist M.P. Lord Ashley (later the seventh earl of Shaftesbury) promoted a Factory Act with the necessary teeth in it. Known as Althorp's Act after the then home secretary, it appointed inspectors to ensure that its stipulations would be observed. In 1840 Shaftesbury pushed through an Act to end the employment of small boys as chimney-sweeps. He was associated with sanitary improvements in common lodging-houses, with a Mines Act forbidding the employment of women and children underground, with reforms in the Poor Law, and with the Ragged Schools. These latter institutions opened at night for the free instruction of all comers, children or adults. As the crusading novelist, Charles Dickens, put it: 'They who are too ragged, wretched filthy and forlorn to enter any other place: who could gain admission into no charity school, and who would be driven from any church door: are invited to come in here, and find some people not depraved willing to teach them something and show them some sympathy.'

(1)

The misery of child workers (1) was a far more common sight than the fortunate children learning dancing at Robert Owen's institution in New Lanark (2).

Other educational work, especially in favour of women's education, was carried on by Elizabeth Fry, wife of a Quaker banker and tea merchant. She also urged better conditions for women in prisons, and for convicts transported to New South Wales.

Edwin Chadwick's work with the Poor Law Commissioners opened his eyes—and his nostrils—to slum conditions in overcrowded cities. Referring to prison conditions described by Howard, the eighteenth-century reformer, he said: 'More filth, worse physical suffering and moral disorder than Howard describes are to be found amongst the cellar populations of the working people of Liverpool, Manchester or Leeds and in large portions of the Metropolis.' A pugnaciously earnest man, Chadwick aroused a great deal of resentment among local authorities, but it was his determination which resulted in the Public Health Act of 1848 and the conquest of cholera, scourge of the slums.

Paradoxically, this very overcrowding made legislation easier. Imposing health or employment regulations on scattered farming communities and itinerant labourers was a daunting task. As Trevelyan observes, 'It is far easier to inspect factories than it would ever have been to inspect the old system of domestic work.'

The Slave Trade
The prosperity of the cotton-mill owners had been built not only on sweated labour at home but on slave labour overseas. Reformers

Charles Dickens drew large audiences in Britain and America when he gave public readings of his books. His novels drew attention to the plight of the urban poor, shown in this engraving by Doré of an alley in Houndsditch.

(1)

wishing to end Britain's part in the supply of such slaves to the American cottonfields made little progress in the later eighteenth century, but by sheer persistence were making themselves more effectively heard by the beginning of the nineteenth.

A decision by the chief justice, Lord Mansfield, in 1772 provided the basis for a long-drawn-out campaign.

In 1765 a lawyer by the name of Lisle turned a half-blind wreck of a slave out on the London streets. He had bought the Negro, known as Jonathan Strong because of his physique and capacity for work, at a Barbados auction and brought him home to England to show off to his acquaintances. Loving to flog and humiliate his servant, he so wrecked Jonathan's health that the man proved incapable of any further work whatsoever, and so was discarded.

Seen queueing at a surgery for free medical treatment, Jonathan was approached by a civil servant, Granville Sharp, who sent him to hospital and later found him a job.

Recovered, Jonathan was seen in the street by his former master, who at once seized and sold him to a plantation-owner shortly to depart for the West Indies. Lisle committed Jonathan to prison to await embarkation; but Jonathan got a message out to Sharp, who had him released from custody, only to be sued for damages by Lisle and the plantation-owner.

Sharp was advised by all his legal contacts to pay up and drop the matter. He was bound to lose the case. But 'I cannot believe', declared Sharp, 'that the law of England is so injurious to natural rights as so many great lawyers are pleased, for political reasons, to assert.'

He fought the case on his own, and finally his opponents dropped their charges. The results of his two years of legal studies were published under the title of *The Injustice and dangerous Tendency of tolerating slavery in England*, and in 1772 Lord Mansfield, though in general no great humanitarian, ruled that in law a slave who set foot on English territory was thereupon free.

Sharp was to devote much of his energy from now on to the anti-slavery movement. But a lot remained to be done.

In September 1781 a trader called the *Zong* sailed from Guinea with over four hundred slaves destined for Jamaica. As usual a number died on the way, and others were reduced by sickness to a

(2)

(1) A slave woman is cruelly parted from her husband in the West Indies.

(2) The crew of a slave ship fire upon the insurrecting slaves from behind a barricade erected on all slave ships for that purpose.

state which would render them unsaleable. The captain decided to throw the sicklier men overboard and let the owners claim insurance. The insurers refused to pay up and were taken to court. After two trials, Lord Mansfield showed himself less benevolent and ruled that the slaves, though human beings, were just chattels: part of a cargo of goods had quite properly been jettisoned to save the bulk of the consignment. 'The case of the slaves', said the chief justice, 'was the same as if horses had been thrown overboard.'

Granville Sharp, horrified by what he considered an offence against man and God, wrote to the Admiralty urging prosecution of the murderers. He failed in this, but did a great deal to publicise the story and awaken public sympathy. In 1787 a committee for the abolition of slavery was formed, and enlisted the support of the young M.P. for Hull, William Wilberforce.

William Pitt the younger approved their aims, but during the French Revolution and the subsequent wars there was little chance of achieving liberal reforms. Supporters of the slave traffic praised it as 'a nursery of seamen'. Wilberforce's 1791 Bill did not get through the Commons until 1804, and then was twice rejected by the Lords. But when Pitt died in 1806 and Fox was in power for nine months before his own death, he added vigorous support. Sadly he did not live to see the triumph of the abolitionists in 1807.

Wilberforce was not satisfied. Although British ships might no longer carry slaves and no British trader might profit from them, there was still the question of men already sold into slavery in various parts of the British Empire. Agitation continued until the Act of 1833 set free all slaves within the Empire. Their owners were compensated by a payment of twenty million pounds.

Slavery in the southern states of America remained, the planter-aristocrats' fears of the economic consequences of abolition being one of the causes of the American Civil War. In September 1862 Abraham Lincoln proclaimed the emancipation of the slaves from 1st January 1863, but it was not until the end of the war that this could be fully implemented.

Parliamentary Reform

The movement of population from rural areas and the creation of many towns which had hardly existed before threw into relief a number of incongruities in the system of Parliamentary representation. 'Rotten boroughs' denuded of all but a handful of electors, and 'pocket boroughs' where the local squire could ensure the election of his own nominee, maintained the predominance of country land-owners in the Commons, while many new industrial areas had no representation whatsoever.

Demands for universal suffrage and for sweeping reforms in Parliament seemed to many apprehensive ministers the preliminary to violent revolution. In February 1817 the Habeas Corpus Act was suspended. In March, weavers from the Manchester region began a march to London to present a reform petition to the Prince Regent himself. Troops broke up the procession only a few miles from Manchester.

Hampden Clubs were springing up all over the country to promote

Granville Sharp went to court to defend the rights of a slave he had taken under his protection and in consequence it was ruled that any slave who set foot in England became a free man.

working-class debate and to press for changes. A member of the London club recorded: 'Instead of attending Divine Service, the Sundays of the people were occupied in reading the works of Cobbett and Paine and other similar publications, that were industriously circulated among them.'

William Cobbett, who pronounced it every man's duty 'to do all that lay in his power to leave his country as good as he had found it', was the outspoken Radical to whom most would-be reformers turned as their spokesman. Each issue of his weekly *Political Register* was eagerly awaited. He demanded reforms of Parliament which would do away with the bribery hitherto taken for granted in elections, allow official and military appointments to be made on merit alone, cut down on the salaries of public employees and remove time-servers from their sinecures, guarantee freedom of the press, and make possible a reduction in the National Debt and taxation as a whole.

First and foremost, every male taxpayer must have a vote, and a man should be able to stand for Parliament without the present substantial property qualification. The duke of Wellington was always a bitter opponent of this clause: he thought it would be a bad day for the country when a gentleman could not buy himself a seat in the House.

The Radical ideals met with little sympathy from the Prince Regent or Parliament, and instead of sending in reasoned petitions the reformers turned to organising large outdoor meetings. If it could be shown that the public were behind them, the Government

(1) Reformers attack the rotten borough system; the names of the boroughs are written on the nests.

(2) The 'Peterloo massacre': the Manchester and Cheshire Yeomanry made a brutal and unwarranted attack on a meeting at St Peter's Fields which had assembled to hear the radical orator Henry Hunt.

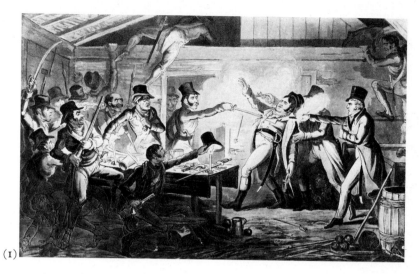

(1) The Cato Street Conspirators attack a police officer.

(2) Sir Robert Peel, the prime minister famed for his repeal of the Corn Law. As home secretary he founded the police force to replace the Bow Street Runners.

(3) John Townsend, a Bow Street Runner, in 1804.

(2)

(3)

would surely have to listen.

The culmination of a series of mass meetings in the summer of 1819 was an assembly on St Peter's Fields, Manchester. The speaker was Henry Hunt, an assiduous lecturer and campaigner who believed that reason and not violence must prevail. On 16th August about eighty thousand people flocked to the scene in cheerful holiday mood. The local magistrates, oblivious to the good humour of the crowd, panicked and sent the local yeomanry to arrest Hunt. The half-trained men panicked in their turn, seized what they claimed were revolutionary banners, and attacked the crowd with sabres. Eleven people were killed, hundreds injured.

Henry Hunt was sentenced to two years in prison. The Government went so far as to congratulate the Manchester magistrates and rushed through the 'Six Acts', giving wide powers of search in private houses and powers to ban public meetings, and slapping a crippling tax on periodicals.

What had begun as a peaceful demonstration ended thus in the massacre of 'Peterloo'—a sour parody of Wellington's victory at Waterloo a few years earlier. It crushed the hopes of many; but inflamed the anger of others. In 1820 a group of extremists planned to murder members of the Cabinet while they were at dinner. Once the deed had been accomplished, the conspirators would proclaim a provisional government.

The Cato Street Conspiracy, so called after the London street where the men met, was reported to the authorities by one of their number who may conceivably have been an *agent provocateur*. Five were hanged, the other five transported for life.

Law and order

The use of troops against fellow citizens was almost bound to result in quasi-military engagements and subsequent hatred. But local and national authorities had no effective alternative. Parish constables and the local watch were not equipped to cope with major disturbances. In London, the Bow Street Runners were badly paid and few in number, and had never been designed as an anti-riot force.

1

At last, in 1829, the Metropolitan Police Force came into being, adequately paid, under a Commissioner at Scotland yard. The original three thousand constables wore top hats and blue frock coats, and were armed only with wooden truncheons. They at once became known as 'peelers' or 'bobbies' after their creator, Sir Robert Peel, then home secretary. Other towns and cities and, more gradually, rural areas followed suit. In 1856 Parliament passed legislation to bring the individual forces into a national network, with the home secretary empowered to inspect them and recommend financial aid to those operating most efficiently.

Catholic emancipation

There was another reform for which reasonable men had been pressing over many decades. This was the removal of disabilities from Roman Catholics, still in force from the Test Act of 1673 in spite of a few eighteenth-century concessions.

In 1823 Daniel O'Connell, an Irish lawyer, founded the Catholic Association to press for abolition of all restrictions, and in 1828 was elected M.P. for County Clare. As a Catholic he was debarred from taking his seat, which sparked off a clamour in Ireland. Neither the duke of Wellington, prime minister between 1827 and 1830, nor Peel, his home secretary, truly favoured the relaxation of the laws, and suspected that O'Connell's tactics were only the beginnings of a campaign for partial separation of Britain and Ireland once more. But to resist such demands wholly would be to invite civil war.

The Catholic Relief Act of 1829 removed most civil disabilities, though disqualifications continued at Oxford, Cambridge and Durham universities until 1871. It was, and still is, forbidden that the sovereign or a regent should be a Catholic.

Wellington's surrender had been a grudging one, and he exacted spiteful penalties for it. The '40-shilling freeholders' of Ireland were deprived of the vote, and the property qualification for voting was set at £10 a year—in effect a disenfranchisement of those people most likely to vote for men such as O'Connell. O'Connell himself was still forbidden to take his seat, on the grounds that the new Act had not been operative when he was elected. He therefore stood once more in County Clare; and won.

The Iron Duke remained obstinately set against any idea of Parliamentary reform. This exasperated the Whigs, and within his own party the duke earned the mistrust of the more liberal-minded Tories and also those who from the start had opposed Catholic emancipation. Shortly after the death of George IV, the Government was defeated in a vote in the Commons, and the new king sent for the Whigs.

'Sailor Billy'

When the then Prince Regent's only child died in 1817, Parliament had urged his four middle-aged, unmarried brothers to seek wives and set about producing heirs. Next in line to George was his brother the duke of York, but the duchess was childless and likely to remain so. The succession must be secured elsewhere.

Among the remaining brothers was William, duke of Clarence,

(2)

(1) Cruikshank's drawing of the early 'bobbies' in top hats and blue frock-coats.

(2) Daniel O'Connell, the Irish Catholic, whose election as M.P. sparked off new demands for Catholic emancipation.

1) In the reign of William IV the reform of Parliament at last took place.

2) The celebratory Reform Banquet held at the Guildhall in 1832.

who served happily in the Royal Navy for eleven years, numbering Nelson among his dearest friends and giving the bride away at Nelson's wedding. At the time of George III's first bout of madness he returned to England, and between 1790 and 1811 lived with the popular actress Mrs Jordan, who presented him with ten children.

They were devoted to each other, and he left her only when it became clear that as a matter of duty he must marry and have a male heir. After pursuing various English ladies and a number of Continental princesses, he married Princess Adelaide of Saxe-Meiningen in 1818. She proved an admirable wife, and showed the greatest affection for his children by Mrs Jordan. She did not, however, produce the desired son: her children were both daughters, and both died in infancy.

When the duke of York died in 1827, this left William next in line; and in 1830 he became king. He at once caused some concern by trying to avoid the coronation ceremonial, which he regarded as a waste of money. The curtailed celebrations incensed many High Tories, but the people in general found him a refreshing change. 'King George had not been dead three days before everybody discovered that he was no loss, and King William a great gain,' wrote the diarist Charles Greville. 'Altogether he seems a kind-hearted, well-meaning, not stupid, burlesque, bustling old fellow, and if he doesn't go mad may make a very decent king . . . his wits will at least last till the new Parliament meets.'

Whatever the bluff eccentricities of 'Sailor Billy', he proved a wise monarch in his dealings with Parliament. Without him, the introduction of essential reforms could have been a lot stormier than it actually was.

(1)

(2)

(1)

The Great Reform Bill

Earl Grey, leader of the Whigs, had been a friend and disciple of Fox. He had long ago declared that Parliament in its existing form did not truly represent the nation, and now he proposed to set this right.

After almost half a century out of office, it was difficult to form a purely Whig government. Grey offered positions to some liberal Tories who had quarrelled with Wellington, including Palmerston and Melbourne. He also approached William Huskisson, an advocate of free trade who had for a time been colonial secretary under Wellington; unfortunately Huskisson made more dramatic history by being knocked over and fatally injured by one of Stephenson's locomotives at the opening of the Liverpool and Manchester Railway.

A Reform Bill framed by Lord John Russell was put before the Commons in March 1831, meeting with noisy abuse from sinecurists of the rotten and pocket boroughs. Passed by one vote, it was niggled at during committee stage—when Bills are discussed clause by clause rather than as a whole—and after defeat on a couple of points Grey decided to resign and call for a general election.

The Whigs were returned with a large majority, and presented a second version of the Bill. This time it passed without too much difficulty, but was thrown out by the House of Lords. A third time the Government tried, and got through the Commons and two readings in the Lords; but Tory peers in committee stage emulated their friends in the lower chamber and wrangled over detail.

Earl Grey visited King William at the Royal Pavilion in Brighton and asked him to create fifty new peers to outvote opponents of the new measures. The king hated the idea and tried to cut the number down. After a see-saw between Grey and Wellington, who was unable to form an administration to carry through a watered-down Bill, after dirt and stones were thrown by the populace at the royal carriage and plans were announced to withhold taxes, the Tories climbed down. Rather than have the House of Lords packed with hastily created Whig peers, put there by a process which would debase the whole concept of the peerage, Wellington himself advised acceptance of the Reform Bill, and it became law in May 1832.

Working-class Radicals found little to be grateful for. The main effect of the Act was to enfranchise industrialists and the upper middle classes. In the boroughs, only householders rated at £10 and more could vote, and in the country only £10 copyholders and £50 leaseholders.

It took several more Acts before the right to vote was extended to other classes of citizen, attaining in 1928 the enfranchisement of all men and women over twenty-one—an age limit lowered in 1969 to eighteen.

(1) 'The Royal Coachman'—Wellington as prime minister in 1829.

(2) A detail from 'Work', a painting by Ford Madox Brown.

Victoria Regina

(1)

England's security as a major power had been established under the rule of a long-lived queen. Britain's greatness and its industrial and trading fortunes were to be consolidated under another. The label 'Victorian' is firmly fixed to the sixty-three-year span which later generations have regarded, according to their own predilections, as an age of stability or smugness, high morality or hypocrisy, material progress or arrogant exploitation, of appalling bad taste in the arts or a happy union of Art and Morality (both, implicitly, with capital letters).

The young princess

In the year of William's marriage to Adelaide, the fifty-year-old duke of Kent made a match with the widowed Princess Victoria of Saxe-Coburg. They produced one daughter, and christened her Alexandrina Victoria—Alexandrina because of financial assistance received by Kent from Tsar Alexander, the princess's godfather, in 1818, and Victoria because of a difference of opinion between Kent and his brother, the Prince Regent. George wanted the second name to be Georgina, Kent said he preferred Elizabeth, whereupon George insisted that she be christened with her mother's name—a fair compromise. For many years of childhood she was known as Drina.

Her father died before she was a year old, heavily in debt. Among his executors was Sir John Conroy, an Irish soldier who had been in his service for some years and who now became comptroller of the duchess of Kent's household. Soon there were rumours that the relationship was less formal than it ought to be, though nobody ever presented any real proof of an immoral liaison. It is more likely that both the duchess and her comptroller loved power, and realised what a strong team they could form together.

Other rumours, assiduously propagated by Conroy, told of plots against the young Victoria. The duchess either believed these, or found it useful to pretend to do so in order to strengthen her supervision of the child. On the grounds that the girl was destined to become queen of England and must be protected and brought up accordingly, her mother refused to let her sleep alone in a room or go anywhere unaccompanied. Both George IV and William IV disliked the widowed duchess and her ambitious adviser. William rightly suspected that the two of them wanted him to die before Victoria reached her majority, so that the duchess might become regent, with Conroy as her *éminence grise*.

In 1835 the princess suffered an attack of typhoid. While she was still weak and depressed during her convalescence Conroy tried to bully her into appointing him as her private secretary, against the

(2)

time when she should succeed to the throne. In spite of her exhaustion she would not give in, even when Conroy presented her with pen and paper and virtually commanded her to sign her consent.

During this argument one faithful friend refused to leave them together. She was the Baroness Lehzen, a Hanoverian lady engaged by the duke of Kent to look after his wife's daughter by her first marriage, and now Victoria's governess. Severe, puritanical and suspicious of all courtiers other than her own intimates, Lehzen remained devoted to her royal charge through all attempted cajolings and pressures.

Another friend on whose judgement the princess relied was her uncle Leopold, widower of the Prince Regent's only daughter. He had helped financially after the duke of Kent's death and was always a favourite visitor to Kensington Palace where the duchess and princess lived; and although his acceptance in 1830 of the throne of newly independent Belgium as King Leopold I meant he could no longer spend much time in England, he and his niece exchanged letters which grew in practical value as she grew older. In 1836 Leopold sent his doctor and confidential adviser, Baron Stockmar, to London to act as Victoria's counsellor.

Among Conroy's clique was Lady Flora Hastings, lady-in-waiting to the duchess. These two persuaded their mistress not merely that she had the right to be declared regent if King William died before Victoria's eighteenth birthday, but that even if he died after that date there was still good cause for a regency: the girl was inexperienced —foolish, even—and needed a strong guiding hand. Fortunately Stockmar and Lehzen were there to provide a counterbalance. And King William knew just what was going on. To the duchess's chagrin, he chose his birthday-party to declare in front of a hundred guests that he meant to live until his niece was of age and that he trusted the Crown would pass direct to her without intervention from 'the person now near me, who is so surrounded by evil counsellors'.

His wish was granted, as was another: he had asked that he might at least be allowed to live through 18th June and see the sun set on one more anniversary of Waterloo—and in fact did not die until 20th June 1837.

The Queen

Victoria was asleep in her mother's bedroom when the news was brought from Windsor to Kensington. At first the porter refused to wake her, but when the lord chamberlain referred to 'the Queen' he realised what had happened and Baroness Lehzen went to fetch Victoria.

At nine o'clock that same morning the prime minister, Lord Melbourne, arrived to learn that Her Majesty Queen Victoria wished him to continue in office. Two hours later she met her Privy Council. There was no sign of the incompetent girl Conroy had tried to depict. She carried off the proceedings with a youthful dignity which awed every man in the room.

Her self-possession could hardly be better exemplified than in the fact that immediately after her coronation she recorded it in meticu-

(3)

(1) The duke of Kent and (2) the duchess of Kent with the young Victoria. The duke was brother to George IV and William IV but died while Victoria was an infant, leaving her as heir to the throne.

(3) William Lamb, Lord Melbourne, Victoria's adored first prime minister.

A detail of Queen Victoria's first privy council. The painter, David Wilkie, purposely altered the queen's black robe to white, to emphasise her youth and innocence.

lous detail in her journal. The entry reveals already her liking for 'my excellent Lord Melbourne', that essentially eighteenth-century Whig aristocrat who now seemed to fall reverently in love with this nineteenth-century princess who had become queen. Of her coronation he assured her: 'You did it beautifully, every part of it, with so much taste; it's a thing you can't give persons advice upon; it must be left to á person.'

This did not prevent Melbourne from offering a great deal of advice in ensuing months. He instructed her in the complexities of official papers and national policy, steered her in the direction which he felt she should take, and discussed political philosophies and the niceties of social life. Nine-tenths of her diary at this time, as Lord David Cecil points out in his biography of Melbourne, is a record of her prime minister's conversation.

But she was capable of making up her own mind on certain matters. When her mother claimed the right to be given the title of Queen Mother, it was Victoria herself who coolly rejected the idea: 'It would do my mother no good, and offend my aunts.' Although the duchess of Kent and her household, including the scheming Conroy, moved into Buckingham Palace with Victoria and moved with her when she went to Windsor, they could not counter the influence of Baroness Lehzen's coterie. Significantly, on the day she became queen, Victoria had declared that henceforth she would have a bedroom of her own.

'Mrs Melbourne'

In 1839 Conroy and Lady Flora Hastings became the centre of a scandal which took some of the bloom off the springtime freshness of the new reign.

On 10th January Lady Flora returned from a holiday in Scotland, accompanied for part of the journey by Sir John. Troubled by griping stomach pains, she went to consult the queen's physician, Sir James Clark, who found her lower abdomen much enlarged. He prescribed some useless palliatives, and Lady Flora was left to hope that the pains would somehow go away of their own accord.

Her misshapen abdomen attracted the attention of other ladies-in-waiting, and rumours of her pregnancy reached the queen's ears. Some contemporaries hinted that Lehzen had started the gossip. Victoria certainly believed it, and confided to her journal the conviction that the 'Monster and demon Incarnate' responsible was Sir John Conroy.

Melbourne advised Victoria to order Lady Flora to submit to a thorough medical examination by Sir James Clark and by a specialist in women's diseases, Sir Charles Mansfield Clarke, which established her innocence. Lady Flora's family demanded fitting public reparation for the indignity, but Melbourne said that the queen had personally apologised for her error and that it was not intended to take the matter further.

The Tory press sought out all the unsavoury details, including a threat by Lady Flora's brother to call the prime minister out to a duel, and used them in a campaign against Melbourne and his influence on the queen. While the uproar was at its confused height Melbourne and the rest of the Whig Cabinet resigned when a majority of only five in an important Commons vote seriously weakened their position in Parliament. Victoria could not believe that her beloved Lord M, on whom she so much relied, was to be replaced by that 'cold, odd man', Sir Robert Peel.

Peel's first demand did nothing to soften the blow. He wished a number of Tory ladies to take the place of the exclusively Whig ladies in the royal household. Victoria regarded this as a personal affront, and refused. In these circumstances Peel was unwilling to form a government, so Melbourne and his colleagues were recalled. The jubilant queen threw herself into a gay round of theatres, concerts and other entertainments, though these were not without their discordant moments: she was more than once hissed in the streets, and at Ascot was jeered as 'Mrs Melbourne'.

In June, Lady Flora Hastings grew weaker and took to her bed. It was now tardily established that the swelling which had caused so much gossip was a malignant tumour. On Melbourne's urging, Victoria cancelled some palace entertainments and visited the dying woman. She came away shocked by Lady Flora's appearance and full of remorse for her own suspicions. On 5th July Lady Flora died.

Shortly afterwards, Conroy was persuaded to resign from the duchess's service, and retired to the Continent. A later comptroller found that he had milked the household accounts by tens of thousands of pounds.

Melbourne's ministry survived until 1841. By then, much as she might still admire him, the queen had another, closer adviser.

Prince Albert

Shortly before William IV's death Victoria had been introduced to a handsome but rather solemn cousin, Prince Albert of Saxe-Coburg-

Gotha. Her mother and her uncle, King Leopold, both wanted her to marry their nephew, but she put off making a decision. In 1839 Leopold pressed the suit more vigorously, and Victoria agreed to Albert's visiting England, though without commitment on her part.

The moment she saw him, her doubts dissolved. Where her diary had once been filled with Melbourne's conversation, it now proclaimed Albert's glories: 'Beautiful blue eyes, an exquisite nose, & a pretty mouth with delicate moustachios & slight but very slight whiskers . . . *most striking*, and he is so amiable and unaffected . . . '

Once she had made up her mind, she informed Melbourne. He advised her on the correct procedure, and on 15th October she, as etiquette demanded, proposed to Albert.

It was as well that from this love match grew such a happy married life, for their public existence was far from comfortable. The English were rather suspicious of this earnest young German, and when he conscientiously set himself to study the British political system his wife's ministers grew equally suspicious of his possible influence on the queen.

King Leopold suggested a peerage for his nephew. Melbourne opposed this. So did the queen, for a different reason: she suggested the splendid title of 'King Consort', but Melbourne was even more horrified. There were arguments about precedence, and Tory peers tried to establish that the prince should rank below the Prince of Wales he was expected in due course to provide for his adopted

A photograph of Queen Victoria and Prince Albert taken in 1854.

country. The expected allowance of £50,000 usually granted to a consort was arbitrarily cut to £30,000.

Just before the queen's first pregnancy became common knowledge, she and Albert were out driving when a deranged youth fired two pistols at her. The possibility that she might die in another such assassination attempt or, like the Prince Regent's heiress, in childbirth disturbed Parliament. In spite of some opposition it was agreed that Albert should be nominated regent in the event of her death.

In all they had four sons and five daughters. Their first-born, the Princess Royal, married the emperor of Germany and became the mother of Kaiser Wilhelm II. The second was Albert Edward, the Prince of Wales for whom the country had been waiting.

The coming of children brought also some quarrels. Albert was appalled to find what a fierce temper his wife had when she was upset. He began to attribute many of their disagreements over the proper management of the nursery to the presence of Lehzen, who after so many years of authority expected to continue her rule over the next generation. Gradually Albert won Victoria over to the view that Lehzen must go. He did not leave it to her to deliver the blow herself, but waited until she and the Prince of Wales were in Scotland and then calmly and courteously sent Lehzen packing.

This tact and firmness were an echo of what had happened a little while before, when Melbourne at last accepted that he could not continue in office. Having heard all the details of the 'Bedchamber Crisis' and foreseeing the damage a repetition might do, the prince, with Melbourne's approval, sent to Sir Robert Peel and asked him not to make an issue of the ladies-in-waiting. Peel knew that many of his followers wished him to give a show of strength by sweeping the ladies out this time; but he bowed to the request, and in return Albert coaxed the queen into offering the resignations of a mere three ladies as a goodwill gesture.

Melbourne, too, made a valuable gesture. Anxious that Victoria should not be unhappy with her new prime minister, he sent a message to Peel recommending a gentle approach. Last time he had not given the queen time to accept him: 'You should always give people time to come round.' And to the queen he wrote, regarding his old habit of chatting to her about his political rivals: 'Lord Melbourne thinks it right to say that he may have spoken upon insufficient grounds, that he may have been mistaken and that the persons in question may turn out to be far better than he has been induced to represent them.' Then, as though symbolically handing over the authority he had so long exercised, and entrusting her absolutely to the care of another: 'The prince understands everything so well.... When you married him you said that he was perfection, which I thought a little overrated, but I really think now that it is in some degree realised.'

(1) A detail from 'The First of May' by Franz Winterhalter, painted for the first birthday of Victoria's seventh child.

(2) The 'penny black', the first postage stamp in the world.

The Corn Laws

The fall of the Whigs had been largely due to a clash over the Corn Laws. Introduced to keep farming communities solvent by imposing duty on imported grain, these in fact kept prices artificially high in the interests of landowners and corn-dealers, while neglecting the

(1)

(2)

need for cheaper food for workers on the land and in industry. In 1839 a National Anti-Corn Law League was founded, preaching that repeal of duty would bring food prices down, leave people more money to spend on other things, and so promote national prosperity.

Protection or Free Trade—it has been a recurring problem in the history of all advanced nations.

Two leading spirits in the League were a Sussex man, Richard Cobden, and a Rochdale Quaker, John Bright. Cobden was a self-made man who prospered as a calico printer in Manchester and used his money and free time to improve his patchy education; Bright was the son of a wealthy mill-owner, and devoted much of his time to local politics and the temperance movement. They joined forces in the Anti-Corn Law Association in Manchester, from which derived the national body. A team of speakers toured the country, and two newspapers and a wide range of pamphlets were published. In the general election of 1841 at which Melbourne was defeated, Cobden was elected M.P. for Stockport. Bright won Durham in 1843.

By 1846 Peel, originally opposed to the repeal of the existing laws, was out-argued by Bright and Cobden and, alarmed at the support they were getting from industrialists throughout the country, put forward a proposal for reducing the duty as a preliminary to complete abolition within three years. Diehard protectionists within his party were outraged. Although Peel could sincerely urge the need for immediate lower-priced imports to offset bad harvests and the terrible 1845 potato blight in Ireland, he was accused of betraying the principles on which his rise to power had been based: accusations most witheringly expressed by the member for Maidstone, Benjamin Disraeli.

Jews were not at this time allowed to sit in Parliament (one of the reformers who were to make this possible in 1858 was John Bright), but as the son of a Christian convert Disraeli was eligible. Derided by opponents and cartoonists, he nevertheless commanded respect by his brilliance in debate, and became the protectionists' main spokesman.

In spite of his best efforts, the repeal of the Corn Laws was carried

(1) Richard Cobden addressing the meeting of the Council of the Anti-Corn Law League.

(2) An Irish mother and son search for potatoes in a field of stubble.

through in June 1846. It came too late to alleviate the effects of the Irish famine, from which it was estimated almost a million people died during the next five years. There was also a great emigration to America, following the eviction of tenants by landlords who were themselves nearly destitute. Those who fled and those who stayed conceived a burning hatred of the English administration, which they passed on to their descendants.

The Great Exhibition

Macaulay, who began to publish his monumental *History of England* in 1848, declared that 'the history of our country during the last hundred and sixty years is eminently the history of physical, of moral, and of intellectual improvement'. This was the ebullient mood in which the Great Exhibition of 1851 was conceived.

Brainchild of Prince Albert, this prototype World's Fair brought together on one site displays of industrial achievement in Britain

A cartoon showing the world-wide attraction of the Great Exhibition.

and other nations invited to participate. The fact that the still unpopular prince was in favour of it put many against it. Protectionists frowned on the international nature of the proposed exhibits and the implication that free exchange of goods and ideas was beneficial to all mankind. Some European monarchs, invited to attend, thought the danger of mob violence and even of assassination too great. Conservationists deplored the destruction of trees in Hyde Park to

Visitors at the hardware section of the exhibition.

make way for the exhibition building, and succeeding in preserving some especially cherished elms which had to be incorporated in the building itself.

Scorn was showered on the concept of a glass palace, designed by Joseph Paxton. In the duke of Devonshire's gardens at Chatsworth he had created an impressive glass conservatory. In Hyde Park he installed a much larger version, covering more than twenty-one acres.

The exhibition was opened by Queen Victoria on 1st May 1851, with Prince Albert beside her. *The Times*, which had been sceptical in the formative stages, praised the display of 'all that is useful or beautiful in nature or in art' as contributing 'to an effect so grand and yet so natural, that it hardly seemed to be put together by design, or to be the work of human artificers'. *The Illustrated London News* lauded Britain as 'a state compared with whose power and dominion the empires of old were but as provinces'.

There was plenty to boast about. In 1848 Britain had produced half the pig-iron in the world, and over the next thirty years managed to treble her output. Her foreign trade was outdistancing that of France, Italy and Germany together, and as yet there was little real competition from the United States. In 1802 William Murdock had illuminated the Boulton and Watt foundry with gas-burners; by 1809 Pall Mall, London, was lit by gas, and the invention of the incandescent mantle spread its use through cities and towns, shops and homes. And already a rival form of light and power was on its way. In 1829 the chemist and physicist, Michael Faraday, awoke the enthusiasm of young audiences in a series of Christmas lectures at the Royal Institution; in 1831 he led the way to the exploitation of electrical energy by his discovery of electro-magnetic induction and between 1845 and 1849 of diamagnetism; and by the time of the Great Exhibition had published many of his *Experimental Researches in Electricity*. Many exhibits in Paxton's 'Crystal Palace' owed their existence to the imaginative development of machine tools in Manchester by Nasmyth and Whitworth: the latter, highly commended at the Exhibition, pioneered the standardisation of accurate gauges and screw-threads.

In Hyde Park there were shilling days and five-shilling days. There were workmen's excursion trains from the North and the Midlands. The Colonel Sibthorp who had denounced the attempted destruction of irreplaceable trees went on to denounce the exploitation of poor people who spent more than they could afford to reach this spot from the provinces. Charles Dickens complained there was far too much to see, and came away lamenting, 'I have a natural horror of sights, and the fusion of so many sights in one has not decreased it.' But, dazed or declamatory, those who saw the Great Exhibition for themselves could not deny it: the thing was a success. The queen was overjoyed at what was demonstrably Albert's personal triumph.

By the time it closed, it had made a profit of over £180,000, with which land was bought in South Kensington for the establishment of colleges and museums. Prince Albert arranged for selected objects from the Exhibition to be preserved in a Museum of Manufactures at Marlborough House, soon enlarged into a Museum of Ornamental

Art. When moved to a more spacious site it became the South Kensington Museum and at last, reconstructed to a new design, was designated the Victoria and Albert Museum. The last major public engagement of the long-widowed queen was the laying of the foundation-stone in 1899.

Sir Joseph Paxton, knighted for his services, supervised the dismantling of his glass hall and its removal to Sydenham, where as the Crystal Palace it remained a landmark for over eighty years.

The Crimean War

Albert's hopes of peace and international brotherhood were soon to be dashed. The tragedy seemed all the darker because its ostensible source was the very birthplace of Christianity.

Since 1740 France had been nominal custodian of the Holy Places in and around Jerusalem, but had neglected her duties. The sultan of Turkey gave the Greek Orthodox Church permission to care for many of the shrines, but in 1850 Louis Napoleon decided to reassert French claims. The sultan agreed that France should have the responsibility for the Nativity Church and the Holy Manger of Bethlehem. Immediately Russia claimed not merely its existing rights as guardian of the Orthodox Church, but the right to be acknowledged as protector of all Christians and Christian shrines throughout the Ottoman Empire.

Three of the Coldstream Guards in the Crimea.

British transport vessels in harbour at Balaclava.

The Turks had no wish for Russian infiltration; the French were suspicious of Tsar Nicholas I and his ambitions; and Britain had for some time been perturbed by Russian activities in Afghanistan which might menace India. Lord Stratford de Redcliffe, British ambassador to Turkey, recommended that the Russian claims should be rejected. Counting on French and British military support, the Turks took his advice.

In July 1853 Russian armies marched into the Turkish-administered Danubian Principalities which form modern Rumania. British and French fleets were hurried to the Dardanelles, but with Austria's help there were still diplomatic attempts to reach a compromise. Since Russia, however, still refused to withdraw her troops, the Turks declared war and in October attacked in Moldavia. A few weeks later a Turkish flotilla was destroyed by the main Russian fleet off Sinope, in the Black Sea.

The prime minister, Lord Aberdeen, still hoped peace by negotiation was possible. His home secretary, the bellicose Lord Palmerston, was sure that threats were the only language the tsar understood. The Cabinet was divided; but after news of the slaughter at Sinope, Britain joined France in issuing an ultimatum to Russia.

Before the opposing armies could come to grips, Austria persuaded Russia to withdraw from the Principalities, which she did in August 1854. But although the declared objective of the allies had thus been achieved, the war rolled on of its own momentum.

A combined force of over sixty thousand British, French and Turks landed on the Crimean peninsula with the task of demolishing the Russian naval base of Sebastopol. The war, said everyone, would be over in a few weeks.

The Russians spoiled this timetable by launching a surprise attack on the British base at Balaclava. After heavy fighting they were worn down by the heavy brigade and the Highlanders' 'thin red line'. But it is by a staggering blunder that the battle is best remembered. Ordered to charge the Russians and recapture some guns, the 'gallant six hundred' of the Light Brigade attacked the wrong position,

A 'thin red line' of Highlanders held off the surprise Russian attack at Balaclava.

seized the wrong guns, and lost a sixth of their number as well as some 130 wounded. Whatever blame may be attached to incompetent commanders, the gallantry of the cavalrymen themselves is unforgettable, and has been preserved in what is probably Tennyson's most famous poem.

The siege dragged on through the terrible months of the Crimean winter. News of military inadequacies reached home: the speeding-up of communications was bringing the war correspondent into his own. Faced by demands for searching inquiries, Lord Aberdeen resigned and handed over to the more determined Palmerston.

Sebastopol fell at last, but it was another year before, faced by an Austrian ultimatum and the growing strength of French and British forces, Russia agreed to take part in peace talks. The Treaty of Paris in 1856 granted near-independence to the two contested Principalities and neutralised the Black Sea, but little else of lasting significance had been achieved—though Russia surrendered her claims to a protectorate over the Christians in Turkey, she certainly did not give up her pretensions in the Near East, and brought Europe to the brink of war over them more than once in the last half of the century.

The lady with the lamp

One of the worst deficiencies revealed during the Crimean campaign was in military medical services. Cholera and dysentery raged through the armies, and when bad weather and fierce fighting combined to fill the hospitals, the authorities had little idea how to cope. Easy-going surgeons allowed nurses to pass the time with personable

(1)

young officers rather than with the seriously sick and wounded.

In November 1854 a determined woman arrived at Scutari, the base hospital near Constantinople, determined to put an end to insanitary conditions and slipshod administration. Having achieved this in a matter of months, she expressed a wish to do the same for the hospitals at Balaclava.

Miss Florence Nightingale had been a social worker in European hospitals and reformatories, and then trained as a nurse in Prussia. She came of good family, had influential connections, and used them to get her own way at Scutari. But no direct authority had been granted her in the Crimea itself, and she faced considerable opposition from nurses who found her discipline too severe, and from Dr John Hall, chief of the medical staff. 'The custom of the service', he reported, 'did not aim to provide facilities, medical or otherwise, up to the lofty standards of Miss Florence Nightingale.'

Nevertheless, by the time she herself had contracted fever and slowly recovered, she had wrought a transformation in the system, and on her return to England continued to press for further essential reforms. She wrote extensively about hospitals and nursing, and badgered those in power until her name became a byword for trouble. But to the soldiers in the Crimea she had been the sympathetic 'lady with the lamp', always at their bedside during the darkest moments. Mrs Gaskell, the novelist, described her at a lecture in Manchester after her return when she was cheered by the audience 'for they feel her as theirs, their brother's nurse, their dead friend's friend—in a way which they don't know how to express'.

A woman's place

'Why have women passion, intellect, moral activity—these three— and a place in society where no one of the three can be exercised?'

This was Florence Nightingale's own indignant cry. Many other women echoed it. But still there were others who agreed with their menfolk that it was not a woman's place to strike boldly out into the world. Queen Victoria admitted that she envied Miss Nightingale for 'being able to do so much good & look after the noble brave heroes', but basically disapproved of ladies in the medical profession —though she herself had been delivered by one—and could hardly

(2)

(1) A ward in the hospital at Scutari where Florence Nightingale's reforms at last gave the wounded a chance of survival.

(2) Florence Nightingale, the lady with the lamp, whose very presence reassured the sick men.

have looked with favour on anyone as determined as Elizabeth Garrett, who, after many setbacks, was admitted to the Society of Apothecaries, opened a dispensary in the Euston Road for women and children, and qualified in 1870 as an M.D. in Paris, because of obstructions put in her way in England. On marriage she retained her maiden name in the form of Dr Elizabeth Garrett Anderson, and in 1908 became the first elected woman mayor in England—of her native Aldeburgh, in Suffolk.

The struggle to improve women's education in general owed a lot in its early stages to men. Christian Socialists such as Charles Kingsley and J. F. D. Maurice, one of the founders of the Working Men's College in 1854, deplored the makeshift education imparted to boarding-school girls by teachers themselves lacking any formal education, and deplored equally the wretched salaries and treatment doled out to girls whose only hope of 'respectable' employment was the drudgery of becoming governess in some private household. They set up a college which was viewed suspiciously by those who thought an all-female establishment would somehow provoke unladylike conduct, but in which Victoria's interest was sufficiently aroused for her to permit its being called Queen's College for Women.

One of its earliest pupils was Frances Mary Buss, who went on to establish the North London Collegiate School for Ladies in 1850. In 1858 Dorothea Beale, after running a school for the daughters of clergymen, became principal and made an impressive success of Cheltenham Ladies' College. Also in Cheltenham, she opened the first residential training college for women, St Hilda's, and later sponsored St Hilda's Hall of Residence in Oxford. The first true hall for women in either of the two great universities was set up in Cambridge by Anne Jemima Clough in 1871, becoming Newnham College in 1880. In 1872 Hitchin College moved to Cambridge and became Girton. Lady Margaret Hall and Somerville soon followed in Oxford.

Still a woman's place was generally considered to be the home. In her authoritative, not to say authoritarian, *Book of Household Management*, Mrs Isabelle Beeton quoted Oliver Goldsmith: 'The modest virgin, the prudent wife, and the careful matron, are much

33

are ferrets! Where can I have dropped them, I wonder?' Alice guessed in a moment that it was looking for the nosegay and the pair of white kid gloves, and she began hunting for them, but they were now nowhere to be seen — everything seemed to have changed since her swim in the pool, and her walk along the river-bank with its fringe of rushes and forget-me-nots, and the glass table and the little door had vanished.

Soon the rabbit noticed Alice, as she stood looking curiously about her; and at once said in a quick angry tone, 'why, Mary Ann! what are you doing out here? Go home this moment, and look on my dressing-table for my gloves and nosegay, and fetch them here, as quick as you can run, do you hear?' and Alice was so much frightened that she ran off at once, without

(1)

(1) A page from the original manuscript of *Alice in Wonderland* (first called Alice's Adventures Under Ground), written and illustrated by Lewis Carroll in 1862–63.

(2) Fire Brigade officers at Girton College, Cambridge in 1887.

(1)

Victorians at Leisure: 'Summer Day in Hyde Park, 1858' by John Ritchie (1) and 'Derby Day' by W. P. Frith (2).

(3) The music-hall songs were not only popular with audiences but sung around the piano by families at home.

more servicable in life than petticoated philosophers, blustering heroines, or virago queens.' She went on to recommend early rising, cleanliness, careful choice of acquaintances, and frugality: 'In marketing, that the best articles are the cheapest, may be laid down as a rule.'

Mrs Beeton also decreed the number and nature of servants which householders of any substance ought to be able to afford. A man earning £1000 a year needed a cook, an upper housemaid, a nurse-maid, an under housemaid, and a manservant. On £500 a year he might manage with a cook, a housemaid and a nursemaid. On the lowest rung, between £150 and £200 a year, he should still run to a maid-of-all-work—'and girl occasionally'.

Pleasure gardens

The respectable middle-class family tended to spend morally uplifting evenings at home. Womenfolk were expected to be proficient in embroidery and sewing, and also in keeping quiet while the head of the household read aloud from some edifying book—or even from some currently best-selling three-volume novel, perhaps borrowed from the circulating library opened by the enterprising

Mr Mudie in 1842.

Outside the home there were other diversions, few of them attended by an unaccompanied lady.

Theatre managers and other organisers of public amusements complained at the time of the Great Exhibition that Hyde Park was taking away all their custom. But some took advantage of the influx of visitors. Walter Batty, a circus-owner, set up a Hippodrome opposite Kensington Gardens, in the very month that the Exhibition opened. There were chariot-races, brass bands, and balloon ascents.

Earlier pleasure gardens were not yet extinct. Vauxhall, with its shaded walks and bandstands, where the music of every well-known composer from 1661 onwards had been played, often in first performances, had been showing signs of decline, and was closed in 1859 as a result of persistent rowdyism and immorality. By then much of its custom had been stolen by Cremorne Gardens, which from 1846 offered nightly masquerades, dancing, puppet shows, circus acts, sideshows and cheap suppers.

There were other supper-rooms in London and provincial cities. In addition to food and drink they offered choirs and soloists, and by the end of the evening there was usually community singing from the audience.

In the more ambitious Variety Saloons, the diner would be given a mixture of opera, comedy and music. These came to an end in 1843 when the Theatres Registry Act laid down that drama should be separated from more material refreshment: premises could be operated as music-halls with food and drink but without legitimate drama, or as legitimate theatres but without food and drink. So the saloons developed through 'Concert Rooms' to the boisterous music-halls which over many decades poured out jokes, comic songs and maudlin songs about the rich and the poor, wives and mothers-in-law, and the follies of foreigners.

(2)

(3)

(1) Acrobats in a Victorian music hall.

Two of the leading stage personalities of the day were Ellen Terry (2) (shown in the role of Guinevere) and Henry Irving (3).

In the 'straight' theatre, Shakespeare was often performed in the pruned versions of Thomas Bowdler, who guaranteed that 'those words and expressions are omitted which cannot with propriety be read aloud in a family', thus adding a new verb to the English language—to 'bowdlerise'. In 1866 young Henry Irving, only twenty-eight but already with ten years' experience behind him, made his début in London; in 1867 first appeared with Ellen Terry and within a few years was the most awe-inspiring of actor-managers. Irving was the first actor to be offered a knighthood, which at first he turned down but accepted in 1895.

The widow of Windsor

In 1857 Palmerston, well apprised of the queen's feelings on the subject, tried to have Albert designated Prince Consort by Parliament. There proved to be a legal snag in this, and impatiently Victoria herself proclaimed him Prince Consort by letters patent.

In 1861 he died of typhoid.

He had never been widely popular, and now the grief-stricken queen herself courted unpopularity. For years she shut herself away, derisively dubbed 'the widow of Windsor', though in fact she spent much of her time on the country estates which she and her husband had fashioned to their own tastes—preponderantly Albert's taste —such as Osborne on the Isle of Wight and Balmoral in Scotland. In the autumn following his death she took six of their children to the top of a Scottish hill where she had ordained the erection of a thirty-five foot cairn in memory of Albert the Great and Good. The view, she noted in her journal, was fine and the day bright—'but no pleasure, no joy! all dead!'

In self-pitying seclusion she continued to deal with affairs of state, as she knew Albert would have wished her to do; but she shunned public appearances. The public, who paid a great deal of money for the upkeep of her large family and establishments, grew restive. Republican murmurings had seldom been stronger. Yet at the same time imperial pride was at its height.

The Empire

During Victoria's reign the British Empire expanded until it could be lauded as the empire 'on which the sun never sets'. There were New Zealand sheep-farmers, Canadians some of whom spoke English and some French, Boer descendants of the Dutch in South Africa, West Indian sugar-planters, tribal chieftains along the river Niger; some were administered by local officials, some by force of arms, some by brilliant entrepreneurs like Cecil Rhodes, who profited from diamonds at Kimberley, gold in the Transvaal, and founded the British South Africa Company under royal charter in 1889, giving his own name to the developing country of Rhodesia.

Of them all, the 'jewel in the Crown' was India.

It was incongruous that this rich possession should be administered, as Cobden complained, by 'a committee of stockholders in Leadenhall Street'; but in the middle of the nineteenth century it was indeed still largely the responsibility of the East India Company, based on

Emigrants embark for the colonies from Liverpool in 1850.

Calcutta, Bombay and Madras. Neighbouring states were hostile or co-operative as it suited them. If any proved especially troublesome, the Company's private armies moved in and, on one pretext or another, annexed them. Idealists at home were not sure of the rightness of the methods, but consoled themselves with the thought that British predominance meant the spread of Western standards and education, and the eventual triumph of Christianity over the heathen.

The fear of having Christianity forced on them and their own

(1)

religious observances flouted led to a mutiny in the Bengal army i⸱
May 1857, sparking off a more widespread rebellion. Ostensibly
protest against the greasing of cartridges with cow fat, which incense⸱
Hindus, or pig fat, which offended Muslims, it was really a long
simmering dislike of the Company's arrogance which now came t⸱
the boil.

Mutineers marched to Delhi and proclaimed allegiance to a⸱
elderly survivor of the old Mogul imperial house. They surrounde⸱
Lucknow and Cawnpore, and in spite of promises to spare Britis⸱
soldiers and their families who surrendered, murdered all those wh⸱
did so at Cawnpore. When British troops recaptured the towns, the⸱
took a bloody revenge. Press reports and letters home told gleefull⸱
of hanging Indians or shooting them from guns. Villagers were pai⸱
to hand over suspected mutineers for summary execution. Shocke⸱
protests in the House of Commons were derided for their 'morbi⸱
sensibility'.

In August 1858 the India Act removed administrative power⸱
from the East India Company to the Crown, and incorporated th⸱
Company's troops in the British Army. The post of secretary ⸱

(1) Amid great slaughter the British recapture Delhi during the Indian Mutiny.

(2) 'Last Stand of the 44th foot at Gandamka, 1842' by W. B. Wollen, an incident during the retreat through Afghanistan.

state for India was created, and instead of a governor-general there was henceforth a viceroy.

Explorers
Not all those who penetrated faraway lands did so purely for commercial gain or military aggrandisement. There were keen geographers anxious to add authentic contours to their maps of the world, adventurers who combined scientific research with a longing to find something simply 'because it was there', as climbers were

(2)

(1) Livingstone's steam launch 'Ma Robert' was specially built for exploring the Zambezi.

(2 & 3) The explorer and translator Richard Burton, and his devoted wife, Isabella Arundell.

(1)

(2)

(3)

later to say of Mount Everest. Also there were missionaries determined to carry the Gospel to the heathen. Some did considerable damage because of their inability to grasp that followers of other creeds could be as sincere as themselves; but others won the love and respect of those with whom they worked.

In December 1840 a Scottish doctor named David Livingstone was sent by the London Missionary Society to Bechuanaland, where he strove against the evils of disease and slavery. He explored the Zambezi and discovered the Victoria Falls. When he returned to England his reports on his findings and a book he published about his travels encouraged the Royal Geographical Society to finance an expedition under Burton and Speke.

Richard Burton (to become Sir Richard in 1886) fell in love with the East during service in India, studied Oriental languages, and towards the end of his life translated *The Arabian Nights*. With John Hanning Speke he went deep into Africa and in 1858 discovered Lake Tanganyika. While Burton was ill, Speke reached Victoria Nyanza, one of the long-sought sources of the river Nile.

Livingstone also longed to find out more about the Nile, and in 1865 set out on another journey, during which he mapped further tracts of the interior. For five years the outside world heard nothing of him. The *New York Herald* sent a Welsh-born reporter, Henry Morton Stanley, to find the great missionary-explorer, and in October 1871 Stanley met him at Ujiji, on the eastern shore of Lake Tanganyika, greeting him with the words: 'Dr Livingstone, I presume?'

They spend a few months together. Livingstone would not return with Stanley, but continued his explorations for another year, growing weaker from illness. He died in May 1873. His grief-stricken servants buried his heart beside Lake Bangweulu and carried his body, wrapped in bark, over a thousand miles to Zanzibar for transport back to London, where he was buried in Westminster Abbey.

The historic meeting of Stanley and
Livingstone six years after Living-
tone's disappearance into the
nterior.

Benjamin Disraeli

The opportunist, expansionist mood of Britain, allied with its evangelical belief in the moral example it could set other nations, had no better exemplar than Benjamin Disraeli. Howled down in his earliest days in Parliament, he had declared 'the time will come when you will hear me'. Now he was making himself heard.

When Earl Russell, formerly Lord John Russell, became prime minister after Palmerston's death in 1865, his first objective was to extend the franchise. Some of his own party were alarmed at the range of his proposals, and the split in their ranks led to Russell's resignation. A Conservative government was formed by Lord Derby, with Disraeli as leader in the House of Commons.

The word 'Conservative' had first been used in preference to 'Tory' by an Irish M.P. in 1833, and was speedily adopted by Peel. In his novels *Sybil* and *Coningsby* Disraeli gave his own interpretation of the principles of Conservatism. As a member of the 'Young England' movement of the early 1840s he advocated a return to the old polarity of property and labour, in a kind of romantic feudalism: he scorned the middlemen represented by Peel, and sought a counterweight to the growing power of the middle classes. Above all was the majesty of the Crown, which should provide the focus not merely for the loyalties of Britain itself but also for the aspirations of other nations which could be drawn closer to it.

In order to 'dish the Whigs', Disraeli in 1867 pushed through a Reform Bill giving wider representation to industrial workers, based on the paying of rates rather than on property qualifications, than the Radicals would have dared to venture. Lord Derby had had his doubts, but Disraeli insisted on making a great 'leap in the dark' rather than tinkering with half-measures. He added about a million voters to the electoral register.

The following year he succeeded Derby, who retired because of illness, but without a workable majority found he had to surrender to a Liberal government under William Ewart Gladstone, his great opponent in Parliamentary debate. For six years Disraeli was in opposition, returning in 1874 at what he termed 'the top of the greasy pole'.

He was a Tory; and the queen had always favoured the Whigs. He was alien in appearance, ornate in speech; and dear departed Albert had pronounced him an impostor. Yet at last Victoria found a man whose flattery, wit, and genuine affection meant to her what the influence of her earlier counsellor, Lord Melbourne, had meant. He offered his perfect devotion in exchange for her perfect confidence. When she acted as he had all along intended she should, he thanked her for her guidance. When she was baffled by his machinations, he joked her into conceding his points. He maintained a shrewd flirtation which played on her as a woman without falsifying his veneration for her as queen.

Above all, 'Dizzy' began to coax the recluse out into public view again, showing her not just to her own people but to the rest of the world as the embodiment of British supremacy. There was no talk nowadays of the divine right of kings, but politicians and the public did come to regard Victoria as near-immortal, if far from infallible.

(I)

(3)

In the 1870s there was a serious depression, when an influx of cheap American wheat and a series of poor harvests in England threatened the country's agriculture with ruin. Refrigerated meat imports challenged local production. Prices tumbled, rents tumbled, land values tumbled. Many farmers and labourers emigrated to join their competitors. Yet achievements seemed still to outweigh setbacks. The Empire grew stronger, and Disraeli brought each fresh triumph to Victoria as a personal gift.

In 1875 the khedive of Egypt found his administration near to bankruptcy, and decided to sell off his shares in the Suez Canal. This waterway had been conceived by Ferdinand de Lesseps while he was French consul in Cairo, and built by him between 1860 and 1869 with money raised largely in France and Egypt. Britain could have bought an interest at the time, but both Palmerston and Gladstone had mistrusted the whole idea. Disraeli, hearing of the opportunity of investing, realised the strategic importance of the canal to British traffic with India, and decided to act. He consulted his Cabinet but had no time to put the matter before Parliament. Raising the money from the Rothschild banking family, he went ahead and was able to announce to Victoria: 'You have it, Madam . . . the entire interest of the khedive is now yours, Madam.' The route to India was safeguarded; Britain was in a position to establish fair rates for her shipping; and she had a foothold in Egypt.

In 1876 Queen Victoria and her prime minister made a mutually admiring exchange. Somewhat peeved by the king of Prussia having set himself up as an emperor, Victoria wondered why she should not be an empress, and in spite of some dissension Disraeli carried through a Royal Titles Bill creating her Empress of India. For himself, he became Lord Beaconsfield, and took pride in being the first to address the new queen-empress as 'Your Imperial Majesty'.

Victoria sent him primroses frequently from Osborne, and he let it be known that they were his favourite flowers. After his death the Primrose League was founded in his memory, dedicated to 'the maintenance of religion, of the constitution of the realm, and of the unity of the British Commonwealth and Empire'.

Benjamin Disraeli (1) shared Queen Victoria's enthusiasm for the Empire. He purchased a controlling interest in the Suez Canal (2) and made the queen empress of India. The cartoon (3) shows him offering her the imperial crown.

William Ewart Gladstone

Just as the Tories had found it expedient to shed a nickname with so many dubious associations, so the Whigs were finding that their old identification with the landed gentry did not help their image in the modern world. Many of them began to adopt the word 'Liberal', and it was under this banner that Gladstone took office as prime minister in 1868.

He was not merely Disraeli's opponent in Parliament but his opposite in most else. Where Disraeli was suave, Gladstone was blunt; Disraeli was a hedonist, Gladstone a puritan; Gladstone treated the queen 'like a public department', Disraeli like a woman. To his followers he became the Grand Old Man; to his detractors a dirty old man, his interest in the humanitarian study of vice and prostitution being interpreted as prurient and hypocritical.

Gladstone, son of a Liverpool merchant, had in his youth contemplated taking holy orders. Instead he turned to politics, at first as a Tory, until his reforming zeal alienated him from the party. As a Tory he attacked Palmerston for his pugnacious dealings with other countries. As a Liberal he was to attack the Conservative Disraeli for his offhanded support of the Turks in their bloodthirsty massacre of Bulgarians. Moral rectitude, nationally and internationally, was Gladstone's creed.

In 1869 he calmed the protests of Irish Catholics against their obligatory contributions towards maintenance of 'the Church of England in Ireland' by disestablishing the Irish Church. This was followed the next year by an Irish Land Act, whereby evicted tenants had to be compensated by their landlords and paid for improvements they had made during their tenancy. Unfortunately there was a clause allowing summary eviction on non-payment of rent, and no clause to set a fair scale of rents, so that it was still a simple matter for a landlord to get rid of anyone when he wished.

In that same year, 1870, came an Education Act framed by W. E. Forster, laying the foundation for compulsory elementary education nationwide, making grants to Church schools, and establishing undenominational 'board schools'.

In 1872 a Ballot Act brought in the principle of the secret ballot, freeing voters from the influence of bribery or intimidation. It had some unexpected repercussions: Irishmen who had so far been scared to vote for Home Rule agitators were now free to elect the men they regarded as truly representative of their views, so that within a few years there was a sizeable Irish contingent in the House of Commons demanding repeal of the Act of Union.

Gladstone gave his full approval to a Licensing Act put through by his home secretary, limiting the sale of alcohol to specified hours and premises. It turned many of the public and most of what we now call the licensed trade against the Liberals, and Gladstone later attributed his loss of the 1874 general election to 'a torrent of beer and gin'.

The Liberal prime minister, William Gladstone, Disraeli's chief opponent. Victoria disliked him so much that she could not bring herself to express regret at his death.

OVERLEAF

(1) 'The Soldier's Farewell' by Robert Collinson.

(2) 'General Gordon's last Stand' by George Joy.

Death in Khartoum

In 1882, with Beaconsfield dead and Gladstone back at the top of the greasy pole, as his old antagonist's ghost might be slyly whispering to him, British forces were sent to Egypt to safeguard the nation's

interests there. Although Egypt owed national allegiance to Turkey, it was effectively controlled by French and British finance, and when the sultan was asked to depose his representative, the khedive, in favour of a son more amenable to Anglo-French pressure, he was easily persuaded. This was too much for nationalist elements, who were led into rebellion by Arabi Pasha, an army officer.

A British fleet bombarded Alexandria, and troops under Sir Garnet Wolseley defeated rebel forces at Tel el Kebir. Britain appointed herself protector of Egypt and installed Sir Evelyn Baring (later Lord Cromer) as administrator.

In the Sudan another revolt broke out. Mohammed Ahmed proclaimed himself Mahdi—the Moslem Messiah—and denounced Sudanese subservience to Egypt. Rather than launch a campaign to subdue the territory, Gladstone decided merely to evacuate isolated garrisons and civilians. The man chosen to command this operation was General Charles Gordon, known as 'Chinese Gordon' from his heroic exploits in China.

Gordon was courageous but stubborn. He had been in the Sudan before, governing it on behalf of the khedive, and felt that with this experience and with God at his side—which he never doubted—he might achieve something nobler than a purely pacific evacuation. Reaching Khartoum, the capital on the river Nile, he sent out requests for troops. To safeguard a rescue operation, or to start an unauthorised war of reconquest? The Cabinet were perturbed by his references to 'smashing the Mahdi'.

Before any of his plans could come to fruition, Khartoum was surrounded by the rebels. The siege lasted for ten months, and in England the public clamoured for a relief expedition to be sent. Gladstone was furious that he should have been put in this position

(1)

by a soldier who had either misunderstood or flouted his instructions.

When at last a relief force set out, it took three months to fight its way to Khartoum. On 26th January 1885, two days before its arrival, the Mahdi's dervishes stormed the town, speared the unfaltering Gordon to death, and massacred those townsfolk who had remained loyal. The last entry in Gordon's diary read: 'I have done my best for the honour of our country. Good bye.' His country and his queen believed him, and for a while it seemed that the prime minister might have to resign. But alarm over Russian activity near the frontiers of India took people's minds off the Sudan, which was abandoned to the Mahdi's doubtful mercy, and Gladstone went on to face conflicts arising from a recurrent problem nearer home.

(3)

Irish Home Rule

Since 1870 a Home Rule Association had been urging dissolution of the union between Great Britain and Ireland, and the establishment of an independent parliament in Dublin. In 1875 a young Anglo-Irish Protestant, Charles Stewart Parnell, entered the House of Commons, and two years later became leader of the Association.

The large Irish contingent set about disrupting the business of the House and seized every opportunity to draw attention to their wrongs. In Ireland itself rents were withheld, landlords and their agents were boycotted—a word derived from an unpopular Captain Boycott who was ostracised by his local community—and 'Moonlighters' spread nightly terror, burning ricks and property and attacking anyone thought to be collaborating with the oppressors. In 1881 Parnell was arrested for supposed complicity in these tactics and put in Kilmainham gaol; but the outbreaks became so much more violent that he had to be released.

On 6th May 1882 a gang of self-styled 'Invincibles' set upon Lord Frederick Cavendish, newly appointed chief secretary for Ireland, and Thomas Burke, permanent under-secretary, in Phoenix Park, Dublin, and stabbed them to death. Parnell condemned the outrage, but public feeling ran high and slowed down conciliatory moves which the Government had been contemplating.

1) General Charles Gordon who was killed by Dervishes two days before a British force reached Khartoum.

2) A memorial service for Gordon is held in Khartoum.

3) The Irish 'Moonlighters' depicted terrorising farmers' daughters.

(1)

(1) St Pancras Hotel and Station from Pentonville Road, 1884. Sir Gilbert Scott built St Pancras between 1868 and 1874.

(2) A young flower-seller outside St Martin-in-the-Fields, 1888.

After two general elections in 1885 and 1886 the Irish increased their number of seats so that they came to hold the balance between the main parties. Whoever wanted their votes would have to grant their wishes.

Gladstone's Home Rule Bill of 1886 proposed a single-chamber parliament in Dublin responsible for all Irish affairs save foreign relations, defence, trade and customs. Unable to stomach the idea of anything more than a limited concession of regional self-government, nearly a hundred of his own party, including the influential Joseph Chamberlain, voted against the proposal. Gladstone went to the country, which chose the Conservatives. The breakaway Liberals became 'Liberal Unionists' and later joined the Conservatives to form the Conservative and Unionist party.

Lord Salisbury reversed the trend towards propitiation of the Irish. Disorder must be quelled. A Crimes Act was passed, authorising trial without jury. Evictions of recalcitrant tenants increased.

The Times published letters claiming to provide evidence of Parnell's part in the Phoenix Park murders, and then had to retract: the 'evidence' was a forgery by a journalist who admitted the fraud and then committed suicide. Parnell's stock rose. Queen Victoria, fiercely opposed to Home Rule and to Gladstone, feared that Parnell's vindication might bring about a Liberal reconciliation and thus threaten Salisbury's ministry.

Parnell proved his own destroyer. For some years his mistress had been Kitty O'Shea, wife of a complaisant Captain O'Shea. In 1890 the captain sued for divorce, naming Parnell as co-respondent. The Catholics who formed the greater part of his following were dismayed, and Gladstone advised Parnell to resign from leadership of the Nationalists. Parnell refused. In June of the following year he married the divorced Kitty, and died in October. His conduct split his own party as effectively as his work for Home Rule had, earlier, split the Liberals.

In 1893 Gladstone, prime minister for the fourth time at the age of eighty-three, presented another Home Rule Bill which got through the House of Commons but was thrown out by the Conservative-dominated Lords.

Jubilees

On 21st June 1887 Queen Victoria attended a thanksgiving service in Westminster Abbey. The accompanying procession of her immediate descendants included the crowned heads of four European countries. It was her Golden Jubilee, and the public turned out to celebrate the fifty years of her reign, willing to let the spectacle sweep away memories of her protracted, unsociable seclusion.

The Diamond Jubilee procession passes through the City in 1897.

(1)

(2)

In 1893 General Kitchener (2) completed the reconquest of the Sudan with the victory at Omdurman (1).

Yet even now, so many years after Albert's death, the queen was reluctant to indulge in anything too spectacular. Whatever her audience might expect of her, she refused to wear the crown and robes of state, and appeared in the familiar black bonnet, allowing only white lace and diamonds as a concession.

Ten years later she reached her Diamond Jubilee. Again she wore her bonnet, this time trimmed with white acacia and diamonds. There were no visiting kings on this occasion: the guests of honour were colonial governors and premiers, with troops from every part of the Empire. 'No State and no Monarch known to history', boomed *The Times*, 'have ever rejoiced in such homage as our colonies will pay to our Queen.'

The following year there was further jubilation when Major-General Kitchener went from success to success in the Sudan. A member of the expedition which had reached Khartoum too late to rescue Gordon, he had the satisfaction in 1898 of sealing the reconquest of rebel territory at the decisive battle of Omdurman, across the Nile from Khartoum. In this engagement the 21st Lancers, among whom was serving the twenty-three-year-old Winston Churchill, launched against the shock-haired 'fuzzy-wuzzies' the last full-scale cavalry charge in British military history. The victor was awarded a baronetcy, then a viscountcy, and ultimately in 1914 an earldom, as Lord Kitchener of Khartoum.

BE UNITED AND INDUSTRIOUS

AMALGAMATED SOCIETY OF ENGINEERS, MACHINISTS, MILLWRIGHTS, SMITHS, AND PATTERN MAKERS.

This is to Certify that _____ was admitted a Member of the _____ Branch on the _____ day of _____ 18_. In witness whereof we have subscribed our names and affixed the Society's Seal.

PRESIDENT.   SECRETARY.

(1)

Trade Unions

The agricultural and industrial depressions of the 1870s and 1880s put workers on the land and in industry in militant mood. Just as concentration of labour in factories had made legislation to control hours and conditions easier, so it made collaboration of workers against their employers easier than in scattered communities. An Agricultural Labourers' Union founded by Joseph Arch in Warwickshire in 1872 made some headway in pressing for higher wages, but was nearly killed off by the depression years. It was in the cities that the real future of the movement lay, shown most dramatically not in the negotiations of individual craft unions but in strikes by unskilled workers.

In 1888 London match girls, working for a pittance and in constant danger of the dreaded 'phossy jaw', poisoning from the yellow phosphorus used for match heads, struck for an increase in wages and, with public sympathy behind them, won. In 1889 came the first large-scale strike of London dockers organised by John Burns, Ben Tillett and Tom Mann. Just when it seemed that the port employers might starve the dockers into submission, contributions came in from home and abroad, including £30,000 from Australia. The dockers were able to stay out until they had won an extra six-

(1) A certificate of trade union membership.

(2) Queen Victoria Street in the City of London, 1897, looking down towards the Royal Exchange.

(2)

(1)

pence an hour—'the dockers' tanner'—and provided an object
lesson for other workers.

Earlier in the century their achievement would have been impossible. The Combination Acts in force during the Napoleonic Wars
forbade workmen to combine in demands for higher wages or fewer
working hours. Ostensibly they applied also to combinations of
masters against men, but while suspension of the Habeas Corpus
Act on grounds of wartime security proved useful in the arrest of
Radicals and argumentative employees, there is no record of it
having been used against cliques of employers.

In 1824 a Parliamentary committee met to consider the abolition
of these restrictions. Francis Place, a tailor of Charing Cross with
strong Radical views, gathered kindred spirits around him in the
library behind his shop, and guided the reforming M.P., Joseph
Hume, in the presentation of evidence. Impressed by the sobriety
and learning of the carefully chosen working-class witnesses, the
committee recommended repeal. Following a wave of strikes, an
Amending Act was passed to forbid molestation or obstruction of
employers or other workers, but still allowed the right of employees
to combine for collective bargaining.

Definition of molestation or obstruction could vary from one
bench of magistrates to another; and there were always those on the
look-out for some technicality on which to attack workmen's groups.
In 1834 George Loveless and five other farm-workers of Tolpuddle
in Dorset were sentenced to seven years' transportation because, in
forming a union branch, they had administered a simple form of
oath, which was common practice but illegal. The jury was packed
with local farmers, delighted at the opportunity of removing these
troublemakers to Australia. The prime minister, Lord Melbourne,

(2)

refused even to consider a petition bearing a quarter of a million signatures; but public outcry against the sentences continued, and in 1836 the 'Tolpuddle Martyrs' were released.

The Chartists

Francis Place also helped William Lovett, a Cornishman, to frame a People's Charter demanding universal male suffrage, equal electoral districts, vote by ballot, abolition of M.P.s' property qualifications, and payment of M.P.s. The enthusiasm shown at mass meetings all over the country caused consternation in Government circles, especially when demonstrations in 1839 and again in 1842 led to riots.

The presentation of the Chartists' petition to Parliament in 1848 was awaited by thousands of special constables from the upper and middle classes, and by troops under the duke of Wellington. In the event it proved very tame. The petition carried less than half the promised signatures, and of these many were spurious.

Those who still believed in the Charter allied themselves with better organised Radical pressure groups, and in due course each demand was met.

(3)

Unrest among the working classes was shown by the public outcry when the Tolpuddle Martyrs (2) were sentenced to transportation for a trivial offence. (1) A huge petition in favour of the martyrs is carried through ranks of demonstrators, 1834.

(3) Chartists attack the Westgate Inn in Newport, 1839.

The TUC

There continued an ebb and flow of restrictive measures against unions, but gradually it was accepted even by their opponents that they were here to stay. In Manchester in 1868 an incipient Trades Union Congress was attended by thirty-four delegates, representing some 118,000 union members. It resolved to use its influence to amend the law in regard to picketing, to secure legal protection of trade societies' funds, and declared it 'highly desirable that the trades of the United Kingdom should hold an annual congress, for the purpose of bringing the trades into closer alliance, and to take action in all Parliamentary matters pertaining to the general interests of the working classes'.

In 1871 Gladstone's administration passed a Trade Union Act

(1) Trade union demonstration at
Manchester.

(2) 'The Bayswater Omnibus, 1895'
by G. W. Joy.

(1)

(2)

to define allowable methods of collective bargaining, to permit unions to hold corporate property and have legal protection for their funds, and to clear up vaguenesses which had made conflicting judgments possible in the courts. Linked with this was, however, a Criminal Law Amendment Act which virtually prohibited picketing.

Under Disraeli this second Act was repealed: peaceful picketing was legalised, and it was laid down that a combination of strikers could not be prosecuted on grounds of criminal conspiracy if the act they were committing was not one which it was illegal for a single person to commit.

The next really alarming challenge came from employers in South Wales. In 1901 the Taff Vale Railway Company brought a claim against the railwaymen's union for financial loss and damage to railway property during a strike. The court ruled that the union was legally responsible for the conduct of its individual members, and awarded the company £23,000. It was obvious that if such actions could succeed, union funds would always be at risk and even a successful strike could prove financially disastrous in the long term.

Neither of the main political parties offered much sympathy, let alone any indication of steps to amend the law. Trade unionists wishing to press for certain Acts of Parliament needed their own spokesmen in that Parliament. The seeds of a Labour Party were being sown.

The Boer Wars

Soon after the abolition of slavery throughout the British Empire, settlers of Dutch descent in the South African province complained that they had been cheated of proper compensation for their slaves, and furthermore that not enough was being done to protect them against raiding Kaffirs, which was what the Dutch in Southern Africa called the Bantu. Thousands of these Boers (farmers) set out on a Great Trek to the interior. Some settled in Natal, but when

Three generations in a family of Boer farmers arm themselves for war.

Gun carriages of the Royal
Artillery cross a pontoon bridge.
The difficult terrain worked in
favour of the more mobile Boers.

Britain annexed that, too, they moved on to join other trekkers beyond the Orange and Vaal rivers.

After some dispute Britain recognised the independence of the Orange Free State and the Transvaal, but the Transvaal was soon appealing for help against the Zulus under their warrior chief Cetewayo. It was granted in return for renewed submission to British authority.

Once the Zulus had been defeated, the Transvaal Boers again clamoured for independence, and unilaterally proclaimed a South African Republic. There followed the brief fiasco of the first Boer War, in which a British force sent from Natal was briskly defeated at the battle of Majuba Hill.

Gladstone, unwilling to commit the country to a war in which he felt much of the right was on the other side, braved the queen's wrath and restored independence to the Transvaal, though Britain was to hold a 'watching brief'.

All might have been well but for the discovery of gold in the Transvaal near what is now Johannesburg.

Miners and adventurers swarmed into the region, until soon there were more 'Uitlanders', or outsiders, than Boers. The country saw the prospect of great wealth but also saw a decline in its austere Dutch Protestant morals. Its leader, Paul Kruger, imposed heavy taxes and freight charges on the newcomers, and allowed a monopoly to sell dynamite to miners at astronomical prices. At the same time he refused the Uitlanders any voting rights, and in legal disputes they found to their cost that the courts used only the Dutch-based Afrikaans language.

Cecil Rhodes, premier of Cape Colony and founder of the British South Africa Company, had a dream of an entirely British Africa. The Boers were in the way of his ambitious Cape-to-Cairo railway. An excellent excuse for taking over the Transvaal would be for the unenfranchised Uitlanders, who contributed so much to the country's prosperity, to rise against Kruger's tyranny and call for aid from freedom-loving neighbours.

The Jameson Raid

It was not difficult for Rhodes in 1895 to ship in arms so that when the moment came the Uitlanders could rebel and set up a provisional government. A company force would then march in across the border, and the British high commissioner at the Cape would at once issue a proclamation ordering both parties to cease hostilities and submit to the arbitration of Her Majesty's Government. It was decided in advance that this arbitration should stipulate immediate elections and a vote for every white adult male.

Questions were to be asked later about the extent to which ministers in London knew of these preparations. A committee of inquiry duly exonerated the colonial secretary, Joseph Chamberlain, from any involvement; but even if he did not originate the conspiracy, he had a shrewd idea of its progress, was in constant communication with the high commissioner, and would have backed the rising if it went well.

In fact things did not go well. The force of about five hundred mounted men waiting on the border were under the command of a Company administrator, Dr Leander Starr Jameson, who was impatient for action. As day by day passed with no message from Johannesburg to say that the Uitlanders had rebelled, Dr Jameson grew more restless. Perhaps in the conviction that a bold gesture would set everything moving, he led his horsemen over the border on 29th December 1895.

The Uitlanders, by now trying to reach a peaceful compromise with Kruger, were appalled. They sent a messenger to halt Jameson, but in euphoric mood the messenger joined the invaders. The Boers rounded them up and contemptuously handed Jameson over to the British, whose high commissioner hurriedly denounced the whole operation.

Jameson was sentenced to fifteen months in prison. Rhodes had to resign his premiership of Cape Colony. But the mood in Britain was one of approval for Rhodes, Jameson, and the ultimate liberation of the predominantly British Uitlanders from Kruger's yoke.

A more enlightened man than Kruger might have used his increased prestige to make a few magnanimous concessions and negotiate reasonably with Britain. Unfortunately a telegram from Kaiser Wilhelm II, congratulating him on having preserved his country's independence without even having to appeal to 'the help of friendly powers' puffed him up so inordinately that he intensified measures against 'aliens', built up his armaments—largely from German sources—and grew more dictatorial.

Lieutenant Roberts won a Victoria Cross firing the last shot at the battle of Colenso, where ten guns were captured by the Boers and the British force had to withdraw with heavy losses.

Sir Alfred Milner, new high commissioner at the Cape, sent home reports of the advisability of intervening if only the Boers would provide some 'flagrant offence' to justify this. Kruger refused to provide anything quite melodramatic enough, grudgingly acceded to discussions of the franchise—and then, alarmed by realisation that British troops were being slyly moved into strategic positions, launched an attack on Natal and the Cape Colony.

'They have declared war on the British Empire,' said *The Times*. 'They must feel her arm and pay the penalty of their aggression.'

Black week

The Orange Free State allied itself with the Transvaal, and prepared not only for enemy reinforcements to arrive but also for aid to come from Germany and the Cape Boers.

Little help was, in the end, offered the Boers, other than anti-British propaganda throughout Europe. But the British did not find the campaign easy. Incompetent leadership resulted in the garrisons of Ladysmith, Kimberley and Mafeking being bottled up from October 1899 onwards, and in the loss of three battles in one 'black week' in December. If the Boers had followed up their early successes and rallied all the Dutch elements in surrounding terri-

(1)

tories they could probably have marched to the Cape and driven their enemy right out of South Africa. Instead, they concentrated on besieging the three towns, and gave Britain time to rush reinforcements to the scene under two new commanders, Lord Kitchener and Lord Roberts.

Kimberley and Ladysmith were relieved in February 1900, Mafeking not until 18th May. With a garrison of just over a thousand men, Colonel Baden-Powell had gallantly held out for two hundred and seventeen days. The news of the relief set people singing and dancing through the London streets, and there were jubilant processions in the provinces. A new word was coined for such unbridled displays of joy—'mafficking'.

Two other new concepts came into being during the next two weary years of the war. When the Boers turned from farming to send small fighting groups against an enemy, they called such a group a 'commando'. These guerrillas, thoroughly at home in their own countryside, defied the formal rules of war by not standing up in brightly coloured lines to be shot at. A man might be a sniper one day, a blandly innocent civilian the next. Kitchener, constantly harassed by these fast-moving irregulars, decided that his only course was to deprive them of all food and shelter. He burned farmsteads and supplies, and packed over a hundred thousand people into concentration camps. Lack of food or sufficient medical supplies resulted in the death of a fifth of the internees, including a large number of children.

At home there was a Liberal outcry against this 'barbarism', and when at last a peace treaty was signed in 1902, £3,000,000 was granted for rebuilding and restocking the farms. In 1906 the Liberals were back in power, and one of their first moves was to grant responsible government to the Boer states.

Reinforcements rushed to South Africa under the command of Lord Roberts (1) and Lord Kitchener relieved the three besieged cities.

(2) Hysterical mob in Piccadilly on the relief of Mafeking. One of the crowd waves the portrait of Baden-Powell, heroic defender of the town for 217 days.

(2)

God save the King

While the war in South Africa dragged on, in England the unthinkable happened. On 22nd January 1901, Queen Victoria died.

She had spent a bleak Christmas at Osborne. By mid-January she was obviously ill, and had difficulty in speaking coherently. The Prince of Wales and the Kaiser hurried to the Isle of Wight, and by the 22nd more of the family had come to gather round the deathbed. Victoria breathed her last at half past six in the evening.

The coffin was carried to the mainland through an array of warships and loaded on to a special train. After a short funeral service at Windsor, Victoria achieved what she had waited for for so long and of which she had written so often in her journal—to be laid to rest beside Albert in the mausoleum she had decreed for them both at Frogmore in Windsor Home Park.

Nobody could really believe the queen was no longer there. And nobody knew quite what to expect from her son. Victoria had always been critical of 'Bertie' and his love of pleasure; half believed that worry over such matters had killed her beloved consort; and refused to allow her son to play any part in affairs of state or to admit him to any of her councils. In this at least she was in the tradition of her Hanoverian ancestors. 'It quite irritates me to see him in the room,' she had once admitted.

Now, at the age of fifty-nine, he was King Edward VII.

(1)

(1) Queen Victoria's funeral; the end of an era.
(2) Prosperous Edwardians afloat at the Henley Regatta.

The Early Twentieth Century

The Early Twentieth Century

Edwardian days are evoked in many novels and memoirs as halcyon times when every man knew his place in the scheme of things and was content, when food was wholesome, the countryside unspoilt, and the pace leisurely. In his autobiography the author and administrator John Buchan (Lord Tweedsmuir) remembered the period as 'unbelievably secure and satisfied. The world was friendly and well bred'. But elsewhere he referred in less nostalgic mood to 'the vulgarity and the worship of wealth which appeared with the new century'.

The pace was in fact anything but leisurely. Worship of wealth there may have been, but also a desperate need for simple subsistence. The population of the British Isles had been about 25 million at the beginning of Victoria's reign; at the beginning of Edward's it was over 40 million. In 1800 there had been about 180 million people in Europe; by the early 1900s the figure was rising over the 400 million mark. Every country had more mouths to feed, every country wanted to sell more goods. Ominously, by the turn of the century German and American steel production had far outstripped Britain's, and their populations were growing faster. Merchant fleets expanded. So did navies and armies.

Steam-power linked British colonies, dominions and protectorates with the homeland: four-fifths of the world's steamships were

Queen Victoria with her son Edward, Prince of Wales, and his wife Alexandra. Edward was sixty years old when he at last succeeded to the throne in 1901.

Edward VII makes his first journey by motorcar in 1899, accompanied by Lord Montagu of Beaulieu. The car is an 1899 Daimler, 12 hp, which could run at 40 mph.

British registered. Steam drove trains over the great mesh of main and branch lines which brought industry closer to its markets within the United Kingdom and closer to the ports. It also opened up new possibilities in work and play: it was feasible for more wage-earners, even in the lower income groups, to travel between city and suburb; businessmen could get about with less waste of working time; and the seaside holiday was in reach of many who could never have contemplated such a luxury if it had been a matter of owning or hiring their own family transport.

London's Underground had opened its first electrified line in 1890, and the network continued to develop through the first decade of the new century. Electric tramways competed with local railways, and in reply the Liverpool to Southport line and Tyneside suburban services, for example, were electrified in 1904.

But the most immediately noticeable force for change was the internal combustion engine. The motor ship was already on the horizon. King Edward himself gave his seal of approval to the motor car. His first two vehicles, however, were not British: he bought a Mercedes and a Renault. In this field Britain was a late starter.

Red flags and mechanical kites

The motor industry in Britain lagged behind Germany, France, and soon the USA, partly because of restrictions imposed by the law that any mechanically propelled vehicle should be preceded by a man on foot carrying a red flag. This Red Flag Act was repealed in 1896, but a speed limit of 12 mph was imposed, rising to 20 mph in 1903.

Although Frederick Lanchester designed a successful all-British car, manufacturers tended for some time to concentrate on the assembly of foreign motor parts or to copy foreign designs. The meeting in 1904 of Charles Stewart Rolls and Henry Royce resulted in a partnership in 1906; their factory at Derby opened in 1908 and set new standards of design and performance. In 1905 the Austin Motor Company went into business; and in that same year a regular motor-bus service was inaugurated in London. The double-decker

(1)

powered vehicles slowly took over from the thousands of horse drawn buses. At first they ran on solid rubber tyres, but the inflatab tyre patented by John Boyd Dunlop, a veterinary surgeon, for us on bicycles was soon adopted for cars, buses and the motor taxi which were also appearing in city streets.

Petroleum at last gave man the power to fly with a reasonabl hope of going in the direction he wished to go. Balloon ascents ha been a popular spectacle since the Montgolfier brothers sent up thei first hot-air balloon in France in 1783, and experiments were carrie out in many countries on the use of gas-filled, rigid airships whic would be dirigible rather than at the mercy of wind and weathe The most successful was the invention of the German Coun Ferdinand von Zeppelin, tried out in 1900, making a twelve-hou passenger run in 1908, and between 1910 and 1914 carrying ove thirty thousand passengers without mishap.

The future belonged, however, to the heavier-than-air machine At Kitty Hawk in America the Wright brothers first got thei powered aeroplane off the ground on 17th December 1903, and tw years later came to Europe to demonstrate their invention. In 190 Louis Blériot made the first crossing of the English Channel by air

A. V. Roe's triplane was the first all-British machine. The firs pilot's certificate granted by the Royal Aero Club was issued t John Moore-Brabazon (Lord Brabazon of Tara), who was to d valuable work in the development of aerial photography.

(2)

(3)

(1) John Moore-Brabazon, pioneer British pilot, at the controls of his Wright aircraft in 1910.

(2) Motor and horse-drawn vehicles mingle in Whitehall, 1910.

(3) A crowded beach in Edwardian times. The increase in leisure and transport made a seaside holiday an annual event for many families.

Significantly, an allocation of funds for aeronautics was introduced into the Army and Navy estimates for 1909.

Voices in the air

The telephone, invented in 1876 by Alexander Graham Bell, an American of Scottish descent, had been introduced into Britain by private companies and taken up by a number of local councils. As the system expanded, independent groups merged into the National Telegraph Company. Ultimately the Post Office, which had controlled all the main trunk lines since 1892, took over the whole operation.

The Post Office also imposed its rule on the newest means of communication. The Wireless Telegraphy Act of 1904 forbade the installation or operation of wireless equipment without a licence from the postmaster-general.

Experiments in the wire-less transmission of messages by radio waves had been carried out in Italy by Guglielmo Marconi, and after taking out a patent he came to England to demonstrate its potentialities to the army and navy. Messages were exchanged between warships eighty miles apart. In 1901 a message was transmitted from Poldhu in Cornwall to Newfoundland.

Operation of wireless transmitters and receivers was greatly improved when in 1904 Professor (later Sir) John Fleming, who had supervised the introduction of incandescent electric lighting into this country on behalf of the Edison Company, invented the thermionic valve.

In that same year a scientific theory of far-reaching importance was expounded, though at the time it meant little to any but the most advanced researchers: Ernest Rutherford and Frederick Soddy stated the general theory of radioactivity. Rutherford, who had been working and lecturing with Soddy at McGill University, Montreal, was appointed professor at Manchester University in 1907 and there, with Niels Bohr, and later as Cavendish professor in the University of Cambridge, continued his work on nuclear physics.

(1) Marconi with the wireless apparatus he demonstrated in England.

(2) An operator works the switchboard of the Purley National Telephone Company Exchange in 1910. The Post Office took over the private telephone companies in 1911.

(3) Fashionable ladies at Ascot, 1910. They wear black in mourning for the death of Edward VII.

(1)

Entente Cordiale

Queen Victoria had misjudged her son. As Prince of Wales he had been addicted to racing, shooting and gambling. He had hobnobbed with the new financial tycoons. Both before and after marriage to the beautiful Danish princess, Alexandra, he had enjoyed the company of pretty, witty women. He established his own country seat at Sandringham in Norfolk, and much preferred it to Windsor or Buckingham Palace, which he referred to during his mother's seclusion as 'the sepulchre'. As King Edward VII he varied his routine and diluted his pleasures as little as possible. He still went shooting, still loved Ascot and Goodwood: he was the first reigning monarch to win the Derby, with his horse Minoru in 1909.

Yet he was not the irresponsible playboy Victoria had feared. His travels as Prince of Wales forged many useful links, and his visit to France as king in 1903 was a personal triumph. At a time when the French were suspicious of British foreign policy and especially antagonistic towards recent treatment of the Boers, he gave a speech in fluent French without a single note, and showed himself so genuinely fond of the country and its people that he overcame all doubts. If not the event of international importance which some admirers have claimed, it eased tensions between two countries

(2)

which had long regarded themselves almost as hereditary enemies, and paved the way for the *Entente Cordiale* of 1904, in which a number of outstanding problems were settled and mutual interests recognised.

Kaiser Wilhelm II, on whom even the affable Edward could make no impression, was far from cordial. Although there was no military alliance between Britain and France, this new friendship, and then in 1907 the formation of a Triple Entente in which Britain agreed Eastern spheres of influence with France's ally, Russia, led Wilhelm and his advisers to complain of encirclement.

(1) Lady Buckingham collecting money on Alexandra Rose Day, 1913.

(2) Edward VII shaking hands with M. Clemenceau during his visit to Paris in 1903, when his bonhomie won him great popularity.

Crisis in the Lords

In home affairs, Edward insisted on knowing everything his ministers were planning, though he was by no means a meddler. When Haldane, secretary of state for War, instituted the Territorial Army in 1907, the king on his own initiative assembled all the lords-lieutenant of the counties and rousingly invited their thorough support. Both he and Queen Alexandra devoted much time to charitable causes, especially those concerned with medicine and the improvement of health services. After his death Alexandra continued this work until her own death in 1925, when nearly a quarter of a million pounds subscribed in her memory was used to extend the district nursing service and provide pensions for queen's nurses.

In 1909 the king faced a constitutional crisis.

After a Liberal victory in 1906, zealous reformers began to push through Bills which shocked the Conservative majority in the House of Lords. The Lords blocked a couple of Bills but allowed through the Trade Disputes Act, reversing the much-deplored Taff Vale judgement. In 1908 old-age pensions were introduced by David Lloyd George, a Welsh solicitor from a working-class home who had entered Parliament in 1890 and was now chancellor of the Exchequer. The president of the Board of Trade, Winston Churchill, who started as a Conservative M.P. but changed his allegiance to the Liberals, was behind legislation to establish labour exchanges. A Trade Boards Act was passed to deal with wage disputes and to eliminate some of the injustices of 'sweated' labour in trades which had so far wriggled through holes in existing factory legislation.

The clash came with Lloyd George's 'People's Budget' of 1909. This proposed a super-tax over and above income tax, a rise in death duties, and a tax on land values, to pay not only for military expenditure in the face of Germany's increasing armaments, but for social reforms not to the peers' tastes. Although it had always been understood that the Lords did not interfere with money Bills, this time they threw the budget out. A general election followed, and the Liberals were returned, though saddled with the problem which had bedevilled them in the previous century—enough Irish Nationalists to hold the balance of power.

At once a Bill was introduced to limit the rejecting or delaying powers of the Lords and to reduce the Parliamentary term from seven to five years. This, too, the Lords threw out, so the prime minister, Herbert Asquith, went to see the king. But it was a new king.

Edward, depressed by tensions in Europe and by the irreconcilable differences between the Lords and Commons, had been further worried by failing health. Early in May 1910 he succumbed to an attack of bronchitis, and was dead within two days. Among the nine reigning monarchs at his funeral was the Kaiser, who had disliked his uncle Edward but got on very well indeed with his cousin George.

King George V was Edward's second son. He had been put to a naval career until the death of his older brother made him second in succession to the throne. He married Princess May of Teck, who had been engaged to that brother, and turned his mind to the affairs of state which must now concern him. He was a staunch, straight-

The funeral of Edward VII, May 1910. George V leads the mourners, flanked by the Kaiser (left), and the Duke of Connaught. The two naval cadets are the Prince of Wales, later Edward VIII (left) and Prince Albert, later George VI.

(1)

(2)

(1) George V and Queen Mary with their children. The baby, Prince John, suffered from epilepsy and died while still a child. The other children from left to right are Princess Mary (later the Princess Royal), Prince George (Duke of Kent), Prince Henry (Duke of Gloucester), Prince Edward (Edward VIII), and Prince Albert (George VI).

(2) King George and Queen Mary at the Durbar in Delhi, 1911, when the king was crowned Emperor of India.

(3) Keir Hardie (bearded) waits to address the crowd in the May Day procession, 1912.

forward man, at first inspiring respect rather than love—a situation which was to change during and after the First World War, when he attracted greater affection from his people than any sovereign since the Hanoverians first came to England.

Asquith asked from him the assurance that, should another election give the Liberals a mandate to proceed with their Parliament Bill and the Lords again threw it out, the king would create enough new Liberal peers—about 250 were needed—to outvote the Conservatives. King George deplored such measures; but consented.

There was another election, which the Liberals won. The Lords gave in, and after some last-ditch struggles the Bill became the Parliament Act of 1911.

Also in 1911 Lloyd George introduced national health insurance, and one of the key demands of the Chartists was granted at last: salaries were to be paid to M.P.s Those who benefited most from this were the members of the young Labour Party.

King George and Queen Mary escaped for a while from strife at home to appear as emperor and empress of India at a magnificent Durbar (Hindustani for a levée or public audience) in Delhi, which was then proclaimed capital of India in place of Calcutta.

The Labour Party

The 1906 election restoring the Liberals to power had also raised the spirits of the Labour Representation Committee, twenty-nine out of their fifty candidates having been elected.

Keir Hardie, a Scottish newspaperboy and miner, who believed in socialism as the only creed to offer 'life for the dying people', became the first Independent Socialist M.P., for West Ham, in 1892, startling the House by arriving complete with cloth cap, tweed jacket and brass band. He was chairman of a conference in 1893 to form an Independent Labour Party, which in February 1900 met other workers' groups and set up a Labour Representation Committee with the task of creating a Labour group at Westminster.

(3)

The first secretary of the LRC was James Ramsay MacDonald, who from poor beginnings in a Scottish fishing village had worked his way through board school and evening classes to become secretary to an M.P. and then a political journalist. In 1911 he became leader of what was now firmly established as the Parliamentary Labour Party, which after the 1910 elections numbered forty-two.

Funds for election campaigns and for the maintenance of Labour members came largely from the trade unions. The payment of official salaries to members eased the strain considerably and made possible a wider representation of socialist views, not tied exclusively to union policy.

Arctic and Antarctic

In 1912 two tragedies shook the country. The first took place in March, but was not discovered and reported back for many months. The second occurred on the night of 14th April and was swiftly reported by the new wireless telegraphy—but not swiftly enough to save more than 703 lives out of 2206.

Britain's splendid new liner, the *Titanic*, was on her maiden

(1) News reaches London of the loss of the great passenger liner *Titanic*, a ship believed to be unsinkable.

(2) When his ship *Endurance* was crushed by icepacks three hundred miles from land, Shackleton made an epic journey in an open boat to save his companions.

(3) Scott's ill-fated expedition reaches the South Pole in 1912. From left to right, standing, Oates, Bowers and Scott; sitting, Wilson and Evans. The whole party perished from cold and starvation on the return journey.

(1)

voyage to New York. Accusations were later levelled against the shipping company and the captain that, in an effort to make a record crossing, the liner had been taken along a route where there had already been warnings of icebergs. Shortly before midnight the *Titanic* struck a berg, and sank within three hours. Her distress signals brought another ship to the scene to pick up survivors; but many more could have been saved if boat drill and the lifeboats themselves had been better organised.

In the nineteenth century American and Scandinavian explorers had made many trips into the Arctic, and an Italian duke made a determined attempt to reach the North Pole. Admiral Peary of the US navy finally got there in 1909. From the time of Captain Cook the Antarctic, too, had beckoned to the adventurous. There were French, Belgian, German and many British expeditions. Ernest Shackleton (knighted in 1909) led the British Antarctic Expedition of 1908–9 and got to within less than a hundred miles of the South Pole. In 1914 he embarked on a complete crossing of the continent, but his ship the *Endurance* was crushed in pack-ice, and the party had to make a gruelling journey to safety in a small boat.

The attainment of the Pole itself was the goal of two men in 1910, the Norwegian, Roald Amundsen, and the Devonian, Captain Robert Falcon Scott. Scott and his companions reached it on 17th January 1912, only to find that Amundsen had been there just a month before. They turned back, slowed by illness and blizzard, and by March were dead. A search-party eight months later found three bodies—Captain Oates, one of the team, had walked out into the night in the hope that they could travel faster without him—and Scott's meticulous records and journal, in which he wrote at the end: 'I do not regret this journey; we took risks, we knew we took them, things have come out against us, therefore we have no cause for complaint.'

(2)

Votes for women

A motion for women's right to vote was introduced as early as 1867 by the philosopher and M.P., John Stuart Mill, but defeated by men confident that the country was safer in male hands. In the more emancipated society of Edwardian days, women began to speak out for themselves; and, when speech availed nothing, turned to aggressive action.

In 1903 Mrs Emmeline Pankhurst established the Women's Social and Political Union to press for female suffrage. Their claims were met with amusement, and the word 'suffragette' became an easy term of derision. Mrs Pankhurst had a meeting with the prime minister at which he made it clear that no action was contemplated to meet the suffragettes' wishes. She and her colleagues, most of them well educated and from good families, thereupon began a campaign of nuisance tactics which intensified as repressive measures were taken. They chained themselves to railings, broke windows, set fire to pillar-boxes, and heckled the public speeches of Government spokesmen. When arrested, some went on hunger strike and were forcibly fed. Descriptions of this ugly process reached the newspapers and the public, and sympathy for the suffragettes began to perturb the Government.

An Act was passed, ostensibly with humanitarian intentions, but soon denounced as the 'Cat and Mouse Act'. Women hunger strikers were to be released from prison when their condition became serious, and then rearrested when they had recuperated or when it suited the authorities.

The distinguished physician Sir Almroth Wright, pioneer of anti-typhoid inoculation and other enlightened methods of combating infection, wrote magisterially to *The Times* to explain women's unsuitability for making rational decisions. 'There are no good women, but only women who have lived under the influence of good men.' Those who chained themselves to railings were sexually thwarted; the middle-aged ones of course going through that phase

(2)

(1) Mrs Pankhurst is carried away by a policeman after the Suffragettes' attack on Buckingham Palace, 1914.

(2) Emily Davison throws herself under the king's horse during the Derby of 1913, to attract attention to the cause of the Suffragettes. She died from her injuries.

A postcard on the Suffragette campaign to win for women the right to vote.

when all women go slightly mad. Their programme, he feared, was simply 'to convert the world into an epicene institution in which men and women shall everywhere work side by side at the self-same tasks and for the self-same pay'.

On 4th June 1913 Emily Davison, a young Northumbrian lady, threw herself under King George's horse at the Derby. She died in hospital. The suffragettes organised a huge funeral procession, at which Mrs Pankhurst was arrested as she was about to get into her carriage.

Militancy increased. Buildings were burned, and paintings in art galleries were slashed, including Velasquez's *Rokeby Venus* in the National Gallery.

But a greater war was threatening.

Sarajevo

Archduke Franz Ferdinand of Austria and his morganatic wife celebrated their fourteenth wedding anniversary on 28th June 1914, combining it with an inspection of Austro-Hungarian troops in Bosnia.

This Balkan state and its neighbour, Hercegovina, had been taken into the Austro-Hungarian Empire from Turkey, and many Serbs and Croats resented an annexation flouting their nationalist aspirations and their racial ties with independent Serbia. Their rancour was played upon by the 'Black Hand' organisation of Serbian officers, who wished to defy the Habsburg Emperor Franz Josef more resolutely than their nervous government could allow.

Franz Ferdinand's visit to Sarajevo was not merely a private anniversary for the archduke: it was also Serbia's national day. The 'Black Hand' supplied a group of students with weapons for an assassination attempt to mark the occasion. When the archduke's open car stopped at a corner on its way out of the town young Gavrilo Princip, standing only a few feet away, saw his chance. He drew his revolver and killed both Franz Ferdinand and his wife.

Austria accused Serbia of complicity in the murders and refused all attempts to discuss the matter. It was the excuse to seize the country for which she had been waiting. On 28th July she declared war.

None of the other great powers had envisaged a major war at this stage. They seemed to shuffle spellbound into it, and then plunge headlong. Russia was pledged to aid Serbia, but the Germans did not really believe she would mobilise. Although Kaiser Wilhelm promised support to Austria if necessary, both he and his chancellor, Bethmann-Hollweg, urged restraint. Germany had been arming at a great rate, preparing one day if necessary to break out of the 'encirclement' of the Triple Entente; but most of Wilhelm's experts predicted that German economic strength would so soon match Britain's that a disruptive war would be unnecessary. Nevertheless, when Russia did begin to mobilise, Germany followed suit. Russia called on France to honour a treaty agreement. France mobilised, and rejected a German request for a guarantee of her neutrality. Germany declared war on Russia on 1st August 1914 and on France on 3rd August.

Recruitment posters of the First World War. The central figure is Lord Kitchener.

For Britain, Sir Edward Grey, the foreign secretary, gave only two assurances: if Germany attacked French ports, the British navy would have to intervene; and if at any stage Belgian neutrality was infringed, Britain would be bound to come to her aid under the 1839 Treaty of London.

The Germans felt safe in ignoring this. After his retirement in 1905 as chief of the General Staff, Count von Schlieffen had exercised his mind by drawing up a blueprint for any future war against France, Russia, and possibly Britain. This Schlieffen plan stipulated a fast attack across Belgium to by-pass French fortifications and strike an immediate knock-out blow. Britain's guarantee to Belgium meant nothing: she would be unable to get a sizeable army in the field before it was all over.

So German troops poured into Belgium. Grey sent an ultimatum demanding their withdrawal. When it was rejected, Britain declared war on Germany on 4th August.

King, Kaiser and Tsar were closely related, and George and Wilhelm were especially good friends. But this was an age of vast, impersonal forces, in which royal relationships, antipathies and affections had lost the importance they possessed in earlier centuries.

The Western Front

The strike across Belgium was not as rapid as strategists had hoped. The Belgians fought gallantly back, and by destroying great stretches of their own railways slowed down the transport of enemy troops and supplies. A French counter-attack was launched through the Ardennes, with appalling loss of life: the flower of the French army was cut down in this very first engagement, and the Germans gathered momentum again, closing in on Paris, until held at last on the river Marne.

The British Expeditionary Force of 130,000 men had advanced from the northern coast of France to a position near the Belgian town of Mons. To the surprise of both sides, two German corps on their way from a victory over the French at Namur met them head on, and for a while were stopped in their tracks. Then Field-Marshal Sir John French, the British commander-in-chief, learned how exposed his small forces were by the French retreat, and decided to retreat also. His men fought dogged delaying actions, until the splitting of the Germans on the Marne allowed them a corridor through which to advance again. Once more there was an almost accidental confrontation between Germans and British, this time at Ypres. Here the British army, like the French before them, suffered the loss of most of their finest men. And here the pattern began to solidify.

Both sides had been confident that the war would be 'over by Christmas'. Instead, men were digging themselves into trenches which ultimately stretched from the Flanders coast to the Swiss border. Here for the next four years they fought over a shell-torn morass and achieved no more than the exchange of a few muddy miles either way.

The names of some Belgian and French towns, villages and hill-sides have been written into British history and the history of the colonies and dominions as indelibly as that of Waterloo: Le Cateau, Beaumont-Hamel, High Wood and Delville Wood, Arras, Amiens and Armentières. Three major battles were fought along the river Somme, the first in 1916, during which sixty thousand British troops died on the first day. The Indians distinguished themselves at Neuve Chapelle, the Canadians at Vimy Ridge in April 1917.

Output of munitions on either side soared, without the deadlock being broken. In 1915 the Germans used poison gas at the second battle of Ypres. In 1916 Britain introduced tanks into the battle of the Somme: awe-inspiring but few in numbers, and so making little real impact until in November 1917 a huge force of them rolled over the barbed wire and machine-gun posts at Cambrai.

In 1917 Sir Douglas Haig, who had taken over as commander-in-chief at the end of 1915, urged on the War Cabinet the need for a massive offensive in Flanders, which he promised could win the war. His own staff disapproved, the French were coping with mutinies and unable to help, and weather and terrain were against it. Haig, however, got his way, on the understanding that if his first assault failed he would not persist.

The first attack did fail. The bombardment which preceded the infantry assault smashed the drainage system of the Flanders plain, so that men and guns stuck in a vast expanse of mud. Haig did not retract. For some three months the battle went on in the quagmire, all for the sake of possessing a strongly defended ridge. When the fighting petered out, the British had taken the ridge and were masters of the ruined village of Passchendaele. British casualties were over 300,000, the Germans' almost 200,000. In the following spring the Germans recaptured the ridge.

Eastern Fronts

In Serbia, cause of the outbreak of war, the first Austrian attacks came to grief in the border mountains. It was not until Germany came to the rescue, and Bulgaria was tempted to join in with an

(1)

(3)

(1) A water cart stuck in the mud near Ypres, 1917.

(2) Troop movements crowd a road during the battle of the Somme, 1917.

(3) An early British tank at the battle of Cambrai.

invasion from the east, that Serbia fell. Its surviving troops escaped to Albania and were evacuated by the Allies, who also sent an expeditionary force to Salonika in Greece to operate against Bulgaria.

The Allies, too, sought friends in return for promises of territorial readjustments after victory. Dissension within the Austro-Hungarian Empire was sown by propaganda assuring minorities of independence when the war was won.

In 1915 Italy entered the war, but by 1917 had been so severely punished by German and Austrian troops that Britain and France had to send reinforcements to hold a defensive line. Rumania joined in April 1916, and was occupied by the Germans within a matter of months.

The major power in the East was Russia, by whom the Western Allies set great store. There was much talk of the forthcoming annihilation of the Central Powers by 'the Russian steamroller'. Unfortunately the steamroller found it difficult to move. There was such a bitter feud between the two main Russian commanders that they could barely make a pretence of acting in consort; and when they did advance into Prussia in August 1914 it was difficult to follow up with supplies because of the difference between Russian and German rail gauges.

The Germans used their railway system to surround the Russian Second Army before its commander realised what was happening. The battle of Tannenberg cost Germany about 13,000 casualties

(1

(3)

against untold thousands of Russian dead and 125,000 prisoners. The commander committed suicide. Then the Germans turned on the isolated First Army, taking almost as many prisoners again but failing to destroy it. The survivors of the battle of the Masurian Lakes made an ignominious escape back to their own frontier.

By the end of December, fighting mainly defensive engagements along an extensive front, Russia was appealing to Britain for help against the Turks, now in the war on the side of the Central Powers. Lord Kitchener, secretary for War, and Winston Churchill, first lord of the Admiralty since 1911, were convinced that an attack on the Dardanelles would not only provide the necessary distraction but also open up an excellent supply route to Russia via the Bosporus. According to Churchill, the navy could do the job on its own without calling on troops from the Western Front.

In February 1915, British marines made a successful landing, but it was not followed up. Several ships were sunk by mines, and when after all it was decided to spare troops for a major assault, the Turks had brought up massive reinforcements. In addition to British detachments, Australian and New Zealand troops training in Egypt were hurried to the Gallipoli peninsula. In spite of courageous attacks—commemorated on 25th April each year as Anzac Day— they were stopped by withering fire from the heights commanding the beaches. Fresh landings were made at Suvla Bay, only to bog down into static trench warfare as indecisive as that in the West. At last Kitchener visited the scene and ordered the abandonment of the campaign.

(4)

(1) The road through Chateau Wood in the Ypres sector, 1917.

(2) Soldiers struggle to draw a field gun through the mud near Zillebeke during the Flanders offensive in 1917.

(3) Winston Churchill had to resign his position as first lord of the Admiralty after the disaster in Gallipoli.

(4) Men resting beneath the shelter of the cliffs along the road from Cape Helles to Gully Ravine, during the Gallipoli campaign.

Churchill, the most vociferous protagonist of the venture, became the scapegoat, and resigned. In early 1916 he served in Belgium as lieutenant-colonel of the 6th Royal Scots Fusiliers; but by 1917 was back in office as minister of Munitions, answerable to a very different prime minister.

The Welsh wizard

'I never believed in costly frontal attacks either in war or politics, if there were a way round.' So, in his *War Memoirs*, David Lloyd George summed up his attitude towards his Parliamentary colleagues and those military commanders whose views failed to coincide with his own. Some admired 'the Welsh wizard' for his verbal and tactical cunning; others regarded him as sly, unprincipled, even treacherous. But after two years of terrible war, still with no end in sight, the country was in the mood for a leader both skilful and vigorous—and even his most ardent opponents could scarcely deny Lloyd George's skill or vigour.

Inside and outside Parliament, criticism of Asquith as an ineffectual prime minister had been growing. In May 1915 he had been manœuvred into forming a coalition of Liberals, Unionists (Conservatives) and Labour to prosecute the war more efficiently; but by the end of the year it was being asked if he were the most capable leader of such a grouping. Behind his back, Lloyd George schemed with Unionist and Labour members. Word of his intentions got around, and many Liberal and Unionist front-benchers rallied to Asquith. 'I would rather die than serve under Lloyd George,' declared Lord Curzon. But Curzon was among those who yielded—naming as one of his conditions that Churchill should not be given office—and Lloyd George, having dispossessed his own leader and split the party so disastrously that it was never to hold power again, became prime minister of a predominantly Unionist coalition in December 1916.

His War Cabinet, unlike its sketchy predecessor, met nearly every day. Many of its directives antagonised the service chiefs, and there was a continual misuse of energy in domestic conflict which might have been employed in fighting the enemy.

A particularly savage animosity existed between Lloyd George and Sir Douglas Haig. As secretary of War, Lloyd George had sus-

(1) After his resignation Churchill served in the army in Belgium; he is shown above with Marshal Foch (on his left) and a group of English and French officers.

(2) Lloyd George, who became prime minister in 1916, addressing a political meeting at Lampeter station, 1919.

1) Sir Douglas Haig inspecting French troops in 1915.

2) A Zeppelin raider, 1916.

pected the commander-in-chief of squandering human life without a qualm, and trusted none of his demands for more men and more freedom of action. Now, as prime minister, he persuaded the War Cabinet in 1917 to authorise the appointment of the French General Nivelle as supreme commander over Haig's head. Haig was persuaded to comply only by the assurance that it was for one operation only, and that if at any time he felt his army was being misused he could appeal direct to his own Government.

The operation specified went wrong. Nivelle had staked all on a decisive victory. Although the Germans fell back on their heavily fortified Hindenburg Line, they inflicted crippling losses on the French soldiers, who refused to continue the assault and settled in defensively along their own lines.

Perhaps it was to score off Nivelle that Haig so strenuously advocated his own scheme for a breakthrough which ended at Passchendaele, breaking his promise not to go on if the first stage failed because his pride would not let him admit the failure.

Lloyd George was equally adept at breaking promises. Once he had decided that he wanted Churchill, he brushed aside all assurances given to Unionists who had agreed to serve with him only if Churchill were kept out; though here his path was made somewhat easier by the Dardanelles Report's exoneration of Churchill of all blame for the Gallipoli failure. He used people when he needed them, dropped them if they proved a hindrance. By guile and forcefulness, emotional bribery and stirring exhortation, he drove the war on, creating ministries to transform the internal economy, and juggling with the conflicting needs of generals who wanted more and more shells yet at the same time clamoured for the release of more men from industry to swell the ranks of the fighting forces and replace the thousands who had been annihilated.

War in the air
Zeppelins appeared over the English coast in December 1914, and in February 1915 dropped bombs on Yarmouth. By April they were attacking London, and later there were hit-and-run raids by heavier-than-air machines. Zeppelins were also used for naval reconnaissance, and smaller balloons for reconnaissance along the Western Front until the new fighter planes made easy targets of them.

301

(2)

Ships of the Royal Navy in the First World War: HMS *Iron Duke* (1), Jellicoe's flagship for two years of the war, had 13·5 inch guns; HMS *Drake* (2) was a cruiser with 6 inch guns.

Britain's aerial combat forces were the Royal Flying Corps and the Royal Naval Air Service, which merged in April 1918 to form the Royal Air Force. RFC squadrons were assigned to specific army corps to report troop movements and guide artillery fire in their individual sectors. The Germans operated in much the same way, and soon there were battles between reconnaissance aircraft transformed into fighting machines. On the ground was mass movement or mass stagnation; in the air, duels between opposing 'aces'. Engine power increased during the war, and technical advances in general opened the way to the expansion of commercial and private flying after the war.

War at sea

Although the German race to build a navy powerful enough to challenge Britain's had been one of the main causes of tension between the two countries in the early years of the century, the two fleets had few major encounters during the whole course of the war. The British navy's main role was to maintain a food and trade blockade on Germany, while keeping a strong force at Scapa Flow in the Orkneys to cope with any sudden enemy sortie from Kiel or Wilhelmshaven.

Early in the war British battle cruisers sank four German ships in a surprise attack on Heligoland. A couple of months later a German squadron shelled Scarborough, Hartlepool and Whitby, and got away without being intercepted. When another squadron put to sea in January 1915 to bombard the English coast again, it met a British

fleet under Admiral Beatty and was driven back to Heligoland. Ranging further afield, a British cruiser squadron tackled five enemy cruisers off the coast of Chile. The German admiral, Graf von Spee, outmanœuvred his attackers and blew up the British flagship. Another cruiser, the *Monmouth*, went down with all hands. The Germans did not lose a man. From the Admiralty, Churchill ordered immediate revenge. Two battle cruisers left England to link up with other ships off the Falkland Islands, and destroyed four of von Spee's five cruisers. The fifth was tracked down and scuttled three months later.

The only truly large-scale engagement was that off Jutland on the evening of 31st May 1916. The Germans had come out in the hope of splitting the British fleet and dealing with it piecemeal, rather as Nelson had operated at Trafalgar. Well aware of these tactics, Admiral Beatty used a small force to lure the Germans into range of Admiral Jellicoe's main fleet. The ruse succeeded, but the exchange of fire was brief, and the opposing forces broke contact. They met again early on 1st June, when the Germans did a great deal of damage before withdrawing. Jellicoe cautiously did not give chase.

British losses were heavier than the Germans', but the encounter alarmed Admiral Scheer and the Kaiser sufficiently to make them keep their fleet in shelter for most of the rest of the war. From now on Germany concentrated on submarine warfare in the hope of starving Britain before being starved by the British blockade.

A large proportion of Britain's food and raw materials had to be brought in by sea. Troops had to be sent to various battlefronts by

(2)

1) Admiral Sir John Jellicoe on board HMS *Iron Duke*.

2) 'Clearing the Seas 1914–18', by C. E. Turner.

(1)

(2)

sea. The German sinking of the *Lusitania* in 1915 with many American passengers aboard had brought outraged protests from the USA, and for a while the U-boat campaign was moderated. But early in 1917 orders were given for it to be stepped up. There was now to be no quarter: all Allied or neutral ships should be sunk on sight.

In one month almost a million tons of shipping went down. Neutrals grew reluctant to undertake shipments to Britain. Harangued by Lloyd George, the Admiralty denied that anything could be done about it. The prime minister surreptitiously consulted junior officers, and came out with a demand for armed convoys. He was given numerous reasons why they wouldn't work. Lloyd George then took arbitrary command of the Admiralty and flatly ordered the introduction of convoys. They were a success. All objections raised before the system had even been tried proved baseless. Lloyd George was right again.

While it lasted, the untrammelled U-boat campaign produced one result which the Germans had foolishly dismissed as irrelevant. On 6th April 1917 the United States of America declared war on Germany.

The last push

America was in the battle, but Russia was out of it. In March 1917, after a series of strikes and riots, the Tsar was persuaded to abdicate. In October, playing on the unwillingness of the people to continue with the war to which the Provisional Government was officially committed, Lenin and the Bolsheviks seized power with the rallying-cry of 'peace, land and bread', and early in December arranged an armistice. Harsh terms were imposed by Germany in the Treaty of Brest-Litovsk, which demanded the surrender of Poland, the Ukraine and other regions, the cessation of socialist propaganda directed at Germany itself, and a payment of 300 million roubles for repatriation of Russian prisoners. The only choice offered the Russians, observed the Austrian delegate to the peace talks, was

(1) Colonel T. E. Lawrence, 'Lawrence of Arabia', painted by Augustus John in 1919. In the eastern theatre of hostilities this one-time archaeologist organised Arab revolt against Germany's Turkish allies.

(2) British soldiers arrive home on leave.

(3) A boat carrying soldiers on leave sails from Boulogne.

(4) A Labour Party poster issued in 1910 and 1929.

"WORKLESS"

'what sauce they shall be eaten with'.

Pressure on their eastern flank removed, the Germans aimed for a quick decision on the Western Front before too many American troops could reach Europe.

Field-Marshal von Hindenburg and his quartermaster-general, Ludendorff, mounted a grand offensive towards the coast. They almost obliterated the British along the Somme, but were unable to take Arras or Amiens. Once again they struck at the Marne, where Americans reinforced the French and held firm. At last the Allied armies were put under one brilliant commander, General Foch, who began a colossal counter-offensive and slowly pushed the enemy back. Half a million Americans added their weight; on 8th August Haig's attack in the Amiens sector resulted in what Ludendorff called 'the black day in the history of the German army'; and as the Hindenburg Line itself crumbled, news came through that the Allies had broken out from Salonika and forced Bulgaria to sue for peace.

On 11th November 1918 representatives of a republican German signed an armistice at Compiègne. Wilhelm II had abdicated and been driven into retirement in Holland, where, in spite of English pleas to 'Hang the Kaiser', he lived on the rich income of his German estates until 1941.

Figures of the dead in all theatres of war are impossible to verify but could not have been less than ten million. Of the six million men who served in the British forces, nearly three-quarters of a million were killed, and some 200,000 from the Empire, one-third of them Indians. The country also found itself with one and a half million seriously wounded survivors, among them many suffering permanent after-effects of poison gas.

Women workers in a munition factory. Over six million women were employed in industry or the services during the First World War.

In recognition of their immense
contribution in war work, women
were at last enfranchised in 1918. (2)
A woman and her family at the poll
at the post-war election.

(?) An unemployed man on a
street corner at Wigan. Despite
Lloyd George's promise of 'a fit
land for heroes' many of the
demobbed soldiers could not find
work.

OVERLEAF (1) 'Bellenglise, or the
breaking of the Hindenburg Line'
by Beadle. (2) 'Putting out his eyes
1919', by G. H. David, illustrates
tactics in aerial warfare. One British
plane attacks a German two-seater
from below while three others
engage it from above.

(1)

)

Fit for heroes

'A fit country for heroes to live in'—that was Lloyd George's post-war promise.

Earlier in 1918 the Representation of the People Act had given the vote to all men over the age of twenty-one and to women over the age of thirty. After what women had shown themselves capable of in war work, it was impossible to withhold the franchise any longer. Ten years later the voting age was reduced to twenty-one for women also.

The electorate had thus trebled. As 'the man who won the war', Lloyd George appealed to old and new voters for ratification of his Coalition Government. Favoured candidates were issued with certificates signed by himself and the Conservative leader, Bonar Law, testifying to their loyalty. Liberals who felt there were higher loyalties than those owed to Lloyd George had to carry on their election campaign without such testimonials. Asquith denounced these as the equivalent of wartime ration coupons, and the name of 'the coupon election' stuck.

Lloyd George and his coalition were returned with an enormous majority.

Peace was in itself such a boon that for a time there were few signs

(1)

of disillusionment. Then it gradually became apparent that the high-sounding promises were not likely to be honoured. After a brief spell of prosperity as industry and commerce got on their feet again, profits began to fall, traders realised that during the war many distant customers had set up their own manufactories and developed their own markets; and, as wages also began to fall, demobilised soldiers found that the only jobs available were underpaid, or intermittent—or that there were no jobs at all. Resentment against 'hard-faced men who had done well out of the war' and the return of the coal-mines and railways to private profiteers after the government supervision of the war years led to a demand for nationalisation, which Lloyd George turned down flat. The example of Soviet Russia encouraged the stirrings of class war. There was an outbreak of strikes, including one by the miners which dragged on for months until they were starved into submission. By the summer of 1921 there were over two million unemployed.

In Europe, a League of Nations was established with headquarters at Geneva in the hope of avoiding all future wars by submitting disputes to international arbitration. It owed much to President Wilson of the USA, who had made its creation one of the essential 'Fourteen Points' in his declaration of America's war aims. The US Senate, however, refused to ratify the peace treaty drawn up at Versailles by the Allies, including Wilson as American delegate, and as this meant rejection also of the Covenant of the League of Nations, the USA never played the part which might have made the League's subsequent history less pitiful.

Among other matters settled at Versailles were huge sums which Germany must pay in reparations, and the redrawing of national frontiers. The Austro-Hungarian Empire was dismembered. A South Slav kingdom of Serbs, Croats and Slovenes came into existence as Yugoslavia. Most significantly for the future, an independent Poland was established, and the aspirations of Czechs and Slovaks were fulfilled in the creation of the new republic of Czechoslovakia.

(2)

(1) Because of the strength of anti-German feeling in the First World War, George V was advised to change the royal name of Saxe-Coburg-Gotha to Windsor.

(2) A meeting of the post-war peace conference at the Quai d'Orsay, Paris, painted by Sir William Orpen. Clemenceau sits between Lloyd George and Woodrow Wilson (in high-backed chair).

(3) 'Row of Sleepers, 1941' by Henry Moore, a war artist who found much inspiration in the plight of civilians during the Blitz.

Crisis Years

Crisis Years

The Easter Rising in Ireland, 1916:
(1) The remains of a car which had
been used as a barricade; (2) The
damage in Earl Street, Dublin.

British Approval of independence for smaller nationalities gave one perennially troublesome faction within the British Isles an excuse to raise its voice yet again. The Irish wanted complete freedom, not just half-measures.

In 1912 Asquith had rewarded the Irish Nationalists whose conditional support kept the Liberals in office by introducing yet another Home Rule Bill. The Unionists, seeing a chance to discomfit the Liberals, came out in support of Ulster Protestants who feared Catholic domination. Sir Edward Carson, a barrister who sat as M.P. for Dublin University, quoted the late Lord Randolph Churchill—'Ulster will fight and Ulster will be right'—and was instrumental in raising a force of eighty thousand volunteers to oppose any attempted imposition of Home Rule on the northern counties.

Officers at the Curragh, the military H.Q. in Dublin, let it be known in 1914 that they would prefer to resign their commissions rather than take part in any operation against these patriotic irregulars. They were assured that their scruples would be respected and that they would not be ordered into action against the Ulstermen.

The Home Rule Bill passed its third reading in May 1914 but was not implemented because of the outbreak of war in Europe. Many Irishmen enlisted and fought bravely for England. Many more planned a fight for independence. Sir Roger Casement, an Irishman who had distinguished himself in the British consular service and retired with a knighthood, was not above enlisting German support. He spent over a year in Germany trying to drum up enthusiasm among prisoners of war for an Irish legion within the German army, and when that failed he appealed for substantial arms shipments to be smuggled into Ireland to support a projected rebellion. Belatedly he realised that the Germans did not take him seriously and that no arms would be forthcoming. He persuaded them at least to land him in Ireland from a U-boat so that he could warn the conspirators. Shortly after disembarking he was arrested.

On Easter Sunday 1916 the rebellion went ahead. The hotheads of the extremist Sinn Fein—'We Ourselves'—who had long since ceased to acknowledge the Nationalist M.P.s as their spokesmen, seized Dublin Post Office after heavy street fighting and proclaimed a republic. It lasted until the Friday of that week, when the rebels surrendered. Fourteen of the leaders were executed, and another, Eamonn de Valera, would have suffered the same fate but for his parentage: his father was Spanish, his mother Irish, and he had been born in the USA. He was sentenced instead to life imprisonment. Casement was hanged for high treason. To silence the pleas of some influential Englishmen for a reprieve, the authorities circulated

Casement's diary, recording details of his sexual perversity.

In 1920 the vexed question of Ulster loyalties was solved—or so it was hoped—by combining six of its counties into Northern Ireland, the other three largely Catholic counties being joined to those of what the Sinn Fein, who had won seventy-three seats in the 1918 election, persisted in calling the Republic of Ireland.

Trouble in the south persisted. Home Rule allowed for only a limited, county council style of Parliament in Dublin. The rebels intensified their terror campaign, and in reprisal the British government recruited tough ex-servicemen into the Royal Irish Constabulary. As sufficient uniforms could not be found in a hurry, the newcomers were supplied with khaki trousers and tunics, and green caps so dark to look almost black. These hated 'Black and Tans' answered violence with violence.

At last the 'provisional government' agreed to accept dominion status as the Irish Free State, renamed Eire in 1936. Full independence as a republic was to come in 1949.

A London street scene, painted by Maurice Greiffenhagen in 1926.

The gay twenties

In 1920 Paul Whiteman, the American 'King of Jazz', brought his orchestra to Britain. Technical advances on pre-war inventions helped the spread of this new music: portable gramophones and the improving quality of recording established it as the all-pervasive sound of the twenties, forerunner of the transistor radios and cassette players of the seventies. Watered down from its vigorous origins in the streets and pleasure houses of New Orleans, it became the dance music of hotels and village halls, pier pavilions, theatres and the frantic parties of the 'bright young things'.

For all classes the most potent entertainment medium of the time was the cinema, from Babylonian edifices complete with Wurlitzer organs to little Gems, Electric Palaces, Mayfairs and Regents in the remotest market towns. Douglas Fairbanks and Rudolph Valentino were the great heart-throbs; Laurel and Hardy, Buster Keaton, Harold Lloyd and the London-born Charles Chaplin the laughter makers. In 1927 the movies became talkies: many stars, owing more to their looks than their diction, did not survive the transition; but new stars were born, and while the newsreels grew ever grimmer throughout the thirties, feature films grew more lavish and tuneful.

Other technical advances opened up new possibilities for the more active. There had been motor racing before the war, but now the fever spread. Setting and breaking speed records became the rage. Henry Segrave and Malcolm Campbell, both knighted in due course, pushed up speeds on land and water. At Daytona beach in Florida, Segrave reached 203 mph in March 1927, to be beaten by Campbell's 206 mph the following February. Segrave attained 232 mph in 1929, but was killed in 1930 when his speedboat overturned on Lake Windermere. Campbell continued setting new records until in 1935 he achieved 301 mph over a measured mile. After the Second World War his son Donald was to follow the same star until, like Segrave, tragically killed in a speedboat crash.

In the air, John Alcock and Arthur Whitten Brown made the first direct flight across the Atlantic in a Vickers Vimy aeroplane in June 1919, taking sixteen hours twenty-seven minutes. That same year a British airship, the *R34*, made a double crossing. Ross Smith flew from London to Australia in 135 hours.

In 1926 Alan Cobham tested the possibilities of long-distance air routes between Croydon and Cape Town, and between England and Australia, and was knighted. He commanded an expedition round Africa by flying-boat and, having studied refuelling problems at stop-overs on long journeys, experimented with refuelling in the air.

Private companies which had started regular passenger and freight services as soon as the war ended found operating costs and compliance with international regulations expensive, and in 1924 joined forces to become, with a government subsidy, Imperial Airways. This operated mainly long-distance flights, while British Airways ran services to and from the Continent. The two amalgamated in 1939 as BOAC—British Overseas Airways Corporation. (Internal and Continental services were hived off again in 1946 as BEA—British European Airways, only to be amalgamated yet again in 1974.)

(1) Charlie Chaplin with Muriel Harvey.

(2) Alcock and Brown stand in front of the plane in which they made the first direct Atlantic flight, 1919.

In 1913 Jacques Schneider, a French flying enthusiast, had instituted the Schneider Trophy for an annual seaplane race. Suspended during the war, contests began again in 1920. Three successive wins, culminating in Flight-Lieutenant Stainforth's 379-mph average in 1931, brought the trophy permanently to Britain.

There were not just more machines in the air, but more voices. So many amateurs were buying wireless parts and assembling sets to listen in to any sort of message which might be floating about in the ether that manufacturers decided to establish a British Broadcasting Company to transmit regular programmes. They appointed a Mr John Reith as manager. He regarded his job as not so much a profession as a vocation, and vowed to offer every household 'all that was best

(1)

(2)

1) Charles Lindbergh, the first man to fly the Atlantic from New York to Paris, arrives at Croydon in 1927.

2) The first Imperial Airways Short Calcutta flying-boat on the Thames at Westminster, in 1928.

(1)

(2)

(1) 'Winter Mine-laying off Iceland' by M. Bone.

(2) 'The Withdrawal from Dunkirk, 1940' by Charles Cundall.

(3) 'Firing Typhoons at Falaise Gap, Normandy, 1944' by Wootton.

(4) 'Tempests attacking Flying-bombs' by W. T. Monnington.

(3)

(4)

(1)

in every department of human knowledge, endeavour and achievement'. The manufacturers, aiming to entertain the public and so sell more wireless sets, found themselves with a Calvinist missionary on their hands.

In 1925 a governmental committee set up to consider the pros and cons of this monopoly recommended its continuance but in a revised form. Late in 1926 the company was reborn as the British Broadcasting Corporation, financed by licence fees from the owners of receivers. Mr Reith, later Sir John and ultimately Lord Reith, was given the title of director-general. Under his jurisdiction, jazz seeped through only in the diluted form provided by tasteful dance bands, regional accents were subdued by BBC English, invisible announcers had to don dinner-jackets and black ties before reading the evening news bulletins, ad-libbing of any kind was forbidden, and the slightest misdemeanour by members of staff meant dismissal: no one involved in a divorce suit, even as an innocent party, could remain on the payroll.

Performers, politicians and many of the public grew to resent Reith's dictatorship. At the same time they had to admire him. The fact that he survived 1926 spoke well for his staying power: for that was the year when the independence of the BBC was at stake, threatened not merely by commercial interests but also by political interference.

The General Strike

Lloyd George's coalition government collapsed in 1922, largely as a result of Conservative alarm at his rashness in bringing the country close to war over a clash between the Turks and the Greeks. His secretary for the Colonies, Winston Churchill, had not helped matters by telling the press of his demand for unqualified military aid from the dominions before even consulting the said dominions.

The Conservatives ruled for a brief spell; then for the first time Labour took a shaky lead with Ramsay MacDonald's minority government. After ten months he called for a general election but

(2)

(1) Listening to an early radio on headphones.

(2) Stanley Baldwin speaking in the market place at Middleton during his victorious election campaign of 1924.

(1)

(2)

Violent class warfare was feared during the general strike; armoured cars escorted supplies throughout the streets (1) and troops guarded bus stations (2) and other strategic points. There was, however, no serious strife, although over three thousand people were charged with acts of violence.

lost it, the decision owing much to the effect on middle-class voters of the 'Zinoviev letter'. This, now generally believed to have been forged by Polish or White Russian *émigrés* in Germany, purported to be from a high Communist functionary urging militant action on the British left wing, and was widely publicised by the Conservatives.

The prime minister from 1924 to 1929 was Stanley Baldwin, a lover of the quiet life at home and abroad. 'Wake me up when that's finished,' he used to say when foreign affairs were being discussed, and in domestic affairs he liked to steer an equable course down the middle of the road. Nevertheless, when the economic crisis worsened and the mine-owners called for longer working hours and lower wages, Baldwin added his voice to theirs: 'All the workers of this country have got to take reductions in wages to help put industry on its feet.'

For some time the Labour movement as a whole had been murmuring about a general strike. Its aims were a bit uncertain—somehow, simultaneously, to liberate the country from the capitalist

319

system, raise wages, shorten hours, and bring about a new brother-hood of man. When negotiations between the Government, mine-owners and miners broke down, it seemed that the moment had come. 'Not a penny off the pay, not a second on the day', became the miners' slogan, and they asked the General Council of the Trades Union Congress to organise a national strike.

Plans were drawn up by a committee including the powerful Ernest Bevin of the dockers' union and Transport Workers' Federation. Builders, printers, transport workers and those in heavy industry were called out in support of the miners in May 1926, restrictions were imposed on gas and electricity supplies, and other trades were held in 'second line' reserve.

Forewarned, the Government had time to set up its own emergency measures. Trains and lorries with essential supplies were driven by volunteers, often accompanied by police guards. Special constables were recruited. Winston Churchill, who had left the Liberals and rejoined the Conservatives, to become chancellor of the Exchequer, advocated a display of troops and tanks in the major cities. He was overruled, and turned his energies to running an official news-sheet, the *British Gazette,* to which the strikers responded with the *British Worker*.

Churchill also urged that the BBC should be commandeered and used as Government spokesman, but the prime minister agreed with Reith that it should remain impartial. Reith interpreted this impartiality according to his own conscience, and there were complaints of bias towards the relaying of Government statements and appeals for volunteers, with little time given to TUC statements. When the archbishop of Canterbury wished to broadcast an appeal for a compromise, Reith refused. But the corporation did scrupulously ban all editorial comment from its bulletins, and at no time permitted any purely propagandist material against the strikers.

After nine days the TUC realised the governmental organisation was better than its own, and called off the strike. The miners refused to surrender and continued on their own until August, when they had to admit defeat. They returned to work with longer hours and lower wages.

The next year a Trades Disputes Act made general strikes illegal, and remained on the statute book until 1946.

Abdication

King George V died on 20th January 1936. His eldest son became King Edward VIII but was never crowned.

The Prince of Wales had made himself personally popular throughout the country and dominions with his easy charm and spontaneity. But he had worried his mother and father by his dislike of official ceremony, and even more by his indifference towards the eligible princesses regularly presented for his approval. He preferred to spend his time alone or with a small circle of friends in an architectural folly in Windsor Park, Fort Belvedere, which he had coaxed his father into presenting to him.

In 1932 one of the guests there was a Mrs Ernest Simpson, an American who had divorced her first husband and married a London

'Bank Holiday, Brighton, 1933' by Charles Cundall.

(1)

(2)

(1) Edward VIII on holiday with
Mrs Wallis Simpson, the twice-
divorced American for whom he
gave up the throne. He was
succeeded by his brother George VI
(2).

stockbroker. Soon Edward was visiting Ernest and Wallis Simpson
in their London home so frequently that rumours about the relationship began to circulate. European and American gossip columnists
ran riot, and many periodicals arriving in Britain did so with large
chunks censored out. The British press remained loyally mute.

In October 1936 Wallis Simpson filed a divorce petition and was
granted a decree *nisi*. King Edward made it plain to his friends that
he intended to marry her.

It was impossible to suppress the facts any longer, and soon the
whole country and the colonies were arguing. To many, especially
to devout members of the Church of England, the idea of their
king's marriage to a twice-divorced woman was unthinkable. A
morganatic marriage was discussed, but Baldwin in the House of
Commons ruled this out: 'There is no such thing as what is called
morganatic marriage known to our law. The lady whom he marries,
by the fact of her marriage to the king, necessarily becomes queen.'
There were only two courses open: the King must set aside either
Mrs Simpson or the throne.

On 10th December 1936, King Edward VIII set his hand to a
document of abdication. He made a farewell broadcast, solemnly
introduced by Sir John Reith, and then fled abroad to stay with the
Rothschilds. The title of duke of Windsor was bestowed on him. Mrs
Simpson's decree absolute came through, and they married on 3rd
June 1937.

Just under a month earlier, Edward's brother, erstwhile duke of
York, had been crowned King George VI in Westminster Abbey.

Peace in our time

The American and European depressions hit defeated Germany
hard, making it a natural breeding-place for conflicting ideologies.
Fear of the spread of Communism, and resentment against the harsh
terms of the Versailles treaty which saddled them with blame for the
war, turned many Germans towards the loudly patriotic, militaristic
National Socialist Party—Nazis for short—led by Adolf Hitler.

Hitler was Austrian born but had served with the German army
during the war, twice winning the Iron Cross. He fostered the idea
that Germany had not really lost the war but had been 'stabbed in
the back'. Like so many demagogues, he found scapegoats on whom
to pin responsibility for all the ills that had befallen the country: in
this case the Communists and, above all, the Jews.

After being appointed chancellor by President Hindenburg in
1933, he imposed a one-party régime, murdering rivals within his
own ranks and persecuting those who did not vociferously applaud
his methods. He set up a secret police, a caucus of bullies and tor-
turers, and began to segregate Jews and deprive them of their rights
as citizens. His concentration camps were ultimately responsible for
the slaughter of over six million Jews from Germany and the countries
which the Nazis were soon to overrun.

Hitler's intentions were made clear in his book *Mein Kampf* (My
Struggle), but the one-time Allies, reluctant to rearm, persuaded
themselves that basically he meant well, that a reinvigorated Germany was a good thing for Europe, and that each of his territorial

(1)

(2)

(3)

(1) Neville Chamberlain meets Hitler in an attempt to avert war, 1938.

(2) British fascists salute Sir Oswald Moseley on May Day at Bermondsey, 1938.

(3) Members of the International Brigade who fought in Spain march down the Embankment, 1939.

demands would be the last. The menace of Soviet Russia worried businessmen and politicians far more than did the well-disciplined Nazi state.

In 1936 German troops reoccupied the Rhineland, which had been under French and British supervision until declared a permanently demilitarised zone. At the same time Italy, under the totalitarian régime of the Duce (Leader) Mussolini and his Fascists, was seizing Abyssinia and defying the feeble protests of the League of Nations. Mussolini and Hitler allied in a European 'Axis', and rehearsed ground troops and air forces in the Spanish Civil War, against the day when they would play their parts in a more widespread conflict. Indiscriminate bombing and machine-gunning of civilians shocked the world; but still nobody was prepared to take strong counter-measures. Winston Churchill warned of the dangers of German rearmament and German ambitions, but he was out of office and out of favour. 'Appeasement' was the watchword: if we made concessions to the aggressors, they would somehow become less aggressive.

In 1938 Hitler went ahead with plans to unify all German-speaking peoples into one glorious Reich which should last a thousand years. He annexed Austria, and then demanded that 'oppressed' Germans in the Sudetenland region of Czechoslovakia should be liberated. His attitude became so fierce that Neville Chamberlain, the British prime minister, flew to Germany to attempt a settlement before a Central European war broke out. Britain and America had been instrumental in establishing independent Czechoslovakia; but America was now pursuing an isolationist policy, and Chamberlain was reluctant to involve Britain in 'a quarrel in a faraway country between people of whom we know nothing'.

The Czechs had a well-equipped army ready for action. But when Hitler and Chamberlain, together with Daladier of France and Mussolini of Italy, reached agreement at Munich in September 1938, it was obvious that nobody was going to help the young republic, and Czechoslovakia surrendered some of its richest land to Germany, on the assurance that the purely Czech and Slovak regions would remain untouched. Chamberlain flew back to London and waved a piece of paper signed by Hitler and himself which represented, he assured cheering crowds and newsreel cameras, 'peace with honour—peace in our time'.

In March 1939 the Germans marched into the heart of Czechoslovakia, and Hitler himself slept in Prague Castle.

Britain had by now begun rearming. A warning system of aerial attack, the new and highly secret radar, was installed along the eastern coastline. Conscription was introduced within a few weeks of Hitler's invasion, and Britain and France gave guarantees to Poland against which the Führer was now making his familiar menacing noises.

Late in August, to the dismay of diplomats who had been trying to establish an Anglo-Soviet entente, Germany and Russia signed a non-aggression pact which, it was learned later, included secret clauses for the division of Poland and spheres of influence in eastern Europe.

Confident that Britain's guarantee would prove as flimsy as her actions over Abyssinia and Czechoslovakia, Hitler invaded Poland on 1st September 1939. On 3rd September, Neville Chamberlain broadcast an announcement to the nation that Britain and France were now at war with Germany.

The phoney war

Once again a British Expeditionary Force was sent to France, sheltering behind the massive fortifications of the French defence barrier, the Maginot Line.

For about seven months little happened along this second-generation Western Front. No practical help could be sent to Poland, which was carved up between Russia and Germany. Russia invaded Finland, and at one point Britain seemed on the verge of taking on Russia as well as the Nazis; but the Finnish War was soon over, and still Hitler made no move towards France. He wanted no war of attrition such as he had experienced for himself in the 1914–18 trenches, and hoped the Allies might compromise as they had so often compromised before. Britain and France were equally reluctant to start shooting, and the RAF contented itself with dropping propaganda leaflets on the enemy. American reporters described it as a 'phoney war'.

In April 1940, shortly after Chamberlain's boast that Hitler had 'missed the bus', the Germans invaded Denmark and Norway, partly to safeguard their supply routes of Swedish ore and partly to establish Norwegian bases from which to break the British naval blockade. A British expedition to Narvik fought gallantly and

RAF pilots scramble to their Hurricanes at Vassincourt, France, 1940.

324

(1)

(2)

Although nearly 400,000 men were evacuated at Dunkirk, many were left dead on the beaches (1) or taken prisoner by the Germans (2).

succeeded in capturing the town, but was withdrawn eleven days later because of the German attack on the Benelux countries and on northern France.

Chamberlain's half-hearted prosecution of the war provoked Labour members into a vote of censure, and one of his own party denounced him in the scathing words of Oliver Cromwell long ago: 'Depart, I say, and let us have done with you. In the name of God, go!'

National unity could be achieved only by a coalition government. Labour and the Liberals refused to serve under Chamberlain. On 13th May a new prime minister, Winston Churchill, rose in the House of Commons and offered the country 'nothing but blood, toil, tears and sweat'.

Clement Attlee, leader of the Labour Party, came into the Cabinet, and by an inspired stroke Churchill made Ernest Bevin minister of Labour. Bevin recruited workers for the factories, stepped up coal production with his conscripted 'Bevin boys', and with his knowledge of the working men among whom he had been raised was able to cajole, bully and organise manpower into ever-increasing productivity throughout the war. At the same time Lord Beaverbrook, as minister of Aircraft Production, forced up the output of fighters.

It was none too soon. On 10th May 1940 Hitler had launched his *blitzkrieg* (lightning war) against Belgium and Holland, bombing Rotterdam almost into extinction and, as in 1914, going round the French fortifications instead of wasting lives on a direct assault. An attempted British and French advance was blocked in Belgium, and by 19th May General Gort, British commander-in-chief, was forced to retreat to the sea. Troops assembled at Dunkirk waited under merciless dive-bombing attacks to be taken off the beaches. The task was not left to the navy alone. Ferryboats, fishing-boats, pleasure craft of every kind rushed out of every creek and harbour. A public house on Felixstowe docks was later to be renamed *The Little Ships* in honour of this patchwork flotilla, whose 600 vessels, added to 200 naval craft, rescued more than 338,000 men, among them 140,000

(1)

(2)

French who would form the nucleus of a Free French army under a little-known but resolute general, Charles de Gaulle.

On 22nd June Marshal Pétain signed an armistice taking shattered France out of the war. Britain stood alone.

The battle of Britain

With France subjugated, Hitler began to plan an invasion of that south-eastern corner of England much used by earlier invaders or featuring in the schemes of those who somehow failed to arrive. He decreed that the RAF should be 'so reduced morally and physically' that it would be incapable of offering significant resistance, and that the Royal Navy's home-based forces should be crippled by air and torpedo attack.

Field-Marshal Hermann Goering was overjoyed at the opportunity of showing what his air force, the *Luftwaffe*, could do. German bombers launched attack after attack on towns and airfields, keeping it up for two months until British fuel supplies were dangerously low and the pilots of the Hurricanes and Spitfires almost worn out. But the Nazis, demoralised by the speed and precision of the defenders—enormously helped by radar's advance warnings—weakened first. 'Never before in the field of human conflict was so much owed by so many to so few', said Churchill of the men of Fighter Command.

Among the most famous planes of the Second World War were the Spitfire fighters (1) and the Lancaster bombers (2).

The invasion was called off, the air attack switched to terror bombing raids on London and other cities. Much that was beautiful was destroyed; but so was the prestige of the *Luftwaffe*.

World war

Fighting was eventually to spread over nearly all Europe, Asia and North Africa, and to threaten Australasia. Italy entered the war on 11th June 1940, hoping for juicy pickings, but proved more of a liability than an asset to her Axis partner. Germany invaded Yugoslavia and Greece. The Afrika Korps came to the aid of Italian forces in East and North Africa and pushed the British back into Egypt. Convoys to Malta were unceasingly attacked from the air.

On 22nd June 1941 Hitler could restrain himself no longer from the attempted fulfilment of his greatest dream. Counting on another surprise *blitzkrieg*, he invaded Russia, which he had always envisaged as a fertile living-space for the master race, with natives fit only to supply slave labour. Britian immediately offered Russia an alliance; and the USA, which had been supplying Britain with arms under a 'Lend-Lease' agreement, offered similar aid to the USSR.

Japan's desire for expansion and the urgent need for raw materials led her to inaugurate a lightning war of her own. On 7th December 1941 waves of Japanese planes from aircraft-carriers attacked the US Pacific fleet in Pearl Harbor, Hawaii, destroying or disabling nineteen ships and over a hundred aircraft. At the same time Japanese troops moved towards Malaya. Two British battleships, the *Prince of Wales* and the *Repulse*, set out to attack the invaders and were sunk by bombers. Hong Kong fell. Singapore, which Churchill had ordered must be defended to the last man, surrendered sixty thousand prisoners into Japanese hands in February 1942. Within a

Goering and his staff gaze across the Channel, July 1940, at the country they expect imminently to invade.

(1)

(1) Mr and Mrs Churchill inspecting bomb damage in the City of London during the Blitz of 1940.

(2) Many Londoners sought safety at nights in the underground stations.

(2)

few months British and Dutch possessions were overrun. Advancing through Burma, the Japanese threatened India.

For once adhering scrupulously to a treaty—the Tripartite Pact of September 1940 between Germany, Italy and Japan—Hitler declared war on the United States. The USA was joined in its declaration of war on Japan by Britain, but decided first to work for the overthrow of Germany and Italy.

With American troops and increased American supplies reaching Britain, the tide began slowly to turn. In August 1942 General Alexander was given a handwritten directive by Churchill in Cairo: 'Your prime and main duty will be to take or destroy at the earliest opportunity the German-Italian army commanded by Field-Marshal Rommel together with all its supplies and establishments in Egypt and Libya.' Alexander held off until sufficient material had been built up, then entrusted the campaign to his Eighth Army commander, General Montgomery. At El Alamein, Montgomery laid down a massive artillery bombardment on 23rd October, followed by an armoured attack, and pursued the routed enemy some 1500 miles across the desert. In November, American and British forces under General Dwight Eisenhower landed in the north-west, assumed control of French Morocco and Algeria, and closed in on the Germans and Italians from the other side.

Churchill and President Roosevelt of the USA met at Casablanca in Morocco and agreed to stand out for unconditional surrender of the enemy. They also decided, in spite of appeals from the hard-pressed Russians for the opening of a Second Front in France, that it was more practicable at this stage to launch an operation from North Africa through Italy into 'the soft under-belly of Europe'.

In July 1943 Allied troops landed in Sicily, and by August had won the whole island. Mussolini was thrown out of office, and a new government hastily arranged an armistice on 3rd September, the day when the Allies set foot on the mainland. The Germans at once took over from the Italian army, freed the imprisoned Mussolini to

(1) Soldiers on patrol pass the Bahe Pagoda during the retaking of Burma, 1945.

(2) Infantrymen search for snipers in Cassino, where fierce fighting took place during the Allied advance up Italy.

328

set him up as head of a puppet government in northern Italy, and pinned the Allied forces down for several wearying months.

At the same time it could be said that the Allies were pinning down German troops, thereby easing pressure on the Russians. After a terrible siege, Stalingrad had been relieved, and as a tribute to the courage of its people King George VI sent Stalin a Sword of Honour. The Germans were being pushed back towards their own country. To finish the job, there must soon be an all-out thrust from the west.

The Second Front

Stalin, Roosevelt and Churchill met in Teheran in November 1943 to co-ordinate plans for a simultaneous squeeze on Germany. They talked also of post-war settlements. Churchill mistrusted Stalin; Roosevelt, anxious to show there was no western line-up against Russia, fell in with Stalin's wishes for a Second Front in France, with no diversions further east. Churchill's arguments were over-ruled. Thus the future of central and eastern European states was delivered into Stalin's hands.

Troops in Britain trained for 'D-day'. Bombers intensified their raids on German cities. Supplies of weapons dropped by parachute or smuggled in to Resistance fighters was stepped up, and sabotage against German-controlled installations in occupied countries increased.

On 6th June 1944 thousands of transports carried an invasion

(2) King George VI with Montgomery on the Normandy beaches, a few days after the Allied landings (1).

army under the supreme command of General Eisenhower to the Normandy beaches. The Germans, who had been fed with false information about a landing near Calais, rushed reinforcements to the area, but could not prevent the Allies forming a solid bridgehead. Prefabricated harbours were towed into position, and supplies flowed through, though it was essential to capture a major port soon: Cherbourg was the first target, Antwerp the ultimate one.

Sections of coastline remained in enemy hands long enough for the launching of Hitler's two pet secret weapons—the V1 flying bomb or 'doodle-bug', and the V2 rocket, which between them killed several thousand men, women and children in London and outlying districts, and were devastatingly used against Antwerp when it was taken.

The Red Army fought its way into Poland, Austria, and Germany itself, and was first to reach Berlin. Hitler, refusing the ignominy of falling into Russian hands, committed suicide in his Chancellery bunker on 30th April 1945, together with the mistress he had at the last moment made his wife. He knew that two days previously Mussolini had been captured by Italian partisans and executed along with his mistress. On 4th May German forces in north-west Germany, Holland and Denmark surrendered to Montgomery on

(1) A V1 flying-bomb, nicknamed the 'doodle-bug', falls near Drury Lane.

(2) King George and Queen Elizabeth visit a badly-bombed area in the East End. Their concern and sympathy boosted morale wherever they went.

(3) Crowds in Whitehall during the VE celebrations in London, May 1945.

Lüneburg Heath. Admiral Dönitz, whom Hitler had nominated as his successor, tried to reach agreement to surrender to the Western Allies while continuing the fight against Russia, but this was rejected. On 7th May he offered unconditional surrender.

On 8th May 1945, VE-day celebrated Victory in Europe. The war against Japan continued until, early in August, the Americans dropped an atomic bomb which killed eighty thousand people and destroyed the city of Hiroshima. A second bomb on Nagasaki hastened Japanese endeavours towards an armistice; and on 14th August 1945 the Second World War was ended.

The share-out

In spite of the League of Nations failure, the Allies had decided in principle on another international peace-keeping body, to be called the United Nations. But as soon as war was over it became clear that the victors were far from united. Countries liberated from the German yoke in eastern Europe now had a Russian yoke imposed on them. Communists in Poland refused to accept the Polish government-in-exile back from London, and set up their own Russian-dominated régime. The Russian-occupied zone of demilitarised Germany was soon reshaped as part of the Communist bloc. An 'iron curtain' was already falling between East and West Europe.

The last meeting of the three war leaders took place at Potsdam, near Berlin, shortly before the dropping of the A-bomb. Roosevelt was not present: he had died in April, and the new president was Harry Truman, who had none of Roosevelt's liking for Stalin. What the Russian dictator must have found bewildering was the disappearance of Winston Churchill in the full flush of victory and his replacement by Clement Attlee.

Welfare state

After victory in Europe, Churchill suggested continuing the coalition government until Japan was defeated. Many of his Labour colleagues favoured this, fearing that an immediate election would give the Conservatives a majority on the strength of Churchill's prestige as war leader. At the Labour Party's annual conference, however, the temper of the delegates was so resolute for change that the most Attlee could offer Churchill was a continuance of the partnership until an October election. Churchill refused such a compromise, resigned, and led a 'caretaker government' until polling in a general election on 5th July.

In an electioneering broadcast, Churchill warned, in the same tones he had used to denounce the Nazis, of the dangers of a socialist Gestapo. His speech caused more laughter than alarm. When the results came through, Labour had 393 seats, the Conservatives 213, Liberals 12 and Independents 22. It was generally accepted that the armed services' vote had been influential in bringing Labour to office. Years later Lord Robens recalled 'the numbers of men home on leave who came on to platforms in their uniforms . . . saying they did not want to resume civilian life under the conditions they had had before they went into the services'.

The basis of Labour's reforming plan was public ownership, with

331

(1)

the nationalisation of key industries and sources of supply. This time there must be none of the post-1918 betrayals: this time there must be fair shares for all. The Bank of England, railways and mines were nationalised, fuel and power came under the state—known, derisively by some, as the Welfare State because of its introduction of a National Health service, a more comprehensive National Insurance, and the National Assistance Act.

Many of these measures were based on proposals in a report published during the war. From 1909 to 1915 a civil servant, W. H. Beveridge, had been administrator of the newly devised labour exchanges. As Sir William Beveridge he was chairman between 1941 and 1942 of a committee on social insurance and allied services whose findings have been known ever since as the Beveridge Report. It recommended flat rate insurance contributions and flat rate benefits against 'interruption and destruction of earning power and for special expenditure arising at birth, marriage or death' to be administered by the state for all citizens irrespective of their salary or status. Many provisions were whittled down before Parliament would accept the report, which was then put on the shelf. A reiterated criticism was that such guarantees of a decent standard of living would mean our being unable to sell our goods competitively abroad.

To this Tom Hopkinson of *Picture Post*, the liveliest magazine of its time, retorted: 'The idea that after this war we are all going straight back to cutting one another's throats in the effort to export more and import less—for the sake of enjoying a lower standard of living and seeing a balance on the right side in the Bank of England's account book—is delirium.'

Unfortunately Britain after the war, if not delirious, was severely handicapped. Although Labour persevered with its social legislation, it found that the account book could not be lightly disregarded. Factories had to be reconverted to peacetime use and compete once more in world markets. American Lend-Lease, generously granted throughout the conflict, was abruptly cut off. Without some kind of loan, the country would go bankrupt.

A team under Lord Keynes, the economist, negotiated a loan of £937,500,000 from the USA, with the proviso that sterling should be made fully convertible against other currencies by mid-1947.

(1) A typical scene in the dreadful winter of 1947; a car runs into a snow drift on the Westerham road, Kent.

(2) The hardship of 1947 was aggravated by a fuel crisis; the people here are queueing for coke— a by-product of gas manufacture— outside the Bow Common Lane gasworks, Poplar.

Although the money was needed primarily for re-equipment of industry, the Americans pressed for a large part of it to be spent buying their films and tobacco. Matters were not helped by the 1946–47 winter, one of the worst in living memory, which brought people and machines to a halt for days on end.

Exports must come first, home expansion last. Britain had won a war; she now had to win the peace.

End of Empire

In March 1947 Lord Mountbatten was sent to India as viceroy to effect a smooth transition from British rule to that of the Indians themselves, for which both Hindus and Muslims had long been clamouring. It was not going to be easy, for, as the Muslim leader Muhammad Ali Jinnah pointed out: 'Hindus and Muslims have two different religious philosophies, social customs, literature. . . . The Muslims are not a minority as the word is commonly understood. Muslims are a nation.' Gandhi, leader of the Indian National Congress, which was largely Hindu, had always deplored any proposed split in the country as a 'vivisection of Mother India'; but in the end there had to be a partition of the main communities into India and Pakistan.

From many other regions there came demands for British withdrawal. Burma became independent. Newfoundland voted to join Canada. Egypt appealed to the United Nations to enforce withdrawal of British troops, and although no formal recommendation was made, Britain left Egypt in 1947.

Anti-British feeling in Arab countries was inflamed by Britain's part in the creation of a Jewish state in Palestine. At the same time the Jews were angered by British restrictions on the expansion of this state. After the First World War a League of Nations mandate had enjoined the British administration to 'place the country under such political, administrative and economic conditions as will secure the establishment of the Jewish national home, while at the same time safeguarding the civil and religious rights of all the inhabitants of Palestine'. Hitler's anti-Semitism had driven many refugees to seek a new life in this national home, but British quota restrictions denied many of them access. Immediately after the Second World

(1)

(1) Lord Mountbatten, last Viceroy of India, speaking to the Constituent Assembly in New Delhi on India's Independence Day.

(2) A ship crammed with 1300 immigrants steams into Haifa harbour three days before British withdrawal from Palestine in 1948. Britain had administered the new state of Israel under a mandate from the League of Nations since 1919.

(2)

Prime minister Clement Attlee opens the Palestine Conference in 1946; Ernest Bevin, foreign secretary, is at his right.

War, outbreaks of terrorist activity marked the emergence of fervently nationalist groups. A United Nations special commission recommended partition between Jewish and Arab communities. In May 1948 Britain withdrew, and the state of Israel was born, to become at once the target of Arab attacks. Opposing states refused to acknowledge the intrinsic existence of Israel or to trade with her. Egypt denied Israel the use of the Suez canal, despite obligations to allow free passage to all shipping in peace and war.

In succeeding years what Harold Macmillan, prime minister between January 1957 and October 1963, called 'the wind of change' began to blow through Africa, Malaya and the West Indies. More colonies and protectorates demanded freedom, though few wished to sever all ties with the UK. The word 'Empire' faded from normal usage in favour of the concept of a Commonwealth of voluntarily associated states. The 900 million people still linked in this way belong to the following countries. (Where names have altered substantially, the earlier version is given in brackets.)

The United Kingdom	Malaysia (Malaya, North
Canada	Borneo—renamed Sahab—
Australia	and Sarawak)
New Zealand	Malta
Barbados	Mauritius
Botswana (Bechuanaland)	Nauru
Cyprus	Nigeria
Fiji	Pakistan (once part of India)
Gambia	Sierra Leone
Ghana (Gold Coast)	Singapore
Guyana (British Guiana)	Sri Lanka (Ceylon)
India	Swaziland
Jamaica	Tanzania (Tanganyika)
Kenya	Trinidad & Tobago
Lesotho (Basutoland)	Uganda
Malawi (Nyasaland)	Tonga
	Western Samoa
	Zambia (Northern Rhodesia)

Among those who once belonged to the Commonwealth but have left are Eire (1949), the Sudan (1956) and British Somaliland, which in 1960 became part of the Somali Democratic Republic. The republican Union of South Africa left in 1961. Rhodesia, known as Southern Rhodesia until the creation of Zambia, made a unilateral declaration of independence (U.D.I.) in 1965. The Crown colony of Aden, once a key base on the route to India, was relinquished to the People's Republic of Yemen in 1967.

Festival

Post-war austerity, personified for many in the bleak features and policies of Sir Stafford Cripps, chancellor of the Exchequer between 1947 and 1950, began to ease as a new decade approached. By early 1950 Britain had a balance of payments surplus, and exports were up 175 per cent on the pre-war figure. It was time for a modicum of rejoicing.

Cripps himself, when president of the Board of Trade in 1945, had given a favourable response to a suggestion that the centenary of Prince Albert's Great Exhibition should be worthily celebrated in 1951. A Government committee recommended an international exhibition 'to demonstrate to the world the recovery of the United Kingdom from the effects of war in the moral, cultural, spiritual, and material fields'. When a Festival Council got down to work, however, it discovered that there was neither money nor space to mount a spectacle of such size, and it was decided to concentrate on a purely national exhibition near the site of a new concert hall south of the Thames.

Newpapers made fun of the whole notion, the Government was attacked for squandering money, the planners found it difficult to get supplies of the right materials, and the pleasure gardens which had simultaneously been devised for Battersea Park suffered from one strike after another.

Yet when King George VI and Queen Elizabeth attended a service of dedication at St Paul's on 3rd May 1951, there was a festive mood in the air. Just as with the Great Exhibition of 1851, the scoffers remained to cheer. Britain suddenly discovered brilliant

The Festival of Britain in 1951 was held on the south bank of the Thames near Waterloo. Many striking examples of modern architecture were erected on the site but the Royal Festival Hall was the only permanent building. Illustrated here is the Skylon, symbol of the festival, beside the Dome of Discovery.

(2)

young designers of furniture, fabrics and ceramics in her midst. Eight and a half million people visited the festival before it closed in September, and were exhilarated by the achievements of which the country showed itself still capable.

In February 1952 George VI was succeeded by his daughter, who had been married since 1947 to the Greek-born Prince Philip, created duke of Edinburgh before his wedding. The mere name of Queen Elizabeth II seemed a happy auspice, and her coronation ushered in what everyone hoped would be a new Elizabethan Age.

The Second World War, like the first, had accelerated the rate of technical development. As far back as 1930 Frank Whittle had taken out a patent for a jet engine, but little official interest was shown until 1937. In 1941 he produced a successful engine for military aircraft. After the war Britain produced one of its most reliable commercial aircraft, the Vickers Viscount, in which a gas turbine powered a propeller; and in the 1950s, after some tragic disasters, the Comet was the first pure jet to go into commercial service.

While work on a hydrogen bomb, even more destructive than the A-bomb, brought a new threat to the world and gave rise to protest marches and demonstrations, Britain led the world in the peaceful use of atomic energy. In the autumn of 1956 Queen Elizabeth opened the first nuclear power station at Calder Hall in Cumberland.

British films during and immediately after the war set new standards; but the film business was menaced by a newcomer far more powerful than sound radio had ever been. In the 1920s John Logie

The year 1953 was memorable for the coronation of Queen Elizabeth II (1) and for the conquest of Everest by Edmund Hillary and Sherpa Tenzing (2) shown at the summit.

Baird had experimented, first in Hastings and later in a house in Soho, London, with transmission of images by radio waves. In 1926 he demonstrated television transmission to the Royal Institute, and early in the war showed colour signals. The BBC inaugurated a limited service from Alexandra Palace in 1936, suspended it during the war, and started again in 1946.

An Independent Television Authority (ITA) was given Parliamentary sanction in 1954 to provide a service financed from advertising revenue, though advertisers were not allowed to influence programme content or introduce slogans into the actual programme as in the USA.

Series, serials and quiz shows kept people at home and resulted in the closure of many cinemas or their conversion into 'bingo' halls. Film companies refused at first to sell their old films to television, but succumbed in the end. Today a large proportion of the remaining studios' output is designed specifically for television.

Suez

In 1956 the United States told the president of Egypt, Colonel Nasser, that it could not give financial assistance on which he had been relying to build a second Aswan dam for irrigation and hydro-electric power from the Nile. Britain, which had been considering a smaller contribution, also backed out. Nasser announced that to raise the money he would have to nationalise the Suez canal.

A third of the vessels using the canal regularly were British. More

(1)

(2)

(3)

The technical advances stimulated by the war were made of more general use in the fifties. Britain harnessed nuclear power to make electricity at the Calder Hall nuclear power station (3) and developed the first commercial jet aircraft, the Comet (2). (1) A British nuclear explosion.

British troops at the Suez Canal, 1956.

than half Britain's oil supplies came by this route. Sir Anthony Eden, Conservative prime minister, saw in the Egyptian president a sinister shadow of those dictators whom he had so strenuously denounced before the war, and accused him of putting his hand on the nation's windpipe. In Parliament there were demands for military intervention. Hugh Gaitskell, leader of the Labour opposition, advocated an appeal to the United Nations. John Foster Dulles, American secretary of State, visited London and, while preaching caution, contrived to leave Eden with the impression that America was not entirely opposed to the use of force if all else failed.

In a secret collaboration, details of which have never been disclosed, Britain and France reached agreement with Israel for joint operations against Egypt. Israel would make a surprise attack on the canal, whereupon Britain and France would send in a peace-keeping force and order both combatants to move back.

The scheme went into action in October. Israel advanced towards the canal, British and French bombers attacked Egyptian airfields, and an invasion fleet made its slow way towards Suez. Airborne landings started on 5th November, by which time Nasser had sunk enough blockships to choke the canal. The military advance was soon halted. An order from the United Nations to cease hostilities might have been ignored. What could not be ignored was a report from Harold Macmillan, chancellor of the Exchequer, that the pound sterling was in a bad way and that British drawings from the International Monetary Fund had been blocked by the USA until the invasion was called off.

Eden notified the French that he had no option but to order a cease-fire. Anglo-French troops along the canal were replaced by a token United Nations force. The waterway remained impassable. Three weeks after the final withdrawal Eden, seriously ill from the effects of an operation he had undergone before the crisis, resigned.

The climb-down infuriated the French. Their resultant mistrust was one element in their unwillingness to accept Britain into the fellowship of nations soon to be formed.

Into Europe

Early post-war signs of Russia's determination to build a bloc of satellite states dismayed her recent allies. The Security Council of the United Nations, charged with determining and recommending action on any breach of international peace, could take no action against aggression unless all five of its permanent members—the United States, Russia, Britain, France and Nationalist China—concurred. One veto immobilised the whole procedure. Every challenge to Russia over its repressive conduct met with a veto. The major powers did not want direct military confrontation; but a 'cold war' of political and economic manœuvring began.

In April 1949 the USA, Canada, and ten Western European nations decided that to combat possible Russian aggression they should set up a defensive North Atlantic Treaty Organisation (NATO). Its original members were the United States, Britain, France, Belgium, Holland, Luxemburg, Italy, Portugal, Denmark, Iceland, Norway and Canada. Later, in 1952, Greece and Turkey joined, and although the disarming of Germany had been one of the Allies' prime tasks, Russia's use of the eastern sector of the dismembered country in her military grouping led to West Germany's inclusion in NATO in 1955.

A united Europe depended not only on armed might. Discussions began on possible unification of agricultural and trade policies, and the elimination of differences in tariffs and taxes. In March 1957 France, West Germany, Holland, Belgium, Luxemburg and Italy agreed by the Treaty of Rome to form a European Economic Community (EEC) or 'Common Market'. Britain debated whether

Edward Heath signs Britain into the Common Market. To his right is the foreign secretary, Sir Alec Douglas-Home; to his left Geoffrey Rippon, chief negotiator of Britain's entry.

Common Market poster, 1973.

to join or not. There were obvious advantages in such a partnership and the wide markets which would be opened up; but many M.P.s and, indeed, many of their constituents were apprehensive of the community's probable development into a political union. Also it would be necessary to drop Commonwealth preference, which seemed a betrayal of one's own family.

Britain suggested that the establishment of a free trade area within Europe need not rule out individual members' right to vary their tariffs on goods from outside the area. The prime minister, Harold Macmillan, encouraged negotiations, but France was suspicious. President de Gaulle put it bluntly: 'I would like you very much to come into the EEC, but from your point of view you cannot come in unless you bring your Commonwealth with you. We cannot have you in if you bring your Commonwealth with you. So I am afraid there can be no agreement.'

In November 1959 Britain played a major part in the formation of a rival consortium of seven countries into the European Free Trade Association (EFTA): Britain, Austria, Denmark, Norway, Portugal, Sweden and Switzerland.

The EEC was still the more tempting prospect. In January 1961 Macmillan met de Gaulle, still in the hope of making special arrangements for Commonwealth countries, but was told that full membership meant adherence to the Treaty of Rome without special concessions. The lord privy seal, Edward Heath, a committed pro-European, continued to negotiate, and by 1963 it was agreed that Britain should make unequivocal application for entry. It was taken for granted that this time all would go smoothly.

Instead, de Gaulle accused Macmillan of deceiving him over a nuclear deal Britain had been making with the USA which would seriously damage the balance of power in Europe; and said 'no' to British membership.

The Labour government of 1964–70 made another attempt in 1967, together with Denmark and Ireland. Although West Germany and other members were anxious for Britain to play her part and counterbalance powerful French influence, France again issued a veto. The Labour prime minister, Harold Wilson, declared that he would try again in due course and would not take 'no' for an answer.

In June 1970 Edward Heath, now leader of the Conservative Party, became prime minister with the avowed intention of carrying Britain into the Common Market. His negotiator, Geoffrey Rippon, brought talks to a satisfactory conclusion in Luxemburg in June 1971.

On 1st January 1973 the United Kingdom became a full partner in that united Europe where, over the centuries, she had fought and won so many battles.

Acknowledgements

Colour illustrations are indicated in italic figures.

The following illustrations are reproduced by gracious permission of Her Majesty the Queen 71 (2), 78, 81, 92, 103 (1), 109 (2), 125, 127 (4), *129, 140*, 142 (2), 148, 159, 164, 183, 204 (1), 238, 240, 266 (2)

Aerofilms 9, *10* (2), 273, 286 (2, 3)

Albertina, Vienna 123 (2)

Ashmolean Museum, Oxford 36 (1)

Basle, Kunstmuseum Print Room 96 (2)

Bern, Burgerbibliothek 53

Bodleian Library, Oxford 19 (2), 108 (1)

D. E. Bower Collection, Chiddingstone Castle 151 (1)

British Airways 315 (2)

British Council 311

British Museum 11, 13 (3), 16 (1), 17 (10), 19 (1), 21, 22, 24 (1, 2), 25, 26 (1, 2), 27 (3), 28 (1, 2), 30 (2, 3), 32, *33*, 34 (1, 2), *36 (2, 3)*, 37, 39, 46 (1), 47, 49 (1), 50 (2), 51 (2), 52 (1), 55, 56 (1), 60, 62, 63, 64 (1), 65, 66 (1), 67 (2), 68 (1), 69 (1), 71 (1), 73, 76, 77, 79, 85 (1), 97 (4), 100 (1, 2), 101, 106 (2), 107 (1), 110 (2), 112 (2), 114, 115, 116 (2), 120, 121, 122 (1, 2), 123 (1), 126 (1), 127 (1), 130, 134, 138, 142 (1), 143, 146 (2), 149 (1), 154, 166, 168, 169, 170, 173, 174, 176, 177, 178 (3), 179 (2), 186 (1), 187, 190 (1), 195, 196 (2), 197, 198, 202 (2), 203, 207 (2), 211, 213 (1), *217*, 218 (1), 219 (2), *221 (4)*, 222 (1), 223, *224*, 225, 226 (1), 228, 229 (2), 232 (1, 2), 233 (1), 235 (2), 243 (2), 251 (1)

British Tourist Authority 18 (2), 30 (1), 102

British Transport Museum *264, 313*

Brunel University Library 227 (2)

Cambridge, by permission of the Master and Fellows of Corpus Christi College 26 (3), 67 (1)

Camera Press 333 (2)

J. Allan Cash 18 (1), 43

De la Tour Collection 294

Department of the Environment 16 (2), 20 (1), 23 (2), *41, 44/45*, 93 (2), *136*

Devizes, Archaeological Museum 12

Devonshire Collection, Chatsworth—reproduced by permission of the Trustees of the Chatsworth Settlement 126 (2)

Elek Books Ltd 210

Ferdinandeum, Innsbruck 113 (1)

R. B. Fleming & Co. 84 (1), 85 (1), *184, 220* (2)

Fox Photos 315 (1), 336 (1)

J. R. Freeman & Co. 58, 93 (1), 131, 160 (2), 173, 178 (3), 196 (1), 200 (1), 202 (3), 207 (2), 218 (1), 223 (2), 229 (2), 232 (1), 235 (2), 275 (2)

The Frick Collection, New York 96 (1)

Giraudon, Paris 35, 38, 51 (1), 64 (3), 74, 111

Girton College Library, Cambridge 251 (2)

Gordon Boys School, Woking *265*

Guildhall Art Gallery, City of London *cover illustration*

Guildhall Library, City of London 150

Michael Holford Library 6, *10* (1), 26 (1), 31, *36 (2, 3)*, *40*, 49 (2), 56 (3), 61 (1), *83, 90*

Holkham Hall, by kind permission of the Earl of Leicester 214

Imperial War Museum 247, 248, 250 (2), 295, 296, 297 (2), 298, 299 (4), 302 (2), 303, 304 (2, 3), *309*, 310 (2), *316, 317*, 324, 325 (1), 326, 327 (1, 3), 328, 329, 330 (1)

Inner Temple Library, London 84 (1)

International Publishing Corporation 292 (3), 323 (1, 3), 330 (2)

Irish Tourist Board 27 (1, 2)

John Johnson Collection, Bodleian Library, Oxford 267

A. F. Kersting 42 (1), 50 (1), 52 (2), 54, 57 (2, 3), 68 (2), 88, 117, 207 (3), 208

Keystone Press Agency 333 (1), 339

Lambeth Palace Library 72

Leicester Museum and Art Gallery *212*

John Leith Photo Library 340

London Museum, by permission of the Trustees 137 (3), 144, 158, 252, *261, 268*, 276 (2)

Lords Gallery *305*

Manchester City Art Galleries 237

Mansell Collection 16 (3), 151 (2), 199, 297 (3), 301 (2)

Metropolitan Museum of Art, New York 112 (1)

Mr and Mrs J. W. Middendorf Collection *185*

National Army Museum 175 (2), 182 (1), 249, 250 (1), 278, 280

National Gallery, London, reproduced by courtesy of the Trustees 70 (2), 108 (2), *133, 189*

National Maritime Museum, London 85 (2), *137 (2)*, 152 (2), 156 (2), 193, 194 (1), 202 (1), 302 (1); Greenwich Hospital Collection 113 (2), 147, 192

National Monuments Record 57 (1)

National Portrait Gallery, London 69 (2), 75, *82*, 84 (2),

89, *91*, *95*, 97 (3), 99 (4), 104 (1), 105, 110 (1), 118, 119, 124, 128, *132*, 135, *141*, 146 (1), 149 (2), 152 (1), 153, 155 (3), *156* (1), 160, 161, 162, 163, 165, 171, 172, 175 (1), 178 (2), 182 (2), 186 (2), 190 (2), 191 (2), 194 (2), 201, 206 (2), 207 (1), 219 (1), 229 (1), 233 (2), 234 (2), 235 (1), 239, 262 (1), 263, 266 (1), 271 (2)

Oslo, University Collections 28 (3), 29 (4)

Ottawa, National Gallery of Canada 186 (3)

Oxford, by permission of the President and Fellows of Corpus Christi College 46 (2)

Oxford, by courtesy of the President and Fellows of St John's College 98 (1)

Paris, Bibliothèque Nationale *48*, 64 (2), 111

Pepys Library, Cambridge 103 (2)

Picturepoint *14/15*, 17 (2), 59, 104 (2)

Pitkin Pictorials 23 (1), 61 (2), 155 (2)

Popperfoto Library 284, 288 (2), 289, 290 (1), 314 (1), 322 (1), 330 (3), 335, 338

By courtesy of the Post Office 287 (2)

Public Record Office, London 42 (2)

Punch 262 (3)

Radio Times Hulton Picture Library 179 (1), 233 (3), 234 (1), 244, 253 (3), 254, 270, 274, 276 (1), 277, 281 (2), 282, 283, 285, 286 (1), 287 (1, 3), 288 (1), 291, 292 (1), 293 (1), 299 (3), 300, 301 (1), 306, 307, 312, 314 (2), 318, 319, 322 (2), 323 (2), 327 (2), 332, 334, 337 (2)

Richmond-on-Thames Borough Council 258 (2, 3)

Rothamsted Experimental Station, Harpenden, 213 (2)

Royal Agricultural Society of England *216*

Royal Anglian Regiment *257*

Royal Commonwealth Society Library 290 (2)

Royal Geographical Society 292 (2), 336 (2)

Frank T. Sabin Ltd *221* (3)

Science Museum, London 107 (1), 218 (2, 3), *220* (*1*), 226 (2), 227 (1)

Walter Scott, Bradford 56 (2)

Scottish National Portrait Gallery 145, 178 (1)

Shakespeare Birthplace Trust 116 (1)

Sheffield City Libraries 222 (2)

Sir John Soane Museum, London *181*

Society of Antiquaries of London 80

Sport and General Press Agency 293 (2)

State Historical Museum, Stockholm 29 (5)

Dr J. K. St Joseph 13 (1, 2), 24 (3)

Tate Gallery, London 191 (1), 200 (2), 205 (1), 209, 253 (2), *269*, 304 (1), *320*

H. Terry-Engell Gallery, London 122 (3)

Toledo Museum of Art, Ohio 99 (3)

Trade Union Congress *272*

United Kingdom Atomic Energy Authority 337 (1, 3)

Reproduced by kind permission of the United Service and Royal Aero Club, on loan to the Imperial War Museum *308*

Victoria and Albert Museum, London 70 (1), 109 (1), *180*, 231 (on loan to Wilberforce House, Hull), 242, 243 (1), 245, 246, *260*

Vienna, Kunsthistorische Museum *87*, 98 (2)

Warburg Institute 18 (3)

Walker Art Gallery, Liverpool 86, *94*, 271 (1)

Wellington Museum, Apsley House (Crown Copyright) 204 (2), 205 (2), 206 (1), 236

West India Committee 230

By kind permission of Lord Willoughby de Broke *188*

Mr Simon Wingfield Digby, Sherborne Castle 107 (2)

Woburn Abbey Collection, by kind permission of His Grace, the Duke of Bedford 106 (1)

Photography by Eileen Tweedy cover, 11, 12, 24 (1), 30 (2), 32, 34 (2), 62 (1), 66 (2), 76, 77, 85 (2), 97 (4), 100 (2), 101, 106 (2), 110 (2), 115 (2), 116 (2), 120, 121, 122, 123, 126 (1), 130, *133*, 134, *137* (*3*), 138, 142 (1), 143, *144*, 146 (2), 149 (1), 150, 166, 168, 169, 170, 176, *177*, 179 (2), *180*, *181*, 182 (1), 186 (1), 187, *188*, *189*, 190 (1), 193, 194 (1), 195, 196 (2), 197, 198, 200 (2), 202 (1, 2), 203, 205 (2), *209*, 211, *213*, *216*, *217*, *220* (*1*), *221*, 222 (1), *224*, 225, 226, 228, 230, 232 (2), 233 (1), 244 (2), 245, 255, *257*, 258, 259, *260*, *261*, 262 (2, 3), *264*, *265*, *267*, *268*, *269*, *272*, 275 (3), 281 (1), 290 (2), 294, 295, 303 (2), *305*, *308*, *309*, 310, *313*, *316*, *317*, *320*

Endpaper illustration:
'Scotland Forever', the charge of the Scots Greys at Waterloo. From the painting by Lady Butler reproduced by kind permission of Leeds City Art Gallery, Temple Newsam House.

Index